Child and adolescent
mental health services

D1471602

000000642

together we stand

THE COMMISSIONING, ROLE AND MANAGEMENT OF CHILD AND ADOLESCENT MENTAL HEALTH SERVICES

London: HMSO

TOGETHER WE STAND

The Commissioning, Role and Management of Child and Adolescent Mental Health Services

EDITORS

Dr Richard Williams

and

Dr Gregory Richardson

AUTHORS

Mr Paul Bates

Dr Zarrina Kurtz

Dr Stuart Cumella

Dr Gregory Richardson

Mr Michael Farrar

Dr Michael Shooter

Dr Michael Kerfoot

Mr Richard White

Dr Richard Williams

ADDITIONAL AUTHORS

The HAS is grateful to the following

Dr Michael Berger

Professor Peter Hill

Mr Bob Sang

Dr David Walk

PROJECT MANAGER

Mr Roderick Montgomery

TOGETHER WE STAND

There is nothing more important than maintaining the mental health of children and young people. Happy stable young people are more likely to become happy stable parents who in turn are able to provide a safe and secure upbringing for their children.

In undertaking this piece of work, Dr Richard Williams has brought together in collaboration experienced people from a wide range of interested professional groups. This is the same challenge – collaborative work across disciplinary and agency boundaries – that faces all those who work with children and young people and is so important to those who care for them.

The title of this thematic review is – Together We Stand. It is by doing just that, by working together that those who provide services can help those who need services. One of the overriding themes of this review is the conclusion that there must be collaboration and cooperation at every level and among all who work with children and young people, if services are to be effective.

The review paints a picture of the services that are currently being provided and suggests ways in which both commissioners and providers can improve them to meet the needs of our children and young people.

I am confident that this review will help all those who work in this field to build a better service for future generations of children and young people.

John Bowis OBE MP
Parliamentary Under Secretary of State
Department of Health
Whitehall
London
April 1995

CHAPTER I

BACKGROUND CONSIDERATIONS

The mental health of children foreshadows the mental health of future generations of adults. Child and adolescent mental health services are a small part of the responsibilities of health and local authorities, but the implications of poor attention to children's and young people's mental health are not only their and their families' continued suffering, but also a continuing spiral of child abuse, juvenile crime, family breakdown and adult mental illness, all of which can lead to more child and adolescent mental health problems.

The 'circular causality' that leads psychologically healthy parents to nurture psychologically healthy children who, in turn, become psychologically healthy parents, is echoed in this document's principal assertion that: *the effective commissioning of child and adolescent mental health services nurtures good provision which, in turn, informs good commissioning.*

The proper collaboration of purchasers and providers is essential in this process. Such collaboration ensures that interacting human factors, such as family discord, child abuse, socio-economic disadvantage, racial and sexual discrimination, learning disabilities, developmental delay, mental illness and severe chronic physical illness, are considered as a whole. We fear that, without proper collaboration, similar circular causality will lead to a downward spiral in the quality of provision and commissioning.

Within the health, social welfare and education services, the multifactorial aetiology of child and adolescent mental health problems means that specialist and complementary skills of different disciplines are required to address them. While this document is primarily concerned with commissioning health services, its authors recognise that many of the contributory and resultant factors of child and adolescent mental health problems are also evident far outside the health field. The emphasis is, therefore, even more squarely placed on close collaboration between agencies in purchasing processes, such as joint commissioning. In turn, this emphasises the need for the many professionals, involved in the provision of child care, to work together. Similarly, purchaser and provider managers must work together to discharge their joint responsibility for ensuring the effective commissioning and delivery of child and adolescent mental health services.

This complex but ultimately rewarding co-operative work cannot be avoided; its need has been highlighted in various reports.

The more recent policies and objectives of a number of government departments, relating to the mental health of young people, are elaborated in the following documents:

Welfare of Children and Young People in Hospital (1991)

Creating a Common Profile for Mental Health (1992)

Choosing with Care; The report of the Committee of Enquiry into the Selection, Development and Management of Staff in Children's Homes (1992)

The Health of the Nation White Paper (1992)

Working Together under the Children Act 1989 (1992)

Protocol for Investment in Health Gain - Mental Health (1993)

Child Protection: Medical Responsibilities (1994)

The Code of Practice on the Identification and Assessment of Special Educational Needs (1994)

Pupils with Problems (1994)

Additionally, the NHS Health Advisory Service (HAS) is aware that the Department of Health has recently published its *Handbook on Child and Adolescent Mental Health* as a component of the Health of the Nation Mental Illness Key Area initiative.

Each makes reference to the mental health needs of children, young people and their carers and the requirement for close collaboration between agencies which work with children and young people.

The profile of child and adolescent mental health services (CAMHS) has also been highlighted by Action for Sick Children's *With Health in Mind,* (1992), the National Association for Health Authorities and Trusts' *Mental Health Services for Children and Young People,* (1992), the Audit Commission's *Children First,* (1993) and the NHS Health Advisory Service document, *Bridges over Troubled Waters,* (1986).

The HAS is also aware that the Audit Commission is planning to undertake an exploration of services for Troubled and Troublesome Youth. This is likely to consider the nature of offending by young people and those services, across a variety of sectors, which respond to young people in trouble.

Comprehensive and balanced child and adolescent mental health services, are required in each locality, for matters such as the placement and treatment of children on adult psychiatric wards, and the uncontrolled behaviour of young people in residential care engender adverse publicity and claims of lack of provision. Ad hoc responses are expensive as they often involve purchasing services at some distance from a young person's family and the cultures of the young people concerned - the very reverse of an active needs-led, community-based service. Deficits in service not only fail the community in the short and medium term, but also herald more intractable problems for the longer term. There is a growing public awareness and commitment to the needs of children and young people who experience mental health problems, and an increasing recognition of the importance of prevention and early intervention.

THE THEMATIC REVIEW

This review arose, in part, from awareness of these background matters. It was also generated by widely held professional and managerial concerns, in the NHS and in the welfare services more broadly, about the state, status and performance of mental health services for children and young people. Visits made by the HAS to services throughout England and Wales have confirmed a high level of uncertainty about child and adolescent mental health services. These services, being by nature diverse, are experienced as confusing by many with managerial responsibilities. The HAS therefore embarked on this review with the intentions of establishing information on the current status and pattern of challenges facing mental health services for children. An important component has been that of generating an understanding of the purchasing and providing processes so that the HAS could then offer guidance.

The information and opinion contained in this document is derived from two main sources. First, up-to-date reviews of research and of professional and managerial practice. Second, and specifically for this document, the visits undertaken by the NHS Health Advisory Service to a number of local services throughout England and Wales. Each was intended not only to aid definition of the current status of purchasing skills and the nature of service provision, but also to identify some of the most significant factors in purchasing and provision which lead to the delivery of services that are considered useful and effective by the populations they serve.

The work has brought the HAS into contact with other groups working on parallel tracks, such as Dr Zarrina Kurtz, Mrs Rosemary Thornes and Dr Stephen Wolkind (Kurtz et al, 1994) and Dr Simon Wallace, Dr June Crown, Professor Anthony Cox and Dr Michael Berger (Wallace et al, 1994), among many others. We have tried to blend our approaches intending that our products should be complementary. Additionally, our approach is similar to that adopted by the Department of Health in its *Handbook on Child and Adolescent Mental Health* produced in support of the Health of the Nation initiative. The HAS advised the Department of Health in producing that text, on the basis of work done in this thematic review, and it is intended that both texts, and that produced by Wallace et al., should be used together by service commissioners and providers.

As readers will learn, this thematic review has been conducted according to a rigorous staged methodology that has enabled findings, hypotheses and recommendations to be examined, tested and refined progressively. The process is summarised in Figure 1.

Figure 1

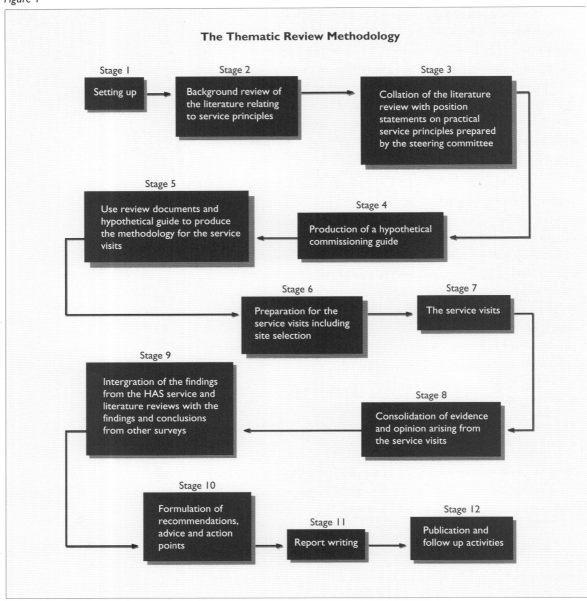

The Thematic Review Methodology

This review has concentrated on matters related to commissioning and managing mental health services for children and adolescents. Service strategy and organisational issues are, therefore, important matters of concern and ways forward in service development are proposed. The HAS is mindful of the roles of the professional bodies with regard to standards of professional practice and training. This review does not deal with these matters directly, but we hope it will provide a strategic and operational framework within which these issues can be integrated with the managerial aspects of service management. Also, this review does not consider the epidemiology and nature of mental health problems and disorders in detail. Orientating chapters offer summarised reviews of these matters and provide brief, contextual information for managers. Readers are referred to other sources for more detailed information and opinion on these matters.

Of necessity, the HAS found it had to choose to highlight matters for particular consideration. The approach adopted then is that of entry to service commissioning and provision from a health service perspective. The HAS is aware of the work which the Audit Commission is preparing with regard to young people who offend and so, while this important topic is referred to here, it is not the prime consideration of this report. Further, the HAS is well advanced in writing a separate review of substance misuse services for young people and so less emphasis is given to them. Despite these, perhaps arbitrary, choices which reflect the need to produce a reasonably concise report, the approach taken overall is based on a belief that mental health services need to be multi-sectoral. The report is vitally concerned with the co-operative and collaborative style which we consider that all the statutory agencies require and it is intended that much of its contents will be helpful to the staff of local authority social services and education departments.

Only in stating that the mental health needs of children and young people must be addressed is this document dogmatic. It sets out guidance in the form of lists of matters to be considered, courses which might be pursued and key tasks. The HAS is aware that there is a wide diversity of styles of service organisation, management and delivery across the UK. There is much to be gained from this and the HAS would not wish to detract from local initiatives or cause antagonism by espousing a single approach. Nevertheless, there are certain overarching guiding issues identified here: services must be well led, directed to explicit purposes and objectives, soundly managed and must be built on effective communication between constituent and related parts.

ACKNOWLEDGEMENTS

The Services

I would like to thank the staff of the many services interviewed in the course of the fieldwork. They gave freely of their time and knowledge. I hope that they recognise the aspects of good practice, derived from discussion with them, and that this report makes them feel their efforts were worthwhile.

The Authors

My special thanks are due to the authors of this document (Annex C). They have formed the backbone of consistency throughout the work of the steering committee by drafting papers, spearheading the service visits and leading in the preparation of this report.

Chapters five and 11 were written by Dr Zarrina Kurtz and particular credit is due to her and to her collaborators in the work which generated these contributions. Chapter five is based on her work, with Dr Stephen Wolkind and Mrs Rosemary Thornes, in conducting a national survey based on self-report questionnaires. These chapters are also informed by Dr Zarrina Kurtz' contributions to the document published by Action for Sick Children in 1992, called *With Health in Mind.* Chapter six is based on work on commissioning conducted, at the behest of the HAS, by Dr Stuart Cumella of the University of Birmingham and Mr Bob Sang of the Kings Fund College.

The Steering Committee and Service Visitors

I cannot thank all of these people sufficiently for their dedication to the task, time and support to me. Biographies for each appear in Annexes D and E.

Within that wider team, Greg Richardson has been a tower of cool, clear-minded, practical strength. He proved an excellent leader throughout. His special efforts and contributions should be recognised and so my particular thanks are offered to him.

Each member of this team of authors, steering committee members and service visitors has ensured that the thematic review has been guided with an appropriately broad perspective which acknowledges and draws on the contributions made by a wide range of professional disciplines in promoting the mental health of children and young people. They have responded to very short deadlines with considerable thought and wisdom, and I trust this document reflects some of their attention and sagacity.

Dr Richard Williams
Director
NHS Health Advisory Service

CHAPTER 2

A Guide to this Review

INTRODUCTION

This review has been written for a wide and diverse professional and managerial group with varying degrees of involvement in the commissioning and provision of child and adolescent mental health services (CAMHS).

Part A reports on the current position relating to both purchasing and delivering child and adolescent mental health services. This part has three intentions.

- To summarise information relating to mental health problems and disorders which should influence the commissioners and providers of services in carrying out their responsibilities.

- To establish the current state of mental health services for younger people.

- To consider lessons learned from current commissioning and providing practice, with a view to improving their quality in the future.

Its origins lie in four main sources of information.

- Epidemiological information derived from established research.

- A survey of purchasing and service provision in England conducted by Dr Zarrina Kurtz, Dr Stephen Wolkind and Mrs Rosemary Thornes, in 1993.

- Surveys of commissioning; (based on analyses of documentation from 90% of health authorities in England and Wales for 1993-94 collected in the NHS Health Advisory Service Library of Commissioning Documentation and conducted by Dr Stuart Cumella); content analysis of a sample of these documents by Mr Bob Sang of the Kings Fund College; and visits to 20 health authorities in England and Wales conducted by Dr Stuart Cumella of the University of Birmingham.

- Visits to services conducted by the HAS in 1994.

Part A is presented in narrative format, and the remaining parts have been presented in a more incisive style using lists, tables and bullets points which individual purchasers and providers should find useful in benchmarking their own progress and in setting local priorities for action.

Part B extracts the principles of commissioning and service provision, drawn from information gained in the course of reviewing the current position. Importantly, Part B offers a simple concept of service composition to assist purchasers in generating a service strategy. This is intended to support commissioners in mapping and benchmarking local provision, and to aid commissioners and providers in understanding the needs for effective collaborative dialogues built on managed interfaces between service components.

Part C then considers commissioning in more detail set against a background of needs assessment, health gain and outcomes. It offers a view of joint commissioning which, in the experience of the HAS, is much talked of and often misunderstood. It also offers a chapter on the importance of specialist services and another, which proposes an Action Plan for commissioners.

The strategic approach described in chapter eight is developed further in Part D, in which the tasks facing services at each of the four tiers in the model are considered.

Part E concludes the report with checklists, references and suggestions for further reading. Also included in Part F, as Annex A, is a summary of expert advice on certain legal matters. These relate to the functioning of child and adolescent mental health services and have been selected from issues about which professionals and managers frequently seek advice.

USING THIS REVIEW

The remainder of this chapter contains suggestions on how particular professionals and managers can derive the most benefit from the document, although to understand the full picture it will be necessary to consider the document as a whole.

Purchasers of Child and Adolescent Mental Health Services

The basics of commissioning child and adolescent mental health services are contained in the Commissioners' Checklist in Part E. This checklist derives from chapter nine on *The Principles of Effective Commissioning of Child and Adolescent Mental Health Services*. Reviews of *Needs Assessment Health Gain and Outcomes*, *Joint Commissioning* and *Commissioning Very Specialised Services* are contained in Part C. Chapter eight, on *A Strategic Approach to Commissioning and Delivering Child and Adolescent Mental Health Services*, provides an overview of the construction of comprehensive services. Chapters five to seven describe the present position in the commissioning and management of child and adolescent mental health services.

Provider Managers of Child and Adolescent Mental Health Services

Chapters five to seven describe the present position and problems of child and adolescent mental health services and Parts B, C and D indicate how some of the current problems might be addressed.

The Providers' Checklist in Part E summarises basic matters. This checklist is based on chapter ten, *The Principles of Providing Child and Adolescent Mental Health Services* and chapter eight, describing *A Strategic Approach to Commissioning and Delivering Child and Adolescent Mental Health Services*. Chapters 15 to 19, offer a practical description of service provision.

Clinical Directors

Clinical Directors responsible for child and adolescent mental health services may, or may not, have an intimate understanding of the problems inherent in providing child and adolescent mental health services. They are encouraged to read chapters eight and 15 to 19 on strategic and management issues which should influence service delivery matters in particular. Chapters nine and ten on the *Principles of Commissioning and Providing Child and Adolescent Mental Health Services* are also important for those engaged in dialogue with purchasers.

Directors of Social Services and their Managers

Judging by the fieldwork, some Directors of Social Services and their senior managers might consider that they invest heavily in child and adolescent mental health services but get little in return. Many have withdrawn social workers from health-based child and adolescent mental health services. In this circumstance, chapter eight describes how child and adolescent mental health services might be provided, with the input of staff from social services departments, benefiting their clients. Chapters nine and 12, which consider *Joint Commissioning*, and the *Commissioners' Checklist*, address co-operation between social services and the health services.

Directors of Education and their Managers

Directors of Education and their senior managers are encouraged to view mental health problems in children and adolescents as a significant responsibility. *The Code of Practice on the Identification and Assessment of Special Educational Needs* provides their staff with an ideal method for recognising children with mental health problems. Chapter eight, and the *Commissioners' Checklist*, provide guidance on the composition of child and adolescent mental health services and chapters nine and 12 suggest how the education, social services and health sectors might commission services jointly.

Paediatricians and the Staff of Child Health Services

Paediatricians see many young people with mental health problems. It is important that they feel supported by, and able to consult and refer to members of local child and adolescent mental health services. They are encouraged to read chapter eight, on *A Strategic Approach to Commissioning and Delivering Child and Adolescent Mental Health Services*. Chapters 15 to 19, on the practicalities of providing child and adolescent mental health services, are particularly relevant to the wider child health services.

Magistrates and Guardians Ad Litem

Magistrates, guardians and others working in the courts often need access to child and adolescent mental health services. Chapters nine and 12 suggests how they might work with health authorities to purchase services.

Members of Child and Adolescent Mental Health Services

This document explains how purchaser and provider managers are being encouraged to approach child and adolescent mental health services. Understanding their approach should help all providers to work with local commissioners and to offer them advice geared to the needs of the children, young people, families and agencies.

DEPARTMENT OF HEALTH AND, WELSH OFFICE INITIATIVES

All of the professionals and managers identified above will also find the following texts informative:

Mental Illness Services - A Strategy for Wales, (Welsh Office, 1989)

The Protocol for Investment in Health Gain - Mental Health (Welsh Health Planning Forum 1993)

A Handbook on Child and Adolescent Mental Health (Department of Health, 1995)

The NHS Executive documents entitled:

a.   *Epidemiologically Based Needs Assessment: Child and Adolescent Mental Health* (Wallace et al., 1995)

b.   Hall, D. and Hill, P., (1994). *Community Child Health Services (and especially Section 3 Child Mental Health: Mild Psychological Pathology). In Health Care Needs Assessment.* Editors Stephens, A. and Raftery, J., Radcliffe Medical Press, Oxford.

CHAPTER 3

1 A series of survey methods has been used to establish a picture of current mental health services for younger people, each has its accent on the components of service provided by the NHS in England and Wales.

2 One survey collected information through questionnaires sent to purchasers and providers. The others involved analysing the contents of commissioning documentation and visits to two samples of purchasers and providers. There is consistency in the findings which indicate that mental health services for children and adolescents are, essentially, unplanned and historically determined. Their distribution is patchy and they are very variable in quality and composition. The work they do seems unrelated in strength or diversity to systematically considered local need.

3 This description does not detract from recognising that work of high quality is being done in many services by many committed staff in a range of disciplines; staff who put considerable energy and zeal into their work. Rather, it suggests that more could be achieved by better understanding and management of services and greater co-ordination of their work.

4 This review explores the definition, nature and epidemiology of mental health problems and mental disorders in childhood and adolescence. The chapters devoted to these matters are brief summaries of an extensive literature and are intended to provide managers with a simplified overview.

5 This review concludes that the overall goal of comprehensive child and adolescent mental health services should be that of delivering seamless, multi-sectoral mental health services for children, adolescents, young people and their families. The services must be effective, sensitive and appropriate to the needs of the local population, and based on achieving the best from partnerships in care.

6 The NHS Health Advisory Service considers that there is now considerable potential for service development based on commissioners seizing opportunities to take a central role. They could achieve a more even distribution of services by co-ordinating the development of strategy, estimating local need, agreeing programmes of service development to meet that need, and by reviewing performance against objectives. In short, much positive forward movement could be achieved by subjecting child and adolescent mental health services to the rigour of the full commissioning process in which professional advisers and the users of services and their carers have clear voices.

7 Based on these findings, this review offers a strategic vision of comprehensive child and adolescent mental health services. Central to the review's recommendations is a concept of composition delivery which is based on four distinct tiers of service organisation. In many districts, areas, counties or boroughs, significant planning and developmental work is needed to achieve comprehensive services, inevitably requiring time to deliver. This calls for progressive and planned programmes of change. Service-mapping in each district, leading to the collation of a resource inventory, conducted jointly by purchasers and providers, is an important step in identifying the aspects or tiers of service which should be the priorities for development. This thematic review will be useful to staff in benchmarking their determination of local priorities.

8 The four tiers of service recommended in this report are not intended as rigid prescriptions of service design, but serve to identify the styles and levels of

specialism of work involved in offering comprehensive, co-ordinated services. Specific objectives and tasks are identified for commissioners and providers, both in general terms and relating to each tier.

9   In many districts, there are aspects of service which are performing well alongside others which are poorly developed or less effective. The profile is very variable. Some purchasers and providers need to achieve development in all tiers of service.

10   Generally, the findings of this review indicate that particular attention needs to be given to:

- Identifying, strengthening and supporting direct contact, Tier 1 services (paragraph 14 considers this matter in more detail).

- Clarifying the components, roles, functioning, leadership, management and communications of current specialist (Tier 2 and 3) child and adolescent mental health services.

- Identifying, sustaining and, where necessary, developing highly specialised (Tier 4) services. These include highly specialised outpatient, day and inpatient services which are capable of dealing with children and young people and their families who have complex and sustained problems and disorders which demand focused interventions and high levels of professional skill.

11   The NHS Health Advisory Service believes that an important principle is that no young person under the age of 16 should be admitted to an adult psychiatric inpatient unit, unless there are major extenuating circumstances. This has significant implications for both purchasers and providers in sustaining, developing and shaping, the provision of in and day facilities, for adolescents especially. Purchasers should devise contractual mechanisms which sustain these very specialised services as, often, they cannot be sufficiently supported by a contract with a single health commissioner.

12   There are a number of themes which run throughout this document:

The first theme recognises the interactional processes of co-operation, collaboration and integration recurring throughout the service visits and reiterated in this review. They apply in all elements and at all levels of service and include:

- Joint commissioning across agencies.

- The ownership and sharing of strategy and agenda for action by the chairs of agencies and their chief executive officers.

- Collaboration at every level of service management and delivery within, and across, agencies.

- Close working relationships between practitioners of a wide variety of disciplines.

The experience of the HAS shows that, where the development of effective partnerships is led from the chairs of the health authorities, the social services and education committees and each of the relevant health trusts, in conjunction with relevant voluntary agencies, then commissioners can have greater confidence in the quality of service provision. These initiatives should be communicated to, and resonate through, all levels of staff in all the organisations involved.

13   A second theme is that of considering the traditional way in which services are distributed by age of the users. The statutory current requirements on, and existing heavy commitments of, local authority agencies are recognised. Nonetheless, the evidence arising from visits to current services suggests that the time is right to consider the creation of youth mental health services offering assessment, care and intervention to older adolescents and young adults; services that are culturally sensitive and appropriate to the position in society of this group. The vision is of integrated child, adolescent and youth mental health services, linking seamlessly with those for adults.

14   The third theme is that of identifying and strengthening the role of staff involved in providing direct contact, primary level (otherwise Tier 1) child and adolescent mental health services. This might do much to relieve the current and acknowledged strain on specialist level services. The high level of demand on primary level services, arising from many quarters, is also recognised. The concept of identifying primary mental health workers is put forward for further consideration as a means of relieving this demand. Postholders would work in intimate contact with first-line services to provide assertive outreach from the specialist tiers. This recommendation is not intended to be prescriptive but to provoke recognition and discussion of the role of first-line services and the support and training that their staff require.

15   Behind each of the key themes identified in this report is the core matter of training. The importance of training cannot be over-estimated. This applies to commissioning, purchasing and provider managers all of whom need familiarity with child and adolescent mental health services in order to undertake their roles. Professional training, and continuing professional development, including the ability of specialists to support the development of less experienced staff, are of central significance to the maintenance and promotion of the quality of services provided. Training should include multi-disciplinary modules set alongside programmes of uni-disciplinary training for each of the professions involved.

16   This review highlights processes and tasks rather than espousing any one model of service organisation. Further work is required on the relative effectiveness and efficiency of the various styles of management of service components, which have emerged, before it would be possible to support one style in preference to others. Whatever model may be chosen, it is important now that the various components of service should have explicit roles and objectives which can be clearly integrated in the provision of improved services for children and young people in each district, area, county or borough.

PART A

The Current Position

Action Points

Service **commissioners** and **providers** should:

- Note the evidence provided by the two national surveys and the HAS service visits which indicates that, currently, commissioning of child and adolescent mental health services is under-developed and that adequate provision is patchy.

- Use this evidence as a benchmark for assessing commissioning and provider activity in their own areas.

CHAPTER 4

The Definition, Epidemiology and Nature of Child and Adolescent Mental Health Problems and Disorders

DEFINITIONS

17   It is important to define terms relating to the mental health of children and
adolescents because experience shows that lack of terminological clarity leads
to confusion and uncertainty about the suffering involved, the treatability of
problems and disorders and, the need to allocate resources.

THE DEFINITION,
EPIDEMIOLOGY AND NATURE
OF CHILD AND ADOLESCENT
MENTAL HEALTH PROBLEMS
AND DISORDERS

A Definition of Mental Health

18   This review has drawn on definitions of *mental health* provided by Professor
Ron Davey, Professor Peter Hill, Dr Zarrina Kurtz, Professor William Parry-Jones
and Mr Peter Wilson.

19   The components of mental health include the following capacities:

   •   The ability to develop psychologically, emotionally, intellectually, and
       spiritually.

   •   The ability to initiate, develop and sustain mutually satisfying personal
       relationships.

   •   The ability to become aware of others and to empathise with them.

   •   The ability to use psychological distress as a developmental process, so
       that it does not hinder or impair further development.

20   Within this broad framework, and incorporating the developmental nature of
both body and mind in childhood and adolescents, mental health in young
people is indicated more specifically by:

   •   A capacity to enter into and sustain mutually satisfying personal
       relationships.

   •   Continuing progression of psychological development.

   •   An ability to play and to learn so that attainments are appropriate for
       age and intellectual level.

   •   A developing moral sense of right and wrong.

   •   The degree of psychological distress and maladaptive behaviour being
       within normal limits for the child's age and context (Hill, 1995).

21   Defined in these ways, mental health is something of an ideal state which all
struggle to attain. The task of maintaining mental health can be aided or
hindered by external circumstances and events, and is dependent upon each
person's potential and experience of life.

Defining Mental Health Problems and Disorders

22   Mental health problems are therefore difficulties or disabilities in these areas
which may arise from any number of congenital, constitutional, environmental,
family or illness factors.

23   There are two terms used in this document. *Mental health problems* is used to
describe a very broad range of emotional or behavioural difficulties which may
cause concern or distress. They are relatively common and encompass *mental
disorders*, which are more severe and/or persistent.

24 There are concerns about using terms such as *mental or psychiatric disorder* in relation to children. First, such terms can be stigmatising, and mark the child as being different. However, unless children with mental health problems are recognised, and some attempt is made to understand and classify their problems, in the context of their social, educational and health needs, it is very difficult to organise helpful interventions for them. The second concern is that the term *mental disorder* may be taken to indicate that the problem is *entirely within the child.* In reality, disorders may arise for a variety of reasons, often interacting. In certain circumstances, a mental or psychiatric disorder, which describes a constellation or syndrome of features, may indicate the reactions of a child or adolescent to external circumstances which, if changed, could largely resolve the problem.

25 To start at the 'normal' end of the spectrum, emotions are an integral part of mental health, be they pleasant or unpleasant. The temporary distress of a child at not being allowed to have sweets at a supermarket checkout may be unpleasant for the child, and probably his or her parent, but it will help him or her to learn what is, and is not, acceptable to the parent, and so help the child to develop within the context of his or her own family. Similarly, a child's anxiety about first going to school may be distressing but, when overcome, gives rise to confidence. The loss of a pet may cause considerable unhappiness but may well help children to deal with loss in the future. Unpleasant emotions do not on their own, therefore, constitute mental health problems.

26 Mental health problems cause concern or distress to those who have them. They may arise from a young person's difficulties in coping with life, developmental difficulty, such as a speech or language disorder, the impact of sensory handicap or an educational difficulty, such as a specific reading disorder, or from social difficulties, including parental violence and sexual abuse or because of illness. It is clear that these problems may arise for reasons, at first sight, unconnected with health matters, and many of them may be far more appropriately addressed by educational or social agencies. In turn, mental health problems and disorders often manifest themselves in difficulties in personal, educational and social functioning, and hence the emphasis in this document on collaboration between the three statutory health, education and social services agencies.

27 One of the problems inherent in distinguishing between mental health problems and disorders and anti-social behaviour is that similar symptoms, complaints or behaviours may be indicative of all of these. Behaviour problems in young people can be viewed as a common pathway by which a variety of underlying circumstances, including mental health problems and disorders, show up. Features which are useful in resolving these challenges to understanding include the nature and constellation of other symptoms, complaints or behaviours, the chronicity of the behaviour and its impact on the child and his or her relatives, friends, teachers and carers. In this report, priority is given to considering services for those children and young people whose mental health problems and disorders give rise to substantial impacts on their lives and relationships.

28 When mental health problems become severe, persistent or associated with other problems, they are termed *emotional and behavioural difficulties* by education authorities. Health service staff may classify them as mental disorders, and, this review uses the definition from the *Tenth International*

*Classification of Disease (ICD10, 1992) "The term disorder is used throughout the
classification, so as to avoid even greater problems inherent in the use of terms such
as disease or illness. Disorder is not an exact term, but it is used here to imply the
existence of a clinically recognizable set of symptoms or behaviour associated in
most cases with distress and with interference with personal functions. Social
deviance or conflict alone, without personal dysfunction, should not be included in
mental disorder."*

29 As a practical illustration of these distinctions, related to children and
adolescents, one author has styled the progression from *problem* to *disorder*
according to the following criteria (after Pearce, J. 1993):

- change in the child's usual behaviour, emotions or thoughts

- persistence of the problem - for at least two weeks

- severe enough to interfere with the child's everyday life

- a disability to the child and or the carers

In coming to opinion on these matters, professionals are recommended to:

- take account of the child's stage of development

- take account of the social cultural context

30 Despite the fact that some problems can be named, this process does not make
them exclusively the province of any one service or profession. Indeed,
different disciplines may label similar conditions in differing ways - hence the
potential for confusion. Additionally, some disorders may include symptoms or
behaviours which appear to lie in another field of description. For example, it is
not at all unusual for young people who have been sexually abused to develop
serious conduct disorders; and the covariance of conduct problems with serious
depressive disorder in adolescents can be strong. The health services cannot
manage mental disorders alone, and there needs to be close collaboration
between agencies to ensure that young people with such disorders have their
social, educational and health needs met. If a young person's disorder derives
primarily from educational difficulties, or has important implications for
educational placement, then the education services should probably be leading
in making provision for the child. If the disorder derives from a social difficulty,
such as disrupted or poor relationships at home, then the social services should
play a prominent role and lead in some circumstances. However, in nearly
every case, some collaboration, including joint assessment and joint funding, will
be necessary to ensure optimal provision for the child or young person.

31 Health services should usually lead when young people have disorders and
illnesses, particularly when they have health-related aspects. It should also be
recognised that it is not unusual for physical illnesses to produce mental health
problems and disorders, especially if they are neurological, or produce organic
mental disorders. Again, the skills of the social and education services will be
necessary to ensure that the developmental needs of the ill child are fully met.
Definition of an exact delineation of responsibility between sectors of care is
not possible in a broad document of this kind. Resolution of this challenging
task should be the subject of active, collaborative planning and continuing
dialogue between commissioners and between providers locally. Strategic
background discussions should offer a backdrop against which individual cases
can be discussed.

32   Schizophrenia, schizotypal and delusional disorders and mood disorders occur
       more commonly in adulthood, but may present for the first time in late
       childhood or adolescence. Fortunately, these illnesses are rare in this age range,
       but the mental health needs of those who develop them between the ages of
       12 and 25 are considerable, and must be addressed, not just in terms of
       immediate intensive treatment, but also with regard to their long-term
       requirements, especially when their illnesses relapse.

33   To an extent, what is meant by *mental health* is culture-bound and will change
       over time and in different situations but, for the most part, it includes freedom
       from problems with emotions, behaviour or social relationships that are
       sufficiently marked or prolonged to lead to suffering or risk to optimal
       development in the child, or to distress or disturbance in the family or
       community (Kurtz 1992a). Mental health for children and young people also
       includes the positive capacity to enjoy and benefit from satisfying relationships
       and educational opportunities and to contribute to society in a number of ways
       including, in due course, in the world of work. Schools have a major
       responsibility for such positive development through the personal and social
       educational curriculum and pastoral and behavioural policies. Education
       services are therefore well placed for early identification and intervention.
       However, a wide range of services can contribute to improving mental health in
       children and adolescents and in achieving these goals. They include, preventive,
       therapeutic, treatment, respite and rehabilitation processes promoted by the
       range of approaches devised by skilled people from a number of disciplines.
       Expertise is often found among lay and voluntary organisations.

34   Again, it is emphasised that the mental health problems and disorders of
       children and young people do not simply or solely relate to the health field;
       neither do they impinge only on narrowly defined health services. A wide
       range of the social, emotional and psychological behaviours of a growing
       number of people occur in the contexts in which children live and interact.
       People, who children encounter, respond in many ways to the children they
       meet or for whom they have responsibility. This results in a broad network of
       associations, causative factors and consequences. No single profession or
       agency can expect to understand all the issues or have pre-eminence in all
       responses. Responding to the mental health problems of children and
       adolescents requires close collaboration between workers in the mental health,
       social, education, juvenile justice and voluntary sectors, among others.

Age Definitions

35   The boundaries of childhood and adolescence are unclear. It is increasingly
       possible to recognise some characteristics of adults which predict that they will
       have difficulties with parenting. Children who may be more vulnerable to
       mental health problems may therefore be identified prior to birth. However,
       child and adolescent mental health services are usually orientated to the needs
       of children after they have been born.

36   The upper age limit is also unclear. Many child and adolescent mental health
       services use the age of 16 or school leaving age as the upper age of the index
       person to whom they will render service. This contrasts with the age of 18 (19
       in certain circumstances) used by the children's sections of social services
       departments and some health service units and 19 by education departments.

Legal definitions compound the problem, the age of consent for heterosexual intercourse being 16 for women, while it is 18 for male homosexual intercourse, voting and joining the armed forces without parental consent. It was recognised in the previous HAS report on adolescent mental health services, (NHS Health Advisory Service, 1986) that the 16 to 25 year-old age group often received mental health services which were not geared to their needs. This group requires tailored provision.

37   The Department of Health recommended flexibility in respect of child health services, but with a tendency towards extending the age range, when, in 1991, it said, *"Flexibility is required in defining childhood. It is generally accepted that children have distinctive health needs under school leaving age (up to age 19) and that adolescents deserve particular attention. In some instances - eg, chronic sickness or disability - the transition to adulthood requires close co-operation between children's departments, and other specialties."* (Welfare of Children and Young People in Hospital, 1991). One of the important features which should be taken into account, in deciding the age range of application of services, is that of the rapid development and change which young people undergo as they grow-up. Services for children and adolescents need to be styled in ways which enable practitioners within them to take into account the impact of development on the presentation, nature and management of problems and disorders. Developmental issues and family relationships also have impact upon the types of services and the facilities required by, and acceptable to, children, young people and parents. Services should be built around staff having a sound understanding of the differing developmental phases of young people, including infancy, young childhood, older childhood, adolescence, and young adulthood, as each poses its own demands. In particular, there is need for increased understanding of adolescence and adolescents and of the normal developmental transitions from childhood to adolescence and on to adulthood (Parry-Jones, 1995).

38   Evidence from the service visits reinforces the long-standing concern of the HAS with youth services. Despite the statutory considerations, which partly define the responsibility of the education and social services authorities, and the organisation, deployment and training of many professionals, the HAS reiterates a recommendation for the generation of services for older young people and young adults. These should be adapted to their circumstances and needs and should relate to mental health services for children and adolescents so that they combine to span an age range of 0 to 25 years. The HAS does not minimise the demands on service organisation and on the collaboration between agencies, in delivering services in this way, but sees the purchaser-provider system as enabling creative, mould-breaking approaches which are tailored to the real needs of those who would use the services.

EPIDEMIOLOGY

39   Rigorous epidemiological studies give fairly consistent figures upon which to base local estimates (Wallace et al 1994).

40   The prevalence of problems, as widely defined here in chapter four, must be considerable and variable. Some sources estimate prevalence as up to 40% of children and adolescents. The overall prevalence of diagnosable mental disorder (now ICD10 or DSM4) in the child population is estimated as up to

25%, with 7-10% having moderate to severe problems (Graham, 1986).
Problems sufficiently severe to be described as disabling were found in 2.1% of
all children aged up to 16, in a national survey of disability carried out by the
OPCS in 1988 (Bone & Meltzer, 1989). Readers are also referred to the work
of Hall and Hill who reviewed the categories, prevalence and incidence of mild
psychological problems in Section 3 of their Chapter on Community Child
Health Services in Health Care Needs Assessment (Stephens and Raftery,
1994).

41   On the basis of these figures, it is now generally accepted that in a total
population of 250,000, of which 20-25% is aged 0 to 18 years, one might
expect between 5,000 and 12,000 children to have a mental health or
psychiatric disorder at any one time. The overall level tends to be higher in the
older age groups because some disorders persist and others arise in older
children (Parry-Jones, 1995). Levels of problems have been found to be twice
as great for children living in inner city environments compared with those living
in rural situations. Commissioners need to be aware of the demographic
profile of the children and young people for whom they hold responsibilities to
ensure that they understand, and can anticipate, the mental disorders which will
arise in the population they serve.

42   Additionally, there is epidemiological information which suggests that the
prevalence of mental health problems in childhood and adolescence is
increasing. Depression is more often recognised in adolescents now and
deliberate self-harm, and particularly substance use and misuse, are increasing.
Readers are referred to the HAS Thematic Review, *Suicide Prevention - The
Challenge Confronted* (HAS, 1994e) for more information on self-harm and
suicide in adolescence.

43   Information indicates that there are differences in the prevalence of child and
adolescent mental health disorders across ethnic groups. However, this is not a
well researched area which requires further study.

THE NATURE OF MENTAL DISORDERS

44   Examples of more mild, but nonetheless impactful and distressing mental health
problems which are frequently the cause of referral to practitioners in the NHS
include:

  •   sleep problems

  •   feeding difficulties

  •   unhappiness, misery, anxiety and social sensitivity

  •   bedwetting

  •   faecal soiling

  •   overactivity

  •   tantrums and oppositional and defiant behaviour problems

  •   abdominal pain without descoverable physical cause (Hall and Hill,
      1994).

45   The nature of mental health disorders in children and young people is
summarised, after *With Health in Mind* (Kurtz, 1992a), by Table 1.

Table 1

A Classification of Mental Disorders	
• Emotional Disorders	eg. phobias, anxiety states and depression. These may be made manifest in physical symptoms such as chronic headache or abdominal pain.
• Conduct Disorders	eg. stealing, defiance, fire-setting, aggression and anti-social behaviour.
• Hyperkinetic Disorders	eg. disturbance of activity and attention, and hyperkinetic conduct disorder.
• Developmental Disorders	eg. delay in acquiring certain skills such as speech, social ability or bladder control. These may affect primarily one area of development or pervade a number of areas as in children with autism and those with pervasive developmental disorders.
• Eating Disorders	eg. pre-school eating problems, anorexia nervosa and bulimia nervosa.
• Habit Disorders	eg. tics, sleeping problems and soiling.
• Post traumatic syndromes	eg. post traumatic stress disorder.
• Somatic disorders	eg. chronic fatigue syndrome.
• Psychotic Disorders	eg. schizophrenia, manic depressive disorder or drug-induced psychoses.

46   Any of these disorders may lead to or be associated with other behaviours, problems or disorders. The association of depressive disorder with conduct problems is increasingly recognised. Conduct disorder is recognised as the precursor par excellence of alcohol, drug and substance misuse. So problems of comorbidity or deliberate self-harm and suicide may arise in many instances.

47   Additionally, it is important to realise that the severity of impact of child and adolescent mental health problems may span a wide range. Some problems can be relatively mild and self-limiting, while, at the other end of the spectrum others can be life-threatening. This latter group can include problems and disorders manifesting in deliberate self-harm, severe eating disorders, abuse, and psychotic conditions. Some children who have a combination of chronic physical illness and mental health problems and disorders may be at risk through non-compliance with treatment for their physical conditions. In between these positions, lie those of a large number of children and adolescents. Many may suffer relatively severe yet treatable problems and disorders in apparent silence.

48   The epidemiology of some of the more common disorders is sketched very briefly here.

   •   Emotional and conduct disorders are the most common and are found, on average, in around 10% of children and 20% of adolescents.

   •   Emotional disorders manifest as persistent fears, anxiety states, phobias, and psychosomatic disorders, or by the expression of distress by physical symptoms. Depression also affects children, at least from school age onwards, and its prevalence increases rapidly in adolescence. Depression lies on a continuum from lowered mood, through misery and into serious depressive disorder. A recent publication, *So Young So Sad So Listen* (Graham and Hughes, 1995) provides a wealth of information which parents, teachers and many managers responsible for planning or developing services will find helpful. The authors estimate that 4 to 5% of children below 12 years of age suffer distress and that 2% of children below 12 years of age suffer depressive symptoms sufficient to warrant a specialist consultation. They also estimate that, in a hypothetical secondary school of 1,000 pupils, their figures would equate to 50 young people being seriously depressed each year, while around 8 children could be seriously depressed and another 16 significantly distressed every year in a primary school of 400 pupils.

- Major depressive disorder is found in about 1% in middle childhood and 2 to 5% in mid-adolescence.

- Conduct disorders include stealing, truancy, aggression, fire-setting, and more persistent delinquency. Delinquency is anti-social behaviour which contravenes the law and is found in 3% of ten to 11 year-olds and is at least, twice as common in urban children. The incidence of first apprehension for criminal activity, mainly offences against property, reaches a peak around the age of 13 to 15 and then declines. Boys are involved seven or eight times more commonly than girls.

- Hyperactivity, in the sense of inattentive restlessness, is a relatively common problem affecting between 10 and 20% of children. When it is the primary and dominating characteristic in a child who is handicapped by it then it becomes the hyperkinetic disorder which affects 1 to 2% of primary school children. However, it is hyperactivity as a phenomenon which has the poor prognosis, being a breeding ground for antisocial behaviour, academic failure and low self-esteem in later childhood. In a recent study, McArdle, O'Brien and Kolvin (1995) showed that the prevalence of pervasive hyperactivity is in the order of 2 to 5% depending on age and urban or rural status.

- Psychotic disorders occur in children from puberty onwards.

- The prevalence of obsessive compulsive disorder in adolescents is in the order of 2%, if a broad definition is taken.

- Suicide is very rare before the age of 12. The rate in 15 to 19 year-olds is 6 per 100,000 for men and 1-2 per 100,000 for women each year. Deliberate self-harm occurs in about 400 per 100,000 each year (cumulatively involving around 3% of adolescents in their teenage years).

- Developmental disorders, such as language delay and autism, can cause severe difficulties. Depending on definition, infantile autism is found in between three and eight children per 10,000 and only 10-15% of these children are likely to be able to lead an independent life. Much less severe, but nonetheless handicapping, conditions include wetting and soiling. These are likely to clear up as the child gets older but are often accompanied by distressing secondary psychological symptoms.

- Severe eating disorders include anorexia nervosa, which occurs in about 1% of 15 to 19 year-old girls and the age of peak incidence is 16. Anorexia nervosa has been found in mid adolescent school populations to occur eight times more commonly in girls who have dieted compared to those who have not. Bulimia nervosa has a greater prevalence, but with a later peak incidence. Both conditions have a much greater prevalence in girls.

- Others include conditions such as tics, which are usually mild and have an excellent outcome are frequent (up to around 10% of both boys and girls). However, they can be severe and constitute a part of a particular syndrome, such as Gilles de la Tourette, which has a much poorer prognosis.

49   The paragraphs in this section review briefly information relating mainly to more established and serious problems and disorders. Readers will find the summaries of more minor problems by Wallace et al. (1995) and Hall and Hill (1994) of assistance in understanding the nature, prevalence and incidence of mild psychological problems and disorders.

Predisposing Factors

50   The following tables list risk factors and are modified after Pearce, J. (1993). Some relate to matters relating to children, others to issues affecting their families and others concern life events.

Table 2

Child Risk Factors
• Genetic influences
• Low IQ and learning disability
• Specific developmental delay
• Communication difficulty
• Difficult temperament
• Physical illness, especially if chronic and/or neurological
• Academic failure
• Low self-esteem

Table 3

Family Risk Factors
• Overt parental conflict
• Family breakdown
• Inconsistent, or unclear discipline
• Hostile and rejecting relationships
• Failure to adapt to child's changing developmental needs
• Abuse - physical, sexual and/or emotional
• Parental psychiatric illness
• Parental criminality, alcoholism and personality disorder
• Death and loss - including loss of friendships

Table 4

Environmental Risk Factors
• Socio-economic disadvantage
• Homelessness
• Disaster
• Discrimination
• Other significant life events

51   Rates of mental health problems and disorder differ according to the type of
environment in which children live and have been shown to relate to a number
of specific factors.   A greater risk of childhood mental health problems and
conditions amounting to disorder are found in:

- *Socio-economic disadvantage*

    An acknowledged risk factor is that which affects families suffering
    socio-economic disadvantage and those where there is family discord.
    These situations are likely to occur when the parents are unemployed,
    divorced, living alone, or homeless. The risk of disorder in the children
    of divorced parents may be increased by a factor of around three.

- *Parental mental disorder*

    Instances when the parents themselves suffer from psychiatric disorder,
    notably maternal depression also raise the risk of disorder in their
    children. For example, about 30% of mothers of pre-school children
    were found to suffer from depression, according to a well respected
    study carried out in an outer London Borough in 1977 (Richman 1977).
    Over half (56.3%) of the children with mild to severe behavioural
    problems had mothers with depression, while the mothers of only 3.3%
    of the children with no problems, were depressed.

- *Abused children*

    Research indicates that about 35% of all physically abused children
    show psychiatric disorders. Often this may take the form of an increase
    in aggressive and violent behaviour. However, it should be recognised
    that there is no one syndrome associated with abuse and a very wide
    range of patterns of response can occur. Some studies have put the
    incidence of disorder as high as 50% and research has found post
    traumatic stress syndromes in a considerable majority of abused
    children. Further study is needed of these areas. Another indicator of
    the impact of abuse is that 4.2 per 1000 children under 18 were on
    local authority child protection registers in England (as at 31 March
    1991) but with variation from 16.4 per 1000 in some Inner London
    Boroughs to 1.2 per 1000 in Hertfordshire. (Department of Health,
    1992).

- *Physical illness*

    Children suffering physical illness, especially chronic conditions such as
    diabetes and cystic fibrosis, and very severe conditions such as
    leukaemia - even after successful treatment are at higher risk of mental
    health problems and disorders (Challen et al, 1988 and 1992 and

Culling and Williams, 1988). Children with sensory deficits such as sight and hearing loss are at special risk and, particularly children who suffer brain injury. The risk of disorder in children with a physical illness has been generally assessed as being twofold and as being three times the average population prevalence if the physical illness is combined with disability. Children with brain disorders may have five times the rate of disorder when compared to the general population and 28% of those with uncomplicated epilepsy and 30% of those with a lesion above the brainstem have been shown to suffer mental disorders. A study of three-year old children showed that significant behaviour disorder was two to three times more frequent in those who had hearing loss due to chronic secretory otitis media compared to the general population at the same age (Barber, Griffiths and Williams, 1992).

- *Children with learning difficulties*

  This is particularly the case when related to reading (Rutter, 1989).

- *Learning disability*

  Rates are particularly high in children with learning disability. It has been found that 40% of children with an IQ below 50 - that is, three to four per 1000 children aged between seven and 16 years, can be expected to have severe mental health problems. (Graham, 1986). Children with an IQ of less than 70 may have a prevalence of disorder which is up to four times that of the general population.

- *Multiply disabled children*

  The extent of multiple disability in children was reported in the 1988 OPCS national survey of disability (Bone and Meltzer 1989). Three and a half percent of 0 to 15 year-olds had disabilities that interfered with their capacity to carry out daily activities. Of these, virtually two-thirds also had a disabling mental health condition.

- *Young offenders*

  Young offenders experience particularly high rates of mental health problems. A diagnosis of a primary mental disorder can be made in a third of young men aged between 16 to 18 years who have been sentenced by a court (Gunn et al, 1991).

52 The intention of this section has been to illustrate the impact of risk factors on the prevalence of disorders. Again readers are referred to Wallace et al. (1995) for a more extended consideration.

RESILIENCE TO PROBLEMS AND DISORDER

53 In recent times, attention has been directed to understanding why it is that many children who suffer adverse circumstances and a combination of the risk factors cited above do not develop problems or a disorder (Garmezy, 1985; Goodyer et al, 1988, 1990; Rutter, 1989, 1990). Research has shown three key groups of factors which appear to protect children and adolescents. They are:

- Self-esteem, sociability and autonomy

- Family compassion, warmth and absence of parental discord

- Social support systems that encourage personal effort and coping

CHAPTER 5

*The National Survey
of Mental Health
Services for Children
and Young People*

54   Services for the mental health of children and young people span health promotion, prevention, identification, diagnosis, treatment, care and rehabilitation. A survey carried out in England, in 1993, shows the extent to which the NHS is joined by the social services, education, the police and the voluntary sector in offering these services. This report is based on answers provided in self-report questionnaires (Kurtz, Thornes & Wolkind, 1994).

55   Parents and family members are all-important as informal carers. Services may be directed at supporting them. In addition, the wider environment and almost every aspect of society and how it is organised - from housing and employment, to leisure facilities - can have a major impact.

56   A number of important services such as antenatal care, are not designated explicitly as addressing mental health, nor perhaps as children's services. However, they form a context for, and have relationships with, the services for children and adolescents that identify mental health as a central concern and have improved mental health as a clear outcome of intervention. The national survey focused upon the latter services while taking account of the former.

57   A chief finding was the remarkable variation across the country both in purchasing and in the pattern of provision of services.

PURCHASING

Strategy

58   Information was based on a 58% response from 122 purchasing authorities, with a good spread across the regions and counties of England and no bias according to urban or rural situation. Just over half of responding authorities had carried out developmental work on a specific strategy for mental health services for children and young people and just over half of these had a strategy in use. In developing a strategy, purchasing authorities reported that they had consulted with the child and adolescent specialist mental health service and, variably, with a range of other relevant departments including acute and/or community paediatrics, adult mental health services, social services, education, the voluntary sector, general practitioners (GPs) and the family health services authority (FHSA). Five authorities reported consulting with all of these and a further 17 (together totalling a third of all respondents), with at least four other departments. Discussions had been held most often with social services (89%) but in only 61% of instances with the local education authority (LEA).

Service Specification

59   In three-fifths of responding authorities, child and adolescent services were specified separately from adult mental health services and in 9% they formed part of a specification for all children's services. The specification was couched in very general terms in 12% of authorities which did not even name or define the child and adolescent mental health service. In 42% of authorities, different elements of the service such as clinical psychology, psychotherapy, counselling or social work were named. A multi-disciplinary approach was identified by 17%, and 15% of authorities highlighted the provision of both community and inpatient care. Further details such as itemised treatments (eg. group therapy, behaviour modification) were mentioned by a third of authorities; less than a

fifth specified the types of problems such as developmental disorders or conduct disorders, that providers would be expected to cover. Ten authorities (7%) included both treatments and types of disorder in their specification.

Contracts

60   A single contract covered community, day and inpatient care for children and for adolescents in a fifth of authorities. Every authority had a contract with named provider units for inpatient care or else mentioned that they used extra-contractual referrals (ECRs) (8%), a block regional contract or a subscription system (7%). However, 30% of the provider units that were named returned information indicating that they had no psychiatric inpatient facilities for children or young people. These contracts could well have been with adult services or with acute hospital units where the child and adolescent psychiatrist has access to beds on the children's ward. Two-thirds of purchasers said they had a contract for day patient care but, once again, in many instances, the provider unit named did not appear to offer this type of care. Treatment on a day basis was often not differentiated from the community services as a whole. In most cases, the work of clinical psychologists was included within wider contracts but separate contracts were specified by 10 authorities. In nine authorities (13%), the main contract included services to be provided in education or social services and a small number were beginning to move towards integrated contracts with other agencies.

Services for Adolescents

61   Older adolescents were included in the same contract as younger age groups in 28% of authorities; in 16% they were included in contracts for adult mental health services by design and, in 17%, by default. There were separate contracts for older adolescents in six authorities but these covered a wider range of inpatient provision than mental health. In 15% of authorities, it was not clear where adolescents were placed.

62   The upper age limit varied from 16 to 21 years. The need for flexibility was frequently acknowledged and the occasional authority (6%) had made provision for this in contracts. A lower cut-off age was often found in contracts for community services, when these were separate from inpatients. Fifteen authorities (22%) classed 16 year-olds as adults unless they were still in full-time education, in which case they were seen by the child and adolescent service. Two authorities felt this to be illogical and were considering the matter as part of a service review. Generally, there was a feeling that this age group missed out on services.

Contracting for Particular Aspects of Mental Health Services

63   Elements of service for children's mental health were included in a variety of contracts, such as those for drug and alcohol services, in 23% of which children and young people were mentioned. In 57% of authorities, contracts for children with learning disabilities mentioned a mental health service input and 33% of authorities made specific mention of the mental health of children and young people in their health promotion contracts. More than a quarter of authorities (29%) either had contracts for preventive services such as Head

Start or they supported the service with a grant. Twenty-six per cent of authorities had additional contracts for psychotherapy, forensic psychiatry and for special services such as bereavement.

The Basis for Purchasing

64 Overall, purchasing was most commonly based on historical provision and this was the sole basis in more than a third (38%) of authorities. Reference to local statistics such as numbers of homeless families and numbers on the child protection register was made by 20% of authorities. Consumer surveys had been used by 16%. A deprivation index was used by four authorities and these were among the seven (10%) that based their specification on a formal needs assessment. In summary, only nine authorities (13%) were purchasing in relation to the needs of their population in some way ie. on the basis of either a formal needs assessment or at least three other indicators of need. Quality standards were included by 32% of purchasers but plans for evaluation were largely undeveloped; 23% felt that co-operation in this with other agencies would be important. The commonest approach was to monitor against listed quality standards (29% of authorities). Others suggested using consumers' views and surveys and discussion with GPs.

Expenditure

65 Financial data was gathered from 28 NHS purchasers. One reason for the poor response related to the difficulty, which many purchasers reported, in separating their spending on child and adolescent services from general expenditure on mental health. However, many purchasers reported that segregated purchasing was a planned future development.

66 When capital charges and GP fundholder (GPFH) reductions were included, the mean contracted expenditure by NHS purchasers was £3.76 million in 1993-94. With other combinations of inclusion/exclusion of capital charges and GPFH reductions, the mean contracted expenditure was between £0.32m and £0.53m. On average, these contracts purchased between three and five services.

Grading Purchaser Development

67 An exploratory exercise was carried out in grading both the purchase and the provision of services into three broad categories representing good, adequate and poor. The criteria used were very elementary, based on what would generally be considered a good service. The scoring system was also kept extremely simple, thus avoiding statistical complication through the addition of weightings - the only scores allocated were 1 and 0, representing 'good' and 'poor'. For each criterion, the research team decided, after full discussion, the distinction between good and poor. Sixty-nine purchasing authorities returned useable information. The other 53 purchasing authorities could not be graded. The highest possible score was 10 and only one authority achieved this score. Four authorities received only one mark. The distribution of purchasing authorities is shown in Figure 2.

Figure 2

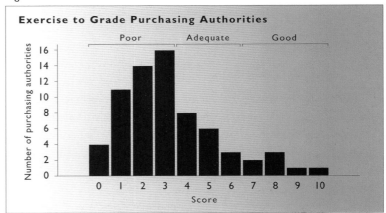

It can be seen that 10% fell into the good category, 25% into adequate and 65% into poor.

PROVISION OF SERVICES: THE STAFFING AND ROLES OF SERVICE COMPONENTS

Child and Adolescent Mental Health Services

68   A response was obtained from 139 (81%) of the 186 services surveyed. The great majority (94%) of child and adolescent mental health services were community-based. One fifth were an integral part of units which also provided inpatient care, while one-tenth also provided day care. Seventy per cent of units provided a clinic service only.

69   Within the community services, 245 consultant psychiatrist whole-time equivalents (WTEs) were employed, with a range of 0 to 7 per department (Table 5). There was less than one WTE consultant in 15% of services and 40% had between one and two. The child population (aged 0 to 18 years) of the districts served by the responding provider units was analysed in relation to the number of WTE consultants and it was found that the number of children per WTE consultant psychiatrist ranged from 6,403 to 244,135 with a mean of 41,180. For a child population of 100,000, the number of WTEs ranged from

Figure 3

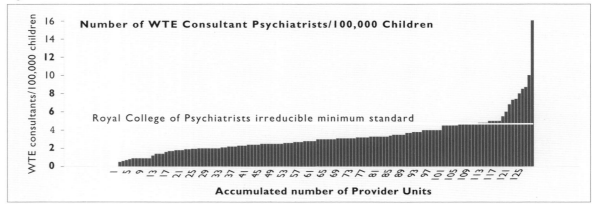

0.41 to 15.62 (Figure 3).

70   Of other professional staff employed, social workers were the most numerous
and worked in a greater proportion of units, with the exception of consultant
psychiatrists. Psychotherapists were unevenly spread across the country, with
92% employed in the four Thames and the, Wessex, Oxford and South
Western regions. Of the 87 units that employed a community psychiatric
nurse, only a third (34%) had even one nurse with specific training in child and
adolescent psychiatric care (ENB 603). Altogether, there were 122 (47%)
community psychiatric nurses with this qualification but 109 out of a total of
260 had done some other post-basic qualification training. However, the type
and level of training varied widely, from counselling and family therapy to drama
and art therapy.

Table 5

Professional Staff in Community Services (n=139)

	Number of staff (wte)		Number of provider units		
	Total	Range in individual units	With (%)	Without	No response
• Consultant psychiatrists	245.2	0 - 7.0	138 (99.3)	1	0
• Junior medical staff	136.4	0 - 8.0	80 (57.6)	58	1
• Non-training medical staff	31.5	0 - 2.1	54 (38.8)	85	0
• Clinical psychologists	146.5	0 - 5.0	96 (69.1)	43	0
• Educational psychologists	52.5	0 - 11.0	15 (10.8)	124	0
• Psychotherapists	91.1	0 - 4.6	61 (43.9)	78	0
• Family therapists	29.9	0 - 3.3	23 (16.5)	116	0
• Outpatient/clinic nurses	259.9	0 - 13.0	87 (62.6)	51	1
• Social workers	304.1	0 - 14.0	113 (81.3)	26	0

71   The survey revealed an almost equal incidence of no change, of a reduction or
of an increase in staffing levels. The greatest change in the last three years has
been the loss of social workers, in 30% of the units. Educational psychologists
had been largely withdrawn by 1990 and only a further 6% of units had been
affected by losses since then. Forty per cent of replies stated that the input of
trainees was necessary to maintain the current level of service.

72   Waiting lists for clinics had increased in 66% of units. In 58% of the units, the
waiting time for a first appointment was reported as between five and 13 weeks
but in 10%, it was more than six months.

Inpatient Care

73   The survey identified a total of 62 NHS inpatient units and information was
received from 37 of these.   A third (32%) had contracts with one purchasing
authority and a further 22% with two. The rest had multiple contracts. There
were differences compared to community mental health services with regard to
staffing, with the employment of ward nurses, and also in relation to medical
staff (Table 6). Almost a third of all consultant psychiatrists (32%) worked in
inpatient units and only 8% of units had less than one WTE consultant; 51% had
two or more WTEs. Ninety-five per cent had junior medical staff in training
and in 69% of units, trainees were necessary to maintain the current level of
service. Only 18% of nurses working in inpatient units had the ENB603
although only four units had no nurse with this qualification.

Table 6

Staffing of Services	Provider Units with these staff (%)	
Staffing in the Child and Adolescent Mental Health Service: Community Units and Inpatient Services		
	Community Services	Inpatient units
• Consultant psychiatrists	99	100
• Junior medical staff	58	95
• Non-training medical staff	39	32
• Clinical psychologists	69	76
• Educational psychologists	11	0
• Psychotherapists	44	32
• Family Therapists	17	19
• Inpatient nurses	0	92
• Outpatient/clinic nurses	63	54
• Social workers	81	70
• Occupational therapists	0	65
• Speech therapists	0	5
• Teachers	0	89

74   Twenty-five per cent of the units catered for both children and adolescents, a further 25% for children only, and 50% for adolescents only. Eighty per cent of the units provided day treatment as well as inpatient care. Sixty per cent functioned on a seven-day basis but only half of the units for children were open at the weekend, while 78% of those accepting adolescents were open at weekends. Most referrals came from GPs, although access to some units was entirely via the specialist child and adolescent mental health team. However, 15% had used private hospitals for inpatient care and 63% occasionally used adult psychiatric wards.

Day Treatment Services

75   Treatment was provided on a day basis by a quarter of provider units overall and was most frequently linked to inpatient facilities. In about 10% of cases, education or social services facilities such as schools for pupils with emotional and behavioural difficulties (EBD) were used. To maximise opportunities for treatment on a day basis, 13% of providers organised a 'package' of outpatient visits. This service was mostly better staffed than the community units, in that 95% had at least one WTE consultant and 89% had junior medical staff. Seventy-eight per cent had a clinical psychologist and 84% a social worker. There were also more community psychiatric nurses, the median being four.

Emergency Cover and Self-Harm

76   Child and adolescent psychiatrists provided emergency cover in 69% of districts. In these 96 districts, 3,702 children and young people had been admitted for deliberate self-harm in the previous 12 months, ranging in age from six to 19 years, but 88% of the psychologists said that there was no specific service, except for follow-up outpatient appointments. Only a small proportion (12%) reported that they had an active input into the substance abuse service, and a further 9% described their input as 'token'.

Services Provided for Others

77   A substantial contribution was made to paediatrics, with a third (36%) of departments providing five or more sessions (half-day duration) per month; of these 8% provided more than 20 sessions a month. However, 19% (32% if non responders are included) of specialist departments provided no services to paediatrics. Figure four shows the number of CAMHS which reported that they provided sessions regularly to paediatric and a range of other children's services. For reasons of clarity CAMHS which provided sessions on an irregular or ad hoc basis are not shown separately in figure four from those which provided no sessions.

Figure 4

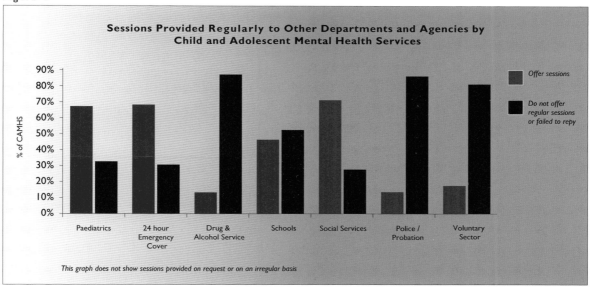

78   Only 11% provided sessions in general practice, the majority on the basis of one session a week. One hundred and thirty-two home visits had been undertaken at the request of the GP in the previous 12 months by the 245 consultants. However, many added that a great many more home visits had been made by members of their staff, especially the community psychiatric nurses.

79   As far as schools were concerned, 28% of services did five or more regular sessions per month, 31% did only occasional or less than five sessions a month, 37% did none in schools.

80   Thirty-five per cent of departments provided more than five sessions a month for social services departments, 43% provided only occasional or less than four sessions a month, and 17% (28% if no responders are included) provided none. Eighteen per cent of departments provided occasional sessions for the police and 8% for the probation service. Thirty-seven per cent did sessions for voluntary sector agencies. In a small number of cases (2%), these comprised between five and 20 sessions a month. Overall, 15% provided no services, or very limited services for other departments. Where a service was provided, it was invariably a small number of sessions in paediatrics or for social services.

Training

81   Eighty-eight per cent of respondents gave the proportion of time that professional staff spent on training, supervising, teaching, team development and staff support as between 10% and 40%, most frequently 10%. For 53%, training was part of their contract; for 30% it was not; and for 7% the situation was unclear. Fifteen per cent provided training just for the students or trainees in their own disciplines, but 62% provided training and support for a wide range of professionals in both the NHS and other agencies.

Referrals

82   Departments varied enormously in the source of their referrals (Table 7). With regard to self-referral, a mixed picture emerged. Fifty-nine per cent of departments had received self-referrals (from child, young person or families) in the previous 12 months, although, in some cases, only re-referrals were accepted. However, these made up percentages ranging from 0% to 62% of total referrals. When analysed in terms of individual clinics, it was found that 45% of clinics were willing to accept self-referral of new patients.

83   The main referrers were GPs from 5% to 90%, with a median value of 42%. There were similar wide variations in percentages of referrals from paediatrics (0% to 60%) and social services departments (0% to 45%).

Table 7

Source of Referrals to Community Child and Adolescent Specialist Mental Health Services (C & AP) and to Clinical Psychology (CP)						
	Services with no referrals from this source (%)		Percentage of referrals			
			Range		Median	
	C & AP	CP	C & AP	CP	C & AP	CP
● General practitioner	0	4	5 - 90	0 - 100	42	30
● Community paediatrics	7	5	0 - 60	0 - 80	10	15
● Hospital paediatrics	5	9	0 - 35	0 - 100	10	15
● Social services	7	15	0 - 45	0 - 75	10	8
● Child, parent or family	41	40	0 - 62	0 - 57	3	1
● Schools	-	21	-	0 - 40	-	4
● Other	38	-	0 - 75	-	2	-

Clinical Psychology Services

84   In some areas, clinical psychology services could be identified as working independently from child and adolescent psychiatry services. In these, 40% of clinical psychology services accepted virtually no self-referrals. However in five services, more than one-third of patients were self-referred and the maximum was 57%. All except seven services received referrals from general practitioners, the proportion ranged from 0% to 100% and the median was 30%. Paediatricians were the second most important source of referral, especially those working in community child health. In five services all referrals were from paediatrics. In twelve services (7%), all referrals were from just two sources, invariably general practitioners and paediatrics. Social services were the

next most important source, accounting for as many as 75% of referrals in some cases, although 15% of departments received no referrals from this source. Teachers, educational psychologists and educational welfare officers also made small numbers of referrals, while 21% of services received no referrals from schools.

85   Some care, on a uni-disciplinary basis, was provided by 67% of clinical psychology services and 25% had separate contracts with GP fundholders. Many clinical psychologists worked regular sessions with acute paediatrics, on the wards (36% of the services) and in outpatients (46%). Figure five shows the number of clinical psychology departments which reported that they provided sessions regularly to paediatric and a range of other children's services. For reasons of clarity, clinical psychology departments which provided sessions on an irregular or ad hoc basis are not shown separately in figure five from those which provided no sessions.

Figure 5

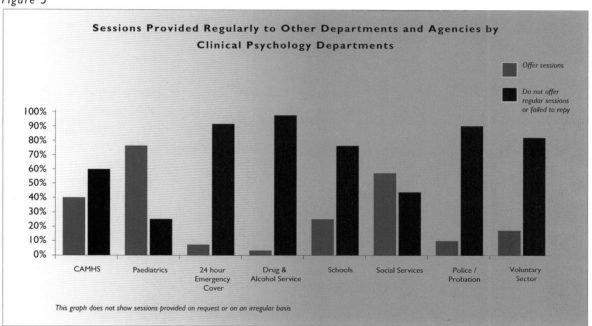

86   Sessions were provided, as required, by 27% in cases of deliberate self-harm and by 29% in cases of emergency admission for abuse. Even more (61%) provided sessions in child development clinics and in 20% of the services this amounted to more than 20 sessions, although a further 16% said they were only occasionally called in. The third most important area of work was for social services, with a regular commitment from 57% of clinical psychology departments. However, 10% said that they provided no sessions and a further 16% were only occasionally called in.

87   Fewer clinical psychologists were involved in schools. Only 8% of services gave more than the occasional session in mainstream schools, but 18% provided regular sessions in special schools for children with learning difficulties, physical disabilities or sensory impairment. The total time provided to schools for children with emotional and behavioural problems was far less since little regular commitment was reported, although 32% provided sessions on an occasional basis.

88   On a smaller scale, sessions were provided for the police and probation services by 10% of services, primarily on an occasional basis, but for some there were regular training sessions. Similarly, 10% of services provided a small input to drug and alcohol services (2% provided a regular input). A third (32%) worked with the voluntary sector, helping in particular with training and management.

89   Training was undertaken by 98% of services and most had at least one clinical psychology trainee. Thirty-nine per cent also provided training for a wide variety of professions, including the police and NHS primary care staff, and in 62% this was part of their contract.

90   In spite of clear indications nationally of growth in this speciality (Hughes, Garralda and Tylee, 1994), 44% of services had seen no change in the number of clinical psychologists, although 30% reported that an increase was planned for the next year. In the previous 12 months, 61% of clinical psychology services had reduced their waiting lists and only 3% reported an increase. However, 35% had a waiting time of more than three months for an appointment for a non-urgent condition, although 10% had a waiting time of four weeks or less.

Costs

91   Costs and expenditure were analysed for nine child and adolescent psychiatry inpatient units and 29 units without beds and for 14 clinical psychology departments. Variation between these was found in the proportion of costs accounted for by staff, by capital expenditure etc, and in average cost per case. The possible causes for variation are discussed in the full report and hypotheses suggested for the determinants of costs and their relation to outcome (Kurtz, Thornes and Wolkind, 1994).

Paediatric Services

92   A response was obtained from the hospital or the community department of paediatrics or both, in the areas of 90% of district health authorities. This indicated that the paediatric profession deals with more children and young people with emotional and behavioural disorders than any other single discipline. Nearly one-third of community paediatricians reported that over 20% of children are referred to them primarily because of emotional and behavioural disorders, while 12% of paediatricians in hospital departments reported this. Seventy-six per cent had managed a child with a serious psychiatric illness - eg anorexia - on their wards in the past year.

93   Hospital and community paediatricians reported differences in their sources of referral, as well as in the proportions that they refer on for specialist consultation. All hospital paediatricians received referrals from GPs and 16% from health visitors and school nurses. While 64% of community paediatricians had referrals from GPs, 83% also received direct referrals from health visitors and school nurses. In addition, over half of the community paediatricians had referrals from teachers and educational psychologists, and 16% took referral directly from parents. In 48% of community departments, the school health service is a more important source of referral than pre-school. Hospital paediatricians also received referrals from the community child health services - this was reported by 28% of units.

94 The range and type of condition treated in both hospital and the community are remarkably similar, community paediatricians having a higher profile of work related to child abuse and to schooling and education, such as school refusal.

95 Many paediatric departments held special clinics for patients whose problems had a major mental health component, for example for enuresis or encopresis, bereavement and cot death. Also mentioned were sleep problems and special input to clinics for childhood cancer, diabetes and cystic fibrosis.

96 Given the level of referrals to paediatricians, it is important to highlight the widespread concern among paediatricians themselves at their lack of training in dealing with children with emotional and behavioural problems. For example, only 39% of hospital paediatricians and 31% of community paediatricians felt adequately prepared by their training for this kind of work. Moreover, at least two-thirds stated that local specialist resources for children's mental health were woefully inadequate, very limited, overwhelmed by referrals, fragmented or with enormous waiting lists. Nearly one-third of community paediatricians felt that there was inadequate provision for the emotional and behavioural difficulties of children with disabilities.

Social Services

97 The table below indicates the range of child and adolescent mental health services provided by social services departments. While 17% of departments were found to have no formal or written policy on assessment and therapeutic services for children with emotional and behavioural problems, all others included these aspects in a policy for children in need, under the Children Act 1989. Forty-six per cent of authorities were either working on, or had already developed, joint policies or joint commissioning with the NHS.

Table 8

Services Provided by Social Services Departments which Related to the Mental Health of Children and Adolescents	
Social services replies from 59/108 departments, covering 62% of DHAs	% of departments providing a service
• Own services or programmes, specifically for children with mental health problems	64
• NHS - Child and family community clinics	58
• NHS - Child development clinics	51
• NHS - Acute paediatric services	49
• Direct input to schools	54
• Voluntary sector	61

98 Major restructuring within social services departments, over the past three years, was evident from the responses received and highlighted the greater emphasis now given to child protection and to formal assessments, with a resulting reduction in ongoing therapeutic work with families. One-tenth of departments mentioned that they had made a clear shift in support of multi-agency or jointly funded work. The views held by social services' staff of current mental health services within the NHS were, however, fairly unfavourable, stressing difficulties in access and concern over the way in which referrals were given priority. Thirty-seven per cent of departments mentioned

uneven development, lack of skills or expertise in certain areas, and insufficient availability of clinical psychology or psychotherapy.

Education

Local Education Authorities

99 The response to the survey from local education authorities (LEAs) was poor (27%), but 59% of those replying had developed a policy for pupils in mainstream education who had, or were at risk of, emotional and behavioural problems. A further 17% were currently reviewing their policy. The majority (over 80%) described a policy based on a staged system for service provision, with individual schools undertaking the first stage of observation and primary intervention, with county-wide or borough-wide support services involved at a second stage. All authorities employed educational welfare officers. But the availability of specialist resources for child and adolescent mental health from other agencies was considered poor or very poor by 66% of LEA respondents.

Educational Psychologists

100 There were wide differences across authorities and in different types of school in the proportion of time which educational psychologists spent on direct work. Educational psychologists working in mainstream schools estimated that they spent an average of 45% (standard deviation 26%) of their time on direct work. In special schools and units for children with emotional and behavioural difficulties, they spent an average of 17% of their time (standard deviation 11%) on direct work. In other special schools, even less time was spent on direct work: an average of 16% in schools for children with learning disabilities, 15% in schools for children with sensory impairment and 15% in schools for children with physical disabilities. In the past three years, the proportion of time spent on direct work had remained unchanged in 51% of services, but it had reduced in 38%. In three-fifths (60%), there were no plans to change the input, but 17% were planning to do more direct work in the next 12 months.

101 Less than half (47%) of educational psychology services worked in child guidance or child and family clinics in which case they spent, on average, only 10% of their time in this setting. Where this input was maintained, the LEA continued to pay for teachers or secretarial staff and, occasionally, social workers.

Special Schools for Children with Emotional and Behavioural Difficulties

102 Responses were received from 165 schools, approximately 55% of those in the country as a whole. In 80% of cases, special schools reported that help from the referring agency was minimal and that they offered inadequate resources. For example, children rarely received visits from specialists from the referring agency. Eighty-six per cent of schools did not feel that the NHS provided the resources that the children needed. Head teachers estimated that 46% of their pupils needed therapeutic help, while 14% of pupils had statements specifying specialist therapeutic help, and only 9% were actually receiving this. Sixty-four per cent of EBD schools had not been visited by a child and adolescent psychiatrist in the past year. To a limited extent, clinical psychologists, counsellors and therapists were employed directly by schools.

Non-Statutory Organisations

103 A detailed survey was carried out by Young Minds in two regions to assess the range and type of services provided by the non-statutory sector. In Yorkshire, 154 independent or semi-independent organisations were found. Of these, 42% were classified as providing a service for a range of general problems of concern to young people. Ninety per cent accepted self-referrals - the most common method of access. Many had strong links with other agencies and a third said they received referrals from all statutory agencies, including the police and the probation service. Sources of funding were varied and few relied entirely on one source. Fifty-one per cent received some local authority funding, including grants from social services, education and housing departments. Six percent specifically mentioned joint funding from health and social services, and 8% received some funding from central government, including the Home Office and the Department of the Environment. Direct charges or contracts were made by 6% of non-statutory services.

DISCUSSION

Some General Conclusions

104 This survey maps out the very wide range of services that contribute to the promotion of the mental health of children and young people and to the treatment of their problems. Information was not collected directly about activity in primary care, although this is clearly an area where problems can be picked up at an early stage and children and families at risk can be identified. These possibilities for early intervention must be exploited and strengthened. However, this will require development in the knowledge and skills of both doctors and nurses working in primary care and an expansion of the employment of specialist therapists and others. There are encouraging initiatives such as a newly available booklet about children's mental health problems for GPs (Hughes, Garralda and Tylee, 1994). The survey reported in this chapter revealed how very little specialists in mental health - child and adolescent psychiatrists and psychologists - currently offer by way of consultation to primary health care teams and also to others such as paediatricians who feel that their expertise needs to be developed.

105 A recurring theme was the need to develop skills in the field of mental health among all who work with children and young people, and to strengthen appropriate training opportunities. In this respect, the time spent in consultation and training by the specialists - child and adolescent psychiatrists and educational and clinical psychologists - is currently very variable. Its value needs to be acknowledged and safeguarded in contracts. It is clear that in other respects also, the work of these specialists is very variable - some providing virtually a primary service and others a more restricted tertiary service. The survey found no evidence that, in general, the level or type of service was based on strategic planning to meet defined needs of the local child population. No relationship was found between the provision of specialists and indicators of likely need such as the Jarman index of deprivation (Figure 6).

Figure 6

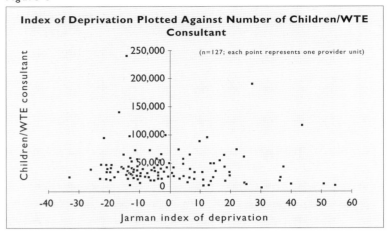

106 This limits the possible ways in which a good or a poor quality service can be evaluated, least of all in terms of cost-effectiveness. However, a preliminary attempt at suggesting criteria that would allow such evaluation has been made as a consequence of this survey. Further work needs to be carried out to validate these criteria and relate them to outcomes for the health of children and young people.

107 This survey leads to the conclusion that commissioning services according to local need is, as yet, undeveloped but provides opportunities to influence service distribution, design and functioning. Other influences are having a major impact upon work in this field. These include the responsibilities of social services for child protection which also signposts a wider need for attention to the emotional and mental well-being of children at risk and their families. Other responsibilities of the social services departments, under the Children Act 1989, and of LEAs, under the Education Acts, have increased the requirement for formal assessments. Frequently, these should include expert mental health input. A significant proportion of children with the greatest needs, in terms of emotional and behavioural disorder, reside in local authority accommodation and in special schools. These newly charted dimensions of need among children and their families stress the importance of the education, social and mental health services working closely together. This should extend to joint commissioning and purchasing of services and an agreed, shared agenda for evaluation.

108 Professionals from whatever discipline who work in these services should regularly take part in multi-disciplinary audit, within a spirit of collaboration, to define and refine their respective skills and roles. Resources are limited and it is essential that they are deployed and developed in the most appropriate and complementary way for the prevention, treatment, care and management of mental health problems in children, young people and their families.

RECOMMENDATIONS ARISING FROM THIS SURVEY

109 The National Survey of Mental Health Services for Children and Young People, reported here, enabled its conductors to make a number of recommendations (Kurtz, Thornes and Wolkind, 1994). They are repeated here as they are consistent with the findings from the other work reported in this review and thus form a base upon which the advice arising from this review is structured.

- It is crucial that purchasing becomes more sophisticated, and is developed in line with a more expert multi-disciplinary assessment of needs. All the relevant disciplines must take part in purchasing decision-making, which should include the views of children and families. Effective services should be clearly and comprehensively specified in primary, secondary and tertiary care.

- The appropriate professional input and the core skills needed in mental health teams working with particular child populations should be defined and specified in contracts. There are significant training implications for every profession currently working in this field.

- There is a case for more realistic use of child and adolescent psychiatrists and clinical psychologists. In any event, the availability of child and adolescent psychiatrists for consultation and training must be increased.

- It is of prime importance that mechanisms are established to ensure that all disciplines in the child mental health field work with regular reference to each other and to agreed, shared objectives.

- Regular clinical audit should be carried out jointly by professionals who work together with particular groups of children, to increase understanding of each other's particular skills and to improve practice by means such as the development of criteria for inter-disciplinary referrals.

- The employment of nurses and occupational therapists should be encouraged, but their training for this type of work should be developed in appropriate ways and adequately funded.

- The role of health visitors in this field should be examined and their expertise in the promotion of child and family health and in preventive programmes should be developed.

- There is urgent need for rational planning of inpatient care. This should be based on further research to identify provision that is appropriate to the needs for inpatient care that differ for children and for young people.

- The general professional training of paediatricians should include a greater component of child mental health.

- The Department for Education's initiative in developing Whole School Behaviour Programmes should be strongly supported and their adoption by every school encouraged.

- Better inter-sectoral understanding of the mental health needs of children in special schools and in residential care must be developed. Joint purchasing agreements should ensure that adequate and appropriate resources are readily and routinely available for children in these settings and for the support and training of teaching and care staff.

- The respective roles of each of the professional disciplines working for the mental health of children and young people should be delineated in a spirit of collaboration by the respective colleges and national bodies, so that improvements can be made in service specification to meet needs and so that staff development can be planned and supported.

- There is an urgent need to improve access for social services department staff to health service expertise in children's mental health for assessments and therapeutic work.

- Complementary provision by voluntary organisations should be supported by appropriate purchasing mechanisms and should be subject to evaluation as are the statutory services. Ways should be found to make full use of, and to support, the highly specialised expertise that resides in voluntary organisations.

- It is vital that finance mechanisms are introduced which allow the costs of child and adolescent mental health to be separated from adult mental health services, and which allow the total expenditure on child and adolescent mental health services to be identified. This data should be made available and included in service audits.

- Exploration of financial data is particularly important in some areas of child and adolescent mental health services where very labour-intensive services are required. There is a need to move towards purchasing and providing child and adolescent mental health services based on data that clearly identifies the components of a cost-effective service.

- All sectors need to confront the central importance of the mental health of children and young people in their particular areas of work and to develop an understanding that they share many objectives and that common investment is likely to be cost-effective. These objectives will be best met if services are regularly reviewed by a planning group on which are represented the three statutory agencies and members from the voluntary sector.

Acknowledgement

110 The work reported in this chapter was conducted by Dr Z Kurtz, Mrs R Thornes and Dr S Wolkind and was supported by a grant from the Department of Health. The HAS is indebted to them for allowing the Steering Committee access to their work and for preparing this chapter.

CHAPTER 6

*The National Survey
of Commissioning of
Child and Adolescent
Mental Health
Services*

BACKGROUND

111 Since the introduction of the NHS reforms, contracts with providers have become the main mechanism by which district health authorities (DHAs) can achieve planned change in the NHS. Recent policy statements have stressed the importance of the commissioning process as a means of improving health care, and have recommended that purchasers develop contracts which focus on the needs of patients, include health gain targets, specify clear service objectives, and provide incentives and sanctions. It has been emphasised that more effective contracts require improved commissioning and purchasing processes, which should include consultation with patients and clinicians, the assessment of local need through improved information systems, an awareness of the results of clinical audit and treatment evaluations, and open and explicit negotiations with providers (Mawhinney & Nichol, 1993).

112 The steps needed to develop effective commissioning and purchasing strategies for mental illness were identified in several of the papers presented at the Consensus Meetings organised by the NHS Health Advisory Service during 1992 (NHS Health Advisory Service 1994 a, b, c, d). Since then, detailed guidance on meeting national objectives for mental health services has been issued by the Department of Health in a *Key Areas Handbook* (Department of Health, 1994), the Welsh Office in a *Protocol for Investment in Health Gain - Mental Health* (Welsh Health Planning Forum, 1993), and the Mental Health Task Force in *Local Systems of Support* (Mental Health Task Force, 1994). Reviews of the needs and provision for people with a severe mental illness have also been published by the Mental Health Foundation (1994) in *Creating Community Care*, and by the Audit Commission in *Finding a Place* (Audit Commission, 1994). None of these recent reviews consider child and adolescent mental health services.

113 In 1993, Ministers extended the remit of the HAS by giving it explicit responsibilities for monitoring the quality of health care and advising purchasers. HAS visits to local services have generated anecdotal information and led to a number of publications on commissioning. These have included one on comprehensive community mental health services (Muth, 1994) and a second on commissioning child and adolescent mental health services (Williams and Farrar, 1994).

114 However, there have been few systematic analyses of the impact of the purchasing process on the quality of services received by people with a mental illness, and none of the initial evaluations of the impact of the NHS reforms included studies of mental health services.

THE HAS REVIEW OF THE COMMISSIONING OF SERVICES FOR VULNERABLE PEOPLE

115 The HAS, therefore, initiated a review of commissioning, strategy and contract documentation and of the commissioning process for mental health services in England and Wales. The intentions of this review were to:

- Clarify and develop the knowledge and opinions of the HAS about the present state of commissioning and purchasing of mental health services.

- Provide baseline information on the realities of commissioning to help create an agenda for purchaser development.

- Provide objective data which will enable the HAS to advise on good practice in commissioning mental health services.

- Identify the tools required by commissioners to develop their own expertise.

- Contribute to the current HAS thematic reviews through specific analyses of the information collected.

116 The review comprised three main investigations:

1. *An Analysis of Commissioning Documentation in England and Wales*

    This study involved a systematic analysis of the contents of health strategies, purchasing plans and contracts for mental health services produced by DHAs in England and Wales for 1993-4 and 1994-5. This work was completed by the Centre for Research and Information into Mental Disability (CRIMD) at the University of Birmingham.

2. *The Analysis of the Commissioning Process*

    This study included 20 health districts in England and Wales, selected at random. In each district, interviews were completed with senior managers and clinicians in the main NHS mental health providers, with the purchasing team for mental health in the DHA, with two GPFH practices, and with purchasers and providers in the local social services department. This work was also completed by CRIMD.

3. *A Review of London Purchasing Plans*

    This study involved an analysis of purchasing plans for mental health services in 1993-4 and 1994-5 prepared by the health authorities comprising the London Implementation Zone (LIZ). This work drew on recent research in the field of purchasing in other sectors, and was completed by the Kings Fund College.

117 The commissioning documentation, assembled for these investigations, forms the *NHS Health Advisory Service's Library of Commissioning*, located at the University of Birmingham, and provides a major resource for the analysis of purchasing in mental health.

118 Ninety-nine (88%) of the health authorities, health commissions and purchasing consortia that were approached returned their documents for 1993-94 to the HAS Library. This chapter summarises the key themes which have emerged from the review of this documentation for 1993-94 and the review of the commissioning process in 1994 relating to child and adolescent mental health services.

STRATEGY DEVELOPMENT

119 This section presents a summary of the findings relating to mental health services generally as they also apply to child and adolescent mental health services.

120 The analysis of purchasing documentation found that over one-third (35%) of health authorities in England and Wales had either completed a strategy for

their mental health services generally during the year preceding the survey, or had a strategy in draft form, while a further 10% had completed preparatory work for a mental health strategy (such as an initial review or needs assessment). The content and style of strategies varied considerably. Some DHAs had completed a comprehensive planning process for their mental health services in general, often using external facilitators. These usually involved systematic consultation with users and carers, reviews of the type and extent of need and the preferred pattern of services for different groups of people with psychiatric disorders, and statements of the principles which should determine the preferred pattern of services.

121 Purchasers with no mental health strategy often included some discussion of mental health issues in their general district health strategies or the annual reports of the Director of Public Health. Nevertheless, it was often difficult to identify the local configuration of mental health services in such districts, or the total expenditure by the DHA on mental health. This was particularly the case where mental health was grouped for contractual purposes with other specialties.

122 The survey of the purchasing process in 20 health districts found a strong commitment by almost all DHAs to develop effective mental health strategies where these were not already in place. But purchasing teams reported that this task was impeded by a number of factors:

- *Lack of expertise*

  Managers and clinicians in the majority of the NHS trusts expressed concern about the limited expertise available to health authorities on mental health issues. DHAs were somewhat more positive about their expertise, although most depended for detailed knowledge of mental health services on a single member of staff.

- *Lack of information*

  Hardly any of the purchasers or providers in the survey had adequate information about numbers of patients in contact with local mental health services and the outcome of their care.

- *Overlapping boundaries*

  Mergers of DHAs since 1991 have resulted in multiple overlaps of boundaries between health districts, social services departments, and NHS providers of mental health services.

- *Issues of co-operation between purchasers and providers*

  Relations between health authorities and the providers of mental health services varied considerably. A small number of DHAs reported that they now had achieved a 'mature relationship' in which their main provider of mental health services was accorded `preferred provider status'. Such health authorities were often co-operating closely with their providers in implementing complex hospital closure programmes. At the other extreme, relationships between some health authorities and their main providers of mental health services were distant.

THE CONTENT OF PURCHASING PLANS FOR CHILD AND ADOLESCENT MENTAL HEALTH SERVICES

123   In this section, the main findings relating to the strategies for child and adolescent mental health services are presented in precised form.

124   Analysis of the purchasing and commissioning documents for 1993-94 indicated that approximately 80% of health authorities and health commissions in England identified services for children and adolescents with psychiatric disorders in their plans. There were differences in the plans presented by English and Welsh Authorities. All of the latter had strategic statements relating to services for children and adolescents and, overall, their plans appeared better developed than those in England. This is seen as reflecting the influence of the Welsh Office document *Mental Illness Services – A Strategy for Wales*. However, as compared with the background scenario relating to mental health services for adults, reported earlier in this chapter, the position of commissioning for child and adolescent mental health services appeared less developed.

125   No consistent model for child and adolescent mental health services emerged from the analysis of purchasing plans in England and Wales, and services for this group were not specified in most of the mental health strategy documents published by DHAs.

126   A minority of health authorities identified the needs of particular subgroups of children and adolescents, including just over one-third (around 36%) which discussed the needs of adolescents with psychiatric disorders, and nearly one-quarter which identified the needs of children who have been assaulted (23%) or sexually-abused (19%) (Figure 7). Smaller numbers identified the mental health needs of children with physical disabilities or illnesses, children in care, and children at risk of substance abuse.

Figure 7

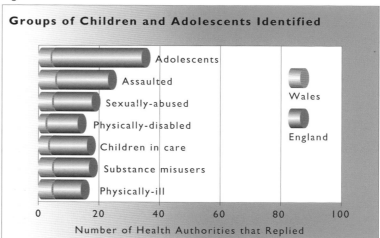

127   The services which were being purchased in 1992-93, as evidenced by contract and other purchasing documents, are summarised by Figure 8.

Figure 8

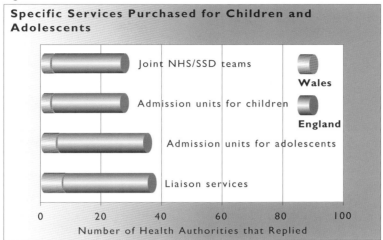

128 Interviews with DHA purchasing teams indicated that the majority were concerned about the effectiveness of current services provided for children and adolescents with mental disorders. This was not usually based on a negative evaluation of the quality of the clinical service, but reflected a perception that the service was grossly under-resourced, with long waiting lists for outpatient appointments, and limited support from non-medical professions and other agencies.

129 Closer consideration of the services proposed in DHA purchasing plans, where they were evident, is summarised in Figure 9. Over one-quarter of health authorities proposed to develop or enhance admission units for adolescents (30%), and liaison psychiatry services for paediatricians and other professions. Approximately one-quarter (24%) proposed to develop joint child and family teams with education authorities and social services. Most such teams would be community-based, and some purchasers identified a need for an early or crisis intervention approach. Other purchasing plans proposed to develop or enhance admission units for children and psychiatric disorders (24%) and specialist day care units (11%). Smaller numbers of purchasers proposed to develop an overdose service for children and adolescents, crisis helplines, and drop-in services. Figure 9 is similar in proportion and content to Figure 8 and this suggests that, in 1993-94, planning for child and adolescent mental health services was not advancing.

Figure 9

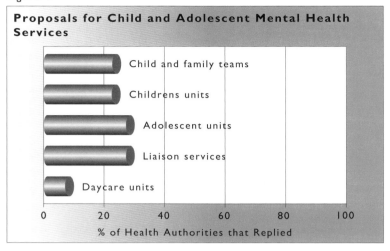

Other Services Relevant to Children and Adolescents

130 DHAs differed in the range of other specialised mental health service provision included in their strategies and purchasing documentation. A summary is offered here as some of these services may be used by children and adolescents. Over three-quarters included proposals for services for alcohol and/or substance misusers (77%), while substantial numbers also identified provision for offenders (68%) and psychotherapy (48%). The remaining psychiatric specialities such as rehabilitation, mother and baby services, neuropsychiatry, eating disorders, and liaison psychiatry were identified by more than one in 10 DHAs. Very few health authorities had purchasing proposals for meeting the mental health needs of homeless people, people with AIDS/HIV, or deaf people.

131 A minority (16%) of DHAs included the mental health needs of people from black and minority ethnic groups in their purchasing documentation, and very few indeed (4%) included any estimate of the local prevalence of mental illness among these groups living in the health district. But just over half (53%) did specify some services to be provided for mentally-ill people from black and minority ethnic groups, including 44% which specified that patients receive information in their own language, 30% which specified that patients receive meals that are appropriate to their religion or culture, and 21% which required facilities for religious observance in hospitals.

132 Rather fewer authorities were then purchasing a specialised service for mentally-ill people from black and minority ethnic groups, or proposed to purchase such a service in the future. One in five included an interpreting service in their purchasing plans, while 10% also purchased a treatment service (usually an individual CPN or psychotherapist) with a specialised remit to treat patients from black or minority ethnic groups.

THE COMMISSIONING PROCESS

133 The analysis of the purchasing process conducted by CRIMD, the detailed content analysis of the documentation for a sample of districts conducted by the Kings Fund College and the experience of the HAS in visiting services, have all contributed to the derivations of interim opinion on the impact of differing styles of approach to commissioning.

The Style of Approach of Purchasers to Commissioning

134 The principal finding from the detailed content analysis of a subset of 12 purchasers' documentation performed for the HAS by the Kings Fund College was that, *"Purchasing style, and the capacity to respond to, and intervene appropriately in, complex networks of relationships, which will be different for different core groups within mental health, are crucial factors in determining the effectiveness of purchasers' plans."*

135 This analysis revealed a tension between the role of purchasers as controllers of local capacity, where the emphasis is on leverage, incentives and disincentives and their potential role as enablers of service development, where the emphasis is on accessibility, flexibility and reliability. The analysis also revealed three broad categories of style of approach on this enabler-controller continuum. These were:

- *Historic/Incremental*
  The approach to commissioning appeared to be based on a relatively uncriticised progression from the past.
- *Rational/Incremental*
  Here authorities appeared to take the reforms arising from the NHS and Community Care Act 1990 as a basis for purchaser-led review and development.
- *Innovative/Progressive*
  In this style, purchasing authorities appeared to have adopted a facilitative, leadership role in achieving local system change.

136 This analysis also concluded that, *"The capability of purchasers to take a leadership role in creating the necessary vision appeared to be crucial. From the documentation, it is clear that this works best when the leadership style is harmonised with the values and principles of the emergent strategy, i.e. when all stakeholders become involved in a `developmental partnership' which is both challenging of past standards and assumptions in respect of goals and means."*

Commissioning Child and Adolescent Mental Health Services

137 When considered against the demanding agenda for commissioners set by *Purchasing for Health*, the evidence from the work of Kurtz, Thornes and Wolkind (chapter five) and the evidence from the analysis presented here, suggests that commissioning had, in 1993-94, yet to make a significant impact on child and adolescent mental health services.

138 There is no doubt that purchasing authorities have faced major challenges since their inauguration in 1991 with many changing their identities and sphere of responsibilities once or twice in the interval. Yet it is evident, from the fieldwork conducted by the HAS (chapter seven) and CRIMD, that many commissioning agencies are increasingly concerned to bring about a more rational approach to the delivery of child and adolescent mental health services and have more ambitious plans for the future. Many are asking for advice and their rate of travel and learning has accelerated. It is also evident that, while there are differences in detail between the findings from the three studies of commissioning reported in chapters five, six and seven (probably explained by their differing methodologies), there are broad issues of agreement relating to

purchasing capacity, style, approach and knowledge arising from them. These
have contributed powerfully to generating the agenda for commissioners which
is the main subject matter of Parts B and C.

CHAPTER 7

Common Concerns
Identified in the
Visits to Services

INTRODUCTION

139   A central component of this review was the service visits that took place between December 1993 and August 1994. In total, 12 specific locations were visited which provided access to a comprehensive range of primary, secondary, and tertiary services from both the statutory and non-statutory health and social welfare sectors. Each visit was undertaken by a small multi-disciplinary team drawn from both purchasing and providing organisations, in order to ensure appropriate consideration of commissioning and service delivery and their contribution towards effective and efficient provision. The visits focused largely on single health commissioning areas but concentrated on the relationship and inputs of health, social services, and education services as commissioners and providers of child and adolescent mental health services.

140   The service had several objectives.

- To elicit the views of professionals involved in the commissioning, provision and usage of child and adolescent mental health services on the current position in each locality, their adequacy, effectiveness, efficiency, and their direction in the future.

- To highlight common themes and concerns in the commissioning and provision of CAMHS.

- To highlight good practice in the commissioning and provision of CAMHS.

142   This chapter sets out common concerns emerging from the visits and is divided into issues relating to commissioning and provision. While the material was collected systematically, it has not been appropriate to analyse it statistically as it is based on a 10% sample of districts. Rather, the information gleaned from this approach to service visits has been used to deepen, enrich and test the findings of the larger and more focused surveys reported in chapters five and six. Hence the conclusions are presented here in summarised form. In order to learn from current practice, this chapter essentially considers problems which were presented recurrently to the visiting teams. Much of the material relating to good practice, which was readily apparent in each of the visits, has been used as a base for the development of guidance in the later sections.

COMMISSIONING

143   In the majority of the districts visited, there was an ineffective approach to commissioning child and adolescent mental health services characterised by combinations of the following:

- Poor dialogue between health, social services, and education commissioners

- Absence of a strategy for CAMHS.

- Absence of an assessment of the mental health needs of children and adolescents.

- Absence of collaboration between commissioners (particularly health) in relation to very specialised supra-district services.

- A low level of understanding and insufficient knowledge of child and adolescent mental health issues and of effective interventions in this field.

- A lack of relevant information and data on CAMHS for both planning and service monitoring purposes.

- Poor contractual arrangements with current providers.

143　In the other visits, a commissioning approach was evident but was unsophisticated and undeveloped, having one or more of the following characteristics:

- Single agency approaches in which each was acting independently of key partner agencies.

- A low level of involvement of users and carers in planning and developing strategy.

- Documentation that bore little resemblance to the reality of provision on the ground.

- Insufficient information to enable the development of performance monitoring or outcome measurement.

- Contractual relationships that hampered the achievement of strategic intent (eg. single year contracts with voluntary sector providers).

- Implementation of strategy that was secretive or inappropriately paced to enable effective management of change by providers.

- A lack of commitment to strategies for CAMHS by senior officers in commissioning organisations, resulting in insufficient time and resource dedicated to implementation.

- Approaches that appeared sufficient but were in their early stages and were untested.

144　The major consequences of such ineffective or undeveloped approaches were:

- CAMHS with little cohesion and co-ordination across agencies and disciplines, characterised by gaps and overlaps in provision of CAMHS by health, social and education services.

- Poor and underdeveloped relationships between different services.

- Vulnerable very specialised services that relied too heavily on extra-contractual referrals for survival.

- Little or no evidence to demonstrate effectiveness or efficiency of existing services.

- Services that may be vulnerable to major incidents of bad practice in relation to the appropriate care of children and adolescents.

145　These consequences have also been described by Vanstraelen and Cottrell (1994) and are explored further in the consideration of common concerns in the provision of services.

PROVISION
Primary Care

146 Typically, GPs regarded child and adolescent mental health services as a secondary specialist resource which, although providing a valuable service, was unlikely to be able to respond quickly. Additionally, some GPs knew little about these services, as they were provided, with little information about the range and scope of services. Professionals in primary care settings, eg. health visitors, social workers, and school nurses, understood that a substantial amount of emotional and behavioural disturbance, particularly among the younger children, was handled by staff outside the specialist mental health services. Therefore, primary care staff were uncertain about what constituted an appropriate referral, or when a problem became serious enough to move from primary to secondary services. Semantic arguments about when a child care or emotional or behavioural problem becomes a mental or psychiatric disorder did not appear to the visiting team to be helpful within primary care settings. Other pragmatic considerations of severity, complexity and responsiveness to intervention or otherwise, seemed more important.

147 The visiting teams came to the opinion that there is a profound need for staff in primary care settings to develop skill and experience in work with children, adolescents and their families in order to address the early manifestations of difficult behaviour. In a number of authorities, this is happening in locality bases, and in schools, but it is largely informal, unstructured, and unco-ordinated. There were examples of primary care staff with these abilities being supported in this work within their own staff group and, more exceptionally, via regular consultation with specialists, such as clinical psychologists or psychiatrists. Many primary care workers appreciated that discussing a concern about a family was often more useful and enabling than making a referral. This work is preventive. Its outcomes will largely be seen in the longer term, and so will be difficult to evaluate with any degree of specificity in the shorter term. These observations on the impact of lack of support to primary care practitioners link with clinical experience, reported by the specialist child and adolescent mental health services, which indicates that, where there were no primary care initiatives of this kind, waiting lists were lengthy, and some families were lost through the frustration of waiting, because the problem appeared to resolve, or was dealt with in other ways (eg. by the child being removed from the home).

148 A summary of the concerns which were expressed by primary health care team members about specialist services is provided by Table 9.

Table 9

Concerns about Provision Expressed by Primary Health Care Professionals
• Problems in the availability and accessibility of CAMHS to provide advice, consultation and accept referrals from the primary care setting.
• Provision of basic information on CAMHS to primary care settings was poor, and feedback was limited.
• If training and support was not available, the demands of children, young people and their families with mental health problems on primary care staff generated problems about role adequacy, role legitimacy and role support (see chapter eight).

149 It is, therefore, of paramount importance that primary health care services are considered to be an important component in the overall provision of child and adolescent mental health services. The specialist components in a network of child and adolescent mental health services should address support for their linkage with primary care services as an important dimension in their work.

Secondary Care

Service Structure

150 The HAS service visits found that the majority of specialist child and adolescent mental health services were provided at what is traditionally termed 'secondary level', through a combination of hospital and community-based outlets. These were often based around a small inpatient facility, with some day patient services, but with the major thrust of the service being towards outpatient work. Several services had to look outside the immediate locality for inpatient facilities. Staffing within services was variable in terms of numbers and professional groupings. In the few services where social workers were still based, they were working wholly as members of the multi-disciplinary team. Often, clinical psychologists were external to the services provided by child and adolescent psychiatrists and other professions, providing sporadic inputs, frequently from a separate departmental base, and occasionally there was competition between other child and adolescent mental health services and clinical psychology departments.

151 Child and adolescent mental health services have traditionally provided a base for established therapeutic practices as well as for more creative and innovative practices. Services which encompass diverse working practices need good, effective management to prevent the staff becoming distanced from one another. The management arrangements revealed by the visits usually included the appointment of an overall service manager from within the trust, with the service being delivered through a clinical team or teams, and often a consultant psychiatrist was the lead clinician. The clinical teams enjoyed a high degree of autonomy and it was apparent that the functioning of the teams, in terms of their cohesiveness, flexibility, and responsiveness to change contributed significantly to the shape of the service. Unclear or inefficient managerial structures evidently created difficulties. The problems which were observed during the visits are summarised by Table 10.

Table 10

The Consequences of Poor Management Structures
• Models of management, service delivery, process etc., were not based on the realities of good clinical practice.
• Structures which were service-orientated rather than needs-led failed, or missed certain groups of patients.
• Manager-practitioner conflict as a consequence of lack of clinical consultation and representation in the contracting process.
• Inefficient or unclear management structures seriously hampered multi-disciplinary working, particularly where team members eg. social workers or teachers, received their line management from outside the specialist service.
• The absence of a clearly documented service business plan appeared to sustain idiosyncratic practice inadvertently which, in turn, created problems and delays in other parts of the service.
• Underuse of existing service resources.
• While continuing to present a community focus in their publicity material, some services were still highly traditional and buildings-led.
• Consultant domination of teams so that staff of other disciplines felt uninvolved or excluded from discussion on service provision.
• Persistent disagreement or disparity between consultants rendered some services leaderless and fragmented, with serious implications for service planning and development.
• Competition between different trust employees with respect to work with families, eg. child guidance personnel competing with clinical psychologists.
• Poor collaboration between different elements of service networks, resulting in duplication and gaps in service provision.
• Elaborate or complicated referral systems and extensive waiting lists which, often unwittingly, had become a means of controlling the flow of clients into some CAMHS.
• Child and adolescent mental health service staff felt overwhelmed by ever increasing referrals, but had not been able to prioritise the many demands on their time.
• The form and content of interventions offered bore little relation to the need to monitor and evaluate them for planning and commissioning.
• The need for expediency and cost-effectiveness was either ignored, or dismissed as being incompatible with responsible professional practice.
• Management of scarce resources seemed secondary to the pursuit of personal therapeutic preferences.
• User involvement in the process of service development and delivery was a token consideration.

Service Delivery

152 The visits provided clear evidence that child and adolescent mental health services have attracted to themselves knowledgeable, keen, and committed workers who, individually and in partnership, showed considerable potential for creativity and innovation in their practice. However laudable these qualities, they clearly needed structures and processes to facilitate their development so

that practice remains flexible and responsive to the overtly prioritised needs of children, adolescents and their families; also to change arising in local circumstances and to developments in professional capacity, practice and thinking. The visits support a picture of limited standardisation of interventions and variations in assessment and treatment styles. This matches findings which have been reported anecdotally by others (eg. Parry-Jones, 1995).

Social Services Departments

153 In the course of the fieldwork, the HAS team usually visited the social services department in each district to meet senior managers and social workers. Many aspects of good practice were observed and, again, these have been subsumed into the chapter which follows. This chapter is concerned with learning the lessons from the problems encountered, which were generally of three types.

- Some social services departments had a narrow view of CAMHS, as evidenced by their preoccupation with parts, rather than the whole, of what the local service can offer.

- Joint planning and other joint initiatives rarely moved beyond the stage of generalised discussion at over-sized meetings. In the rare instances where planning had been translated into joint action, the results had been encouraging and satisfying for all concerned.

- Child protection issues often dominated the agendas of social workers in CAMHS teams and its statutory importance sometimes diverted them from other kinds of work within CAMHS.

Education Departments

154 Teams made contact with the education departments in most visits and the problems encountered appeared to fall into two broad categories.

- The feeling in many education and health services was that links were poor, and liaison was too infrequent to be truly effective.

- The education department had its own statutory responsibilities for children with emotional and behavioural difficulties and a programme of projects and initiatives for them. Some appeared to be playing a lone hand in which the department appeared not to recognise the need to liaise with other sectors.

The Voluntary Sector

155 Traditionally, the voluntary sector has played a major role in the provision of child care services. Often, non-statutory organisations have taken the lead in introducing and evaluating new techniques and methods of service delivery. However, the service visits revealed that child and adolescent mental health services often seemed to work in ignorance of the scope and potential within the voluntary sector. Frequently, the involvement of voluntary sector organisations in discussion and planning was token, and appeared as an afterthought.

Very Specialised Care

156 Very specialised services are provided by health, social and education services for relatively few, but nonetheless very troubled, children and young people, who have complex psychological problems and psychiatric disorders. Services of this type are exemplified by those offering focused interventions to more than one member of a family, sexually and physically abused children and their families, children and adolescents with life-threatening or chronic physical illness, young people after major trauma, young people with severe eating disorders and those suffering refractory chronic fatigue syndrome. These services may be provided by outpatient clinics staffed by professionals with special experience but also, and importantly, include day patient and most inpatient units for children and adolescents. Staff working in these services experience high levels of strain, need to keep abreast of developments in technique and should maintain contact with others doing similar work elsewhere. They, therefore, need regular opportunities for training and support and, in return, are a powerful source of training for others. Frequently, they may be based around day and inpatient units which should, ideally, act as resource centres for a wide area.

157 In the course of the service visits, the HAS again found many examples of good practice but these appeared unplanned and built around individuals with special experience and zeal. The problems encountered are listed in Table 11.

Table 11

Concerns About the Provision of Very Specialised Services

• Difficulties in relationships with local CAMHS:
   - difficulties of liaison with referrers;
   - difficulties of discharge planning;
   - disinclination to share specialist skills with secondary services.

• The vulnerability of very specialised services in the internal market:
   - lack of contracts for services created difficulties of financial and service planning;
   - financial insecurity hampered development of new services and restricted their capacity to disseminate specialist skills.

• Inappropriate use of very specialised services in providing a source of less specialised interventions in districts with under-developed secondary level services.
• Inappropriate use of local specialist services to provide more specialised care: - eg. non-use of very specialised services, on grounds of their cost or insufficient capacity, led to disruption of local CAMHS through disproportionate time and effort being diverted to difficult or extremely challenging cases.
• Poor systems of quality control and performance monitoring: - the absence of commissioning mechanisms often resulted in very specialised services not being subject to questions on monitoring of their activity, effectiveness, and efficiency.

RESEARCH AND DEVELOPMENT IN CHILD AND ADOLESCENT MENTAL HEALTH SERVICES

158 Academic centres were included in a number of the field visits, and the investment of certain universities, trusts, organisations and individuals reaped considerable rewards in the understanding and management of mental health problems in children and adolescents and in the training of mental health professionals. However, once again, there was an absence of a coherent commissioning approach to research and development in child and adolescent mental health services at local, regional and national levels. This said, some national co-ordination is accorded by the national mental health research and development funded projects in child and adolescent mental health.

159 The lack of coherence partly derived from the fact that research by one statutory agency often has relevance to another, for example Professor Rutter's work on young people in secondary schools, *Fifteen Thousand Hours* (Rutter, 1979), had implications for educational planning as much as health planning. Hence joint commissioning of research and development, as well as a national overview to ensure coverage of significant gaps in knowledge and prevention of repetition of work, is required if useful observations are to be made on children, young people and their families functioning in all their contexts.

160 Research was often only occurring in high-cost, low-volume services with very specialist expertise, but there were some outstanding examples of staff from specialist facilities sharing their expertise with primary and secondary workers, and producing practice-changing research at the same time.

161 There was no evidence from any of the field visits of the application of health economics research to child and adolescent mental health services.

PART B

The Principles

Action Points

Commissioners (GPFHs, HAs, SSDs and Education Departments) should use the conceptual model set out in the Strategic Approach and the guidance on the Principles of Commissioning CAMHS to:

- Map, assess and audit current provision.
- Plan any necessary investment and disinvestment.
- Understand the relationships of key providers in an effective network of CAMHS.
- Inform more effective dialogues with partner commissioners.
- Diagnose system failures and blocks.
- Introduce a discrete contracting framework for CAMHS.

Providers should use the conceptual model set out in the Strategic Approach and the Principles of Providing CAMHS to:

- Understand their position and role in the network of CAMHS as a whole.
- Build and develop necessary links with other providers.
- Invest in training to maximise the contributions of providers in each tier.
- Focus each tier of provision on the appropriate patient/client groups.
- Benchmark current practice and service policies and procedures.

CHAPTER 8

A Strategic Approach
to Commissioning
and Delivering Child
and Adolescent
Mental Health
Services

BACKGROUND

162   Goldberg & Huxley (1980) drew attention to the filtering mechanisms which operate in the provision of psychiatric services for adults. Until recently, this concept has not been used in child and adolescent mental health, nor developed as a basis for service delivery. In 1994, Cox (personal communication) and Hill (1994), on behalf of the Royal College of Psychiatrists, introduced a strategic approach to child and adolescent mental health service based on tiers of service. The HAS elaborated a similar model on the basis of its work and this has, subsequently, been developed in discussions with Cox and Hill to produce a strategic approach based on the same number of tiers. This approach recognises four tiers of provision for children and young people across all agencies and deliberately avoids the health service categories of primary, secondary and tertiary. It has another advantage too, that of dovetailing with the Department for Education's Code of Practice for the identification and assessment of special educational needs.

163   The two main purposes of this model of service are, first, to integrate the many elements of a truly comprehensive service for children, adolescents and young people into an understandable whole. Second, it is intended, through encouraging the development of service networks, to support those working with children, young people and families so that they are enabled in their work, and their skills are increased. This should also reduce the contentious problem of referring reluctant families to services whose stigma they resent, and reduce the problem of the staff of specialist services being and (or feeling) overwhelmed by referrals for problems which may be more helpfully addressed in the community by other service components.

164   In the model described here, a child and adolescent mental health service is seen as consisting of a range of primary and specialised services purchased by the health, social services and education sectors. Similarly, the providers consist of a range of services, at a range of levels of expertise, provided by primary healthcare, secondary healthcare, education, social services, voluntary sector and private sector organisations. This, a comprehensive service is likely to be delivered by a number of different providers.

THE STRATEGIC APPROACH

Tier One - Primary or Direct Contact Services

165   Tier I consists of professionals, such as GPs, social workers, voluntary sector workers, school staff, police officers, school medical officers, school nurses, health visitors etc, who are not necessarily employed for the prime purpose of promoting mental health, but who directly and indirectly influence the mental health of children and young people through their work with them. They are usually the first point of contact between a child or family and the child care or health agencies.

166   It is suggested, in this review, that the objectives of closing the gap between Tier I and the more specialised child and adolescent mental health services might be promoted in many areas by the appointment of a *primary mental health worker.* Such a person would be a member of the more specialised child and adolescent mental health service with the specific brief to act as a first contact for discussions, referral, advice, liaison and consultation. The tasks of this worker are described in chapter 16.

167 Contracts with the specialist child and adolescent mental health services should recognise the needs of general practitioners, other child care agencies and the criminal justice systems for work to be done by individual members of child and adolescent mental health services, by teams from within the specialist service or by multi-disciplinary elements of the service overall (Richardson, 1994). Examples might include agreements between the probation service and the health commissioners for a number of court reports per year to be provided by a specific member of, or team with the child and adolescent mental health service or agreements between social services departments and health commissioners for a number of risk assessments by specified service staff.

168 For Tier 1 services, the access point to the more specialised child and adolescent mental health services should be by explicit routes negotiated and instituted locally.

169 In some instances, and for strategic reasons, services may decide to establish referral processes based on an overt division of labour (such a decision would take into account the capabilities of elements of the service and the organisational management model of those elements in Tiers 2 and 3, outlined below). In such a system, cases of certain types from defined localities, or identified referral sources, will be routed to one profession or a group of professions. In other instances, shared referrals will be made to a multi-disciplinary team in a child and adolescent health service. The team, or senior members of the service (depending on the internal service organisational model used), might consider referrals in conjunction with primary health care workers, who are members of that team, alongside referrals from elsewhere. Through its discussion of referrals, or the discussion of open cases, the team or service could then advise on and allocate the appropriate intervention.

170 Given the spread of providers (and the differing departments within individual providing organisations) which may be appropriately involved, it is most important that referral mechanisms should be clearly and overtly negotiated, defined and monitored. It should also be recognised that the first intervention by specialist services may be to collate information from other agencies, such as school and social services, to understand what interventions are already being made and how they should be jointly organised for the benefit of the children, young people or their families.

Tier Two - Interventions Offered by Individual Specialist Child and Adolescent Mental Health Professionals

171 This tier is represented by individual specialist mental health workers, who work with children, adolescents and their families. Frequently, they will be members of multi-disciplinary child and adolescent mental health teams through which their work is co-ordinated, or otherwise members of part of the network of child and adolescent mental health service components. This work may take place at the specialist service base but could also be conducted in the homes and schools of the children concerned, or in health centres or social services establishments. At this level, specialist staff work as individual mental health professionals performing the tasks required in Tier 2. These are described in chapter 17.

172 Tier 2, in the social and education services, may be represented by specifically tasked social workers, pupil support teachers or educational psychologists.

They are likely to have a major impact on the mental health of those coming in contact with them and should have had specific training to conduct these tasks.

173 In child health care, Tier 2 is provided by paediatricians (hospital and community) and their teams. They should have a close working relationship with their mental health counterparts. It may well be that the role of clinical psychologists is important in this respect, given their contributions to both child and adolescent mental health and child health services.

Tier Three - Interventions Offered by Teams of Staff from Specialist Child and Adolescent Mental Health Services

174 Tier 3 consists of services which are more specialised, often by virtue of the complexity of problems presented to them. In this tier, members of multi-disciplinary mental health services will often work in specific therapeutic teams, such that the co-ordinated interventions of several professionals can address the many facets of the problem or bring sufficient skill to bear on specific problems such as eating disorders, substance misuse, traumatic stress, developmental disorders, affective disorders etc. Examples are the complex issues arising from child protection cases which may require a psychologist, social worker and a psychiatrist to work together on a case, or where the complexities of a family's mutually destructive interactions may require the input of the members of a family therapy team who are practised in working together. Meeting the needs of young people who misuse drugs, alcohol and other substances may also require the establishment of a specific team. Supervision, support and joint working are also essential parts of the training of mental health professionals and some of their training needs may be met by established teams of staff working together.

Tier Four - Very Specialised Interventions and Care

175 This tier provides for highly specific and complex problems which require considerable resources. These include, for example, inpatient psychiatric provision for adolescents, secure provision, specialist facilities for those with sensory handicaps, very specialised services (outpatient and inpatient) for young people with severe eating disorders, specialised neuropsychiatric out-day and inpatient services and consultation services for rare paediatric disorders. Such services are required occasionally (and not always predictably) in small districts but, when they are, they are essential. Mergers of districts into larger commissioning agencies may help to resolve some of the problems experienced within smaller districts in the past.

176 Tier 4 services are also provided by the social and education services for clients and pupils with problems of similar levels of complexity. In these circumstances, joint working and co-operation are necessary to meet the health, educational and social needs of young people requiring these services.

The Model

177 A schematic diagram of how a tiered service might be conceived is presented in
     Figure 10. As with all schemata it has its drawbacks. It is emphasised that the
     professionals, teams and services listed at each tier are examples only, and there
     are likely to be other professionals operating at each level, or professionals listed
     who may not be working in an identified tier. It must also be recognised that
     other child care systems such as the education or paediatric services will
     overlap and interact with services strategically organised in this way. This figure
     artificially centralises the place of health-based child and adolescent mental
     health services. It is important that, through the understanding and
     reinforcement of staff in all such services, these overlapping systems dovetail.

Figure 10

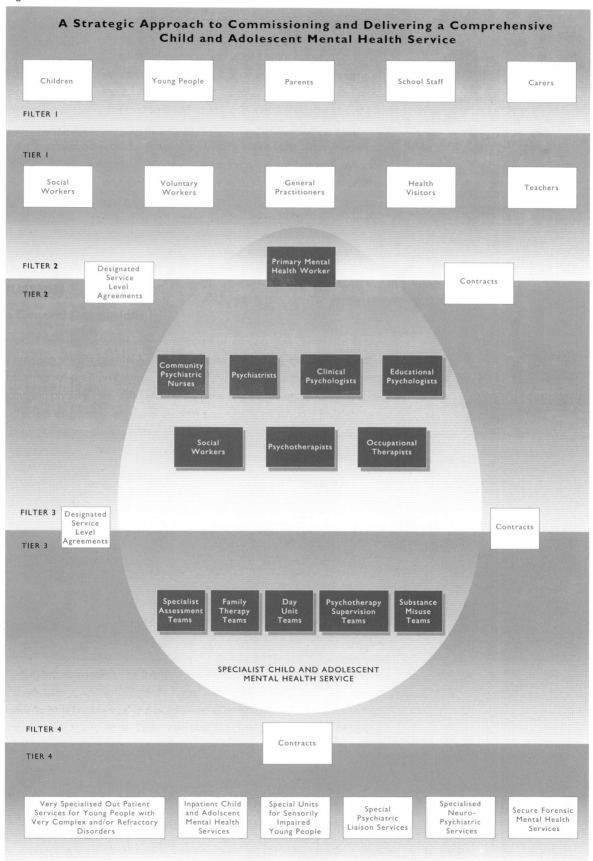

A Strategic Approach to Commissioning and Delivering a Comprehensive Child and Adolescent Mental Health Service

178 It should be emphasised that the model described here is intended to present a strategic approach to service commissioning and provision. This model is not intended to imply a single approach to the way in which the components of a service should be organised, work or be managed. Nonetheless, this model does provide a framework which commissioners could use to conceptualise the service components required. It also offers a strategic approach to commissioning and service provision which ensures better co-ordination and integration of the various components of a comprehensive service, however they are arranged or managed.

179 The notion of a primary mental health worker arises from the observations made in this report. The intention of this proposal is that of strengthening the identification of primary level components of child and adolescent mental health services which are in direct contact with children, adolescents and families (Tier 1). As envisaged here, a core task for these primary mental health workers would be that of supporting and being consulted by professionals offering Tier 1 services. These staff would be integral members of the specialist multi-disciplinary child and adolescent mental health service, also fulfilling some of the roles designated at Tier 2. Primary mental health workers could also work in Tier 3. However, they should have less onerous work demands at both Tiers 2 and 3 to allow them to fulfil their main role. Primary mental health workers will need to be specifically trained to undertake this work.

180 This schema must not be taken as an absolute blueprint. Tiers 1-3 child and adolescent mental health services must be provided in all localities. So, to serve a population of over 200,000, it will be necessary to have a comprehensive specialist child and adolescent mental health service which has the capacity to provide Tier 2 and 3 services which link well with a variety of identified Tier 1 services. The specialist services should at least have access to sufficient resources at Tier 4. Depending on geographical, and other local factors and the style of service organisation employed (eg the single integrated service or separate service component models), these services may be organised into one, two or more child and adolescent mental health teams to provide services at Tier 2, and these may combine certain of their membership to provide Tier 3 services.

The Relationship of this Strategic Approach to the Department for Education's Code of Practice of 1994.

181 A somewhat similar model was introduced into the education service, with effect from September 1994, by the Code of Practice for the Identification and Assessment of Special Educational Needs. This is a statutory instrument, and one to which all services and agencies must have regard.

182 The Code recommends five stages for identifying, assessing and responding to the needs of children whose educational progress or adjustment in school are giving cause for concern. This group of children with special educational needs is estimated to comprise some 20 per cent of the school population and includes those with emotional or behavioural difficulties.

183 In Stages 1 and 2 of the Code, a school should draw largely on its own resources and expertise to respond to children's difficulties, while also keeping parents informed. However, if a problem were to continue to persist (Stage 3),

the Code recommends that the school should seek outside support or advice. This may be from within the education service, usually in the form of specialist advisers or support teams and/or the educational psychology service. Alternatively, or in addition, a school may turn to health or social service personnel for assistance.

184 If a problem were to persist despite intervention at Stage 3, a formal referral to the local education authority (LEA) usually follows (Stage 4). The LEA must then consider whether a full, multi-disciplinary assessment is indicated (which includes seeking advice from the health and social services). Such an assessment may result in the LEA producing a statement of the child's special educational needs - and providing the extra resources to meet those needs (Stage 5).

185 The Code's Stage 1 has a similarity to Tier 1 in the model presented in this chapter, equating teachers, with GPs and other primary health care team members, as primary contact workers. However, schools are expected by the Code to have the resources and expertise to respond at this Stage and, indeed, at Stage 2. Therefore, in most (but not necessarily all) circumstances, Stage 3 of the Code becomes the point when the possibility of contact with a member of a specialist child and adolescent mental health service would be considered. Furthermore, given the existence of specialist advisors and behaviour support teams in most LEAs together with educational psychologists, it would seem appropriate that a referral to the Tier 2 level of the child and adolescent mental health service might often come from one of the specialists employed by the education service.

186 The discussions and agreement about the details of referral guidelines, and the dovetailing of the two models, are essentially something for local action, although the fact that LEAs have no direct responsibility for schools' implementation of the Code at Stages 1 to 3 increases the difficulty for health services. Nonetheless, health services have a statutory duty to 'have regard to' the Code, and the quality of co-ordination will inevitably be dependent on the ease of local communication.

MANAGING THE STRATEGIC APPROACH

187 The strategic framework presented here is seen as having considerable value to both purchasers and providers. Its advantages are summarised in Table 12. Table 13 in chapter nine may also be useful to purchasers and providers in converting theory into practice.

Table 12

Advantages of the Tiered Approach to Purchasing and Providing Child and Adolescent Mental Health Services	
Purchasers are enabled to	Providers are enabled to
• Assess and audit current provision	• Understand their position and role in the CAMHS as a whole
• Plan necessary investment and disinvestment	• Build and develop necessary links with other providers and between each tier
• Understand the relationship of key providers in an effective CAMHS system	• Invest in training to convert existing services to this framework
• Use the framework for dialogue with other commissioners (eg general practitioner fundholders)	• Achieve better outcomes through devoting resources to earlier interventions
• Diagnose system failures and blocks	• Focus each tier of provision on the appropriate client group
• Avoid duplication of services	• Better integrate and co-ordinate service delivery by a range of specialist components

Turning Theory into Practice

230   The HAS service vists suggest that three matters are of particular significance in developing child and adolescent mental health services:

- Basing service directions and roles on overt joint strategy

- Leading and managing staff

- Tackling challenges to effective functioning

231   The following paragraphs consider each of these issues in outline and begin by offering a view of the steps in formulating a strategy.

Steps to Formulate a Response Strategy

232   *The Protocol for Investment in Health Gain - Mental Health* (Welsh Health Planning Forum, 1993) illustrates the steps required in formulating an outline strategy. These apply well to child and adolescent mental health services and appear here in Figure 11.

Figure 11

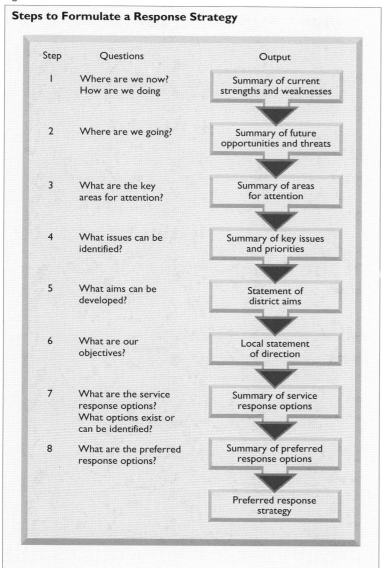

Steps to Formulate a Response Strategy

Step	Questions	Output
1	Where are we now? How are we doing	Summary of current strengths and weaknesses
2	Where are we going?	Summary of future opportunities and threats
3	What are the key areas for attention?	Summary of areas for attention
4	What issues can be identified?	Summary of key issues and priorities
5	What aims can be developed?	Statement of district aims
6	What are our objectives?	Local statement of direction
7	What are the service response options? What options exist or can be identified?	Summary of service response options
8	What are the preferred response options?	Summary of preferred response options
		Preferred response strategy

Leading and Managing Staff

233   One of the key challenges is that of leading, managing and training staff. There has been considerable research into how to make this sort of approach work in practice. (Shaw et al., 1978). This is expressed here in terms of the requirements needed to ensure that the 'task' (working with children, adolescents who have mental health problems and disorders, and their families) is undertaken effectively at each level. These include:

Role Support

234   At each tier, the personnel working in the service must feel supported in their particular 'task' by those they work with in all tiers who have complementary and specialist skills.

Role Adequacy

235   At each tier, staff must feel adequately trained to undertake the 'task' to the level required. Basic and post-basic training is therefore essential.

Role Legitimacy

236   At each tier, staff must feel the task they are being asked to undertake is legitimately their job and not that of other people.

Motivation

237   At each tier, staff must wish to work with the particular groups of patients which have problems requiring that level of complexity of service; they must also derive some satisfaction from involvement in the 'task'.

Self-esteem

238   As well as feeling competent to undertake the task, staff must feel they are respected for what they do. Staff also need to gain a sense of achievement and success from their job.

Service Policy

239   Service policy is crucially important. The policy of the service overall must be supportive to the work on the 'task' it is being asked to undertake. This ensures a commitment of time and resource to it. Without this, the tasks allocated to individuals may be impossible to achieve.

Challenges to Effective Functioning

240   There are further challenges that must be understood if the framework is to be helpful in developing comprehensive child and adolescent mental health services.

- Children, young people and families may not make access to services in the way that the theoretical framework suggests. Examples of this may be:

  — becoming 'stuck' in primary care settings through inability to access appropriate specialised services;

  — making first contacts with social service departments;

  — making first contacts through the accident and emergency services; and

  — making first contacts via the criminal justice system.

- Most commissioners are faced with an existing profile of services. If they wish to move towards a different composition of service, they may need to develop a strategy for disinvestment and reinvestment. This may be achieved by:

  – strategic use of bridging finance;

  – investment in training to develop the required skill mix; and

  – estate management, if locations are to change.

- In recent years, the Department of Health and the Welsh Office have stressed the importance of specialist mental health services adopting a focus for their efforts on people with more severe disorders. At the same time services are being encouraged towards their becoming primary care led. Consequently there is an increasing accent on the provision of specialist services for people with serious disorders alongside primary care services in the community. Historically, the focus of child and adolescent mental health services has always been towards community services. Nevertheless, commissioners, purchasers and providers should consider similarly the balance of their allocation of resources in child and adolescent mental health services to:

  – prevention;

  – recognition of and intervention with children with more minor problems and disorders;

  – recognition and management of children and adolescents who have more serious disorders and illnesses;

  – consultation and liaison services; and

  – training and research.

  A balanced service will include the capacity to respond to all these demands. In practice, the allocation of staff time and expertise to each of these endeavours should be monitored and actively managed to ensure that resource, where limited, is most effectively and appropriately used. This calls for local discussion and agreement between commissioners, purchasers and providers.

199 These challenges require the framework to be flexible to and for its development through local networks. Co-ordination of the commissioners from the range of statutory agencies is essential if the contributions of the providers of the differing elements of the service and those from different agencies are to be understood and integrated within the overall framework.

CHAPTER 9

The Principles of Effective Commissioning of Child and Adolescent Mental Health Services

COMMISSIONING AND PURCHASING

THE PRINCIPLES OF
EFFECTIVE
COMMISSIONING OF
CHILD AND
ADOLESCENT MENTAL
HEALTH SERVICES

200 There is a tendency to use these words interchangeably. The guideline document, *Purchasing for Health,* refers generically to the term *purchasing.* In this review, *commissioning* is the umbrella term, emphasising strategy. We take it to mean a strategically driven process by which purchasers (health authorities, GP fundholders, social services departments and education departments) provide services for their local population. *Purchasing* refers to the various technical procedures carried out by purchasers to secure and monitor the services they are buying from providers. *Contracting,* a sub-division of purchasing, is the process by which services are purchased. In effect, commissioning encompasses purchasing and contracting and also implies a greater range of tasks because it is led by strategy and involves attempts to monitor, define and manage the market, thus creating a circular process.

201 Since the NHS and Community Care Act 1990 there has been a dynamic force in the system responsible for moving the *purchasing* of health care as close to the patients as possible. This has lead to organisations such as health authorities, family health service authorities (FHSAs) and GP fundholders experiencing shifts in the scope of their role as both *commissioners* and *purchasers.* EL(94)79 *Towards a Primary Care-Led NHS,* sets out an agenda that sees 'new' health authorities an amalgamation of the old health authorities and FHSAs taking the responsibility for *commissioning* at a strategic level, informed by the public and the providers (including GPs), while increasing the direct responsibility of GP Fundholders as *purchasers.* The change process attributable to this initiative means that in the future, health authorities will act primarily as the commissioners, while retaining some direct purchasing (increasingly of more specialised services), and GP fundholders will act primarily as the major direct purchasers while retaining the role of informing commissioning decisions. In *order to accommodate this change process, the thematic review uses the terms commissioning and purchasing to describe the functions rather than to prescribe them to any one agency.*

202 It is also important to recognise the differences of approach which are being taken, generally, by local and health authorities. The former, with conspicuous responsibilities for care management, are required to purchase packages of care for individuals, while health authorities buy sectors of care for populations. One result of this difference is that the assessment of individuals is, at least in part, a purchasing role in the case of local authorities, while it lies, almost entirely, within the provider province in the NHS. Health authorities are being urged to move away from the extra-contractual referral of individual or small numbers of cases. This involves a variety of techniques, including consortium and lead purchasing or the delegation of established ECR budgets to providers, with the intention of redistributing the financial risks. Despite these differences in approach, which must be surmounted through jointly agreed strategies and priorities, and through the co-ordination of care for individuals, local authorities and health purchasers are being encouraged towards joint commissioning. Substantial sections of this review are concerned with elaborating an idealised cycle of events for commissioners and then interpreting these in relationship to the particular requirements of young people with mental health problems and disorders.

An Idealised View of the Commissioning Process

203 The work of the HAS, through its Library of Commissioning has revealed a number of authorities where purchasing capacity appears to be developing rapidly and effectively. Observations of their approaches to their tasks has enabled the HAS to compile a hypothetical view of an idealised commissioning process. This is described in Figure 12. Each phase of the processes illustrated here requires dialogue between purchasers and providers as well as consultation with partner commissioning agencies from other sectors of care and with the partners/clients/users of services and their carers.

Figure 12

204 Determination of priorities within a setting of limited and constrained resources is a demanding matter. Figure 13 illustrates the steps which might be taken in the idealised commissioning process to balance perceived need, clinical capacity, and the views of service users and carers with current provision to generate an agenda for service developments.

Figure 13

205   In their interim paper on commissioning child and adolescent mental health services, Williams and Farrar (1994) identified historical factors which they believe have contributed to the current position of mental health services for young people. Their position is that, effectively applied, the role of commissioning could be a powerful force in tackling some of the problems of provision inherited from the past. There is no reason why the idealised approach identified in this chapter, perhaps modified to meet the demands of realism locally, should not be applied to child and adolescent mental health services.

KEY PRINCIPLES

206   An analysis of HAS' findings indicates that there are certain key matters which should command the attention of purchasing agencies in applying a commissioning framework to the services they specify. These, aggregated here, are similar to the seven stepping stones upon which *Purchasing for Health* bases its definition of effective commissioning (Mawhinney and Nicol, 1993). So, the seven stepping stones are used as the basis of organisation of the remainder of this chapter. In brief, the HAS conclusions are:

- It is important to ensure that the activities of, and resources allocated to, child and adolescent mental health services are co-ordinated across agency boundaries.

- It is essential that those agencies responsible for the care of children at risk of suffering mental health problems and disorders should be involved in commissioning child and adolescent mental health services, so that there is a longer term *strategic approach jointly agreed,* between the health, social and the education services and the voluntary agencies.

- In order to achieve the strategic goals, commissioning agencies must hold *effective contracts* with providers that allow for the measurement and management of performance.

- Commissioning agencies must have, or have access to, a *sound knowledge base* on the mental health requirements of children and adolescents and on the relative effectiveness of potential interventions (where the research evidence exists).

- Commissioning agencies must *be responsive to the needs of their local population* to ensure that child and adolescent mental health services are developed from a relevant strategy with appropriate priorities.

- The development of mental health services for children and adolescents will be enhanced and promoted within the context of *good working relationships between commissioners and service providers.*

- Commissioners must act collaboratively with other commissioners and organisations to form *healthy alliances* that promote consistent and coherent policy aimed at providing a comprehensive prevention, assessment and treatment service for children and adolescents.

- In order to develop an effective commissioning approach to child and adolescent mental health services, commissioning agencies themselves must have the appropriate *organisational capacity and capability.*

A STRATEGIC APPROACH

207 It is important that commissioners develop a longer-term strategic approach to
child and adolescent mental health services that ensures:

- Organisational fit with child and adolescent health, and general adult
  mental health services, and the strategies for those services.

- A wide range of appropriate health, social care, educational and
  voluntary sector inputs.

- Continuity of input that must be capable of addressing the transition
  from childhood to adolescence and on into adulthood.

- A comprehensive range of co-ordinated service inputs that operate
  within the auspices of educational, children's and mental health
  legislation and the guidance issued relating to the law (including the
  Department for Education's Code of Practice relating to the Education
  Act 1993).

- Clear identification of an agreement of each agency's primary
  responsibilities and what services should be provided through co-
  operative arrangements.

- A balance of service inputs capable of meeting individual needs and
  rights.

- Recognition of the legitimate roles and responsibilities of not only
  children and young people but also their parents, guardians and carers,
  in which their contribution to service planning and evaluation is
  encouraged.

- That the potentially insecure financial basis of delivering high-cost, low-
  volume very specialised services is recognised and addressed with
  appropriate and responsible contractual mechanisms.

- That service inputs represent value for money and are based, wherever
  possible, on sound evaluated practice offering demonstrable health gain
  or health maintenance (see chapters four and 11).

- The inclusion of short-term goals and targets (eg development of
  clinical audit, healthcare or outcome measures such as weight gain for
  those suffering from anorexia, return to school for those with school
  refusal).

- The inclusion of longer term targets (eg reduction of suicides in the 11
  to 18 age group).

- The inclusion of resources for research and development.

- The inclusion of resources for staff training.

208 Commissioners may consider that the Children's Action Planning Framework
provides a vehicle for their strategic approach. If this is adopted locally, then
consideration should be given as to how the full range of those agencies with
purchasing or funding responsibilities for child and adolescent mental health
services are involved in the process.

EFFECTIVENESS THROUGH CONTRACTING

209 Contracts for specialist child and adolescent mental health services need to recognise the wide diversity of roles of these services without losing focus. This is a significant challenge to purchasers and providers alike. Contracts that merely specify and measure direct work with children and their families will be insufficient. Contracts must value indirect work, including policy advisory, consultation and liaison roles (chapter ten) and also recognise the importance of circumstances when professionals will need to work together in teams. In many child and adolescent mental health services, there may be a need for planning change strategically and managing it over a realistic time. Contracts which are renegotiated and renewed annually divert both managerial and clinical staff into an annual cycle of preparing for the next contract round. A balance needs to be found between this and propelling the development of services. It is suggested that it may well be appropriate, in many services, for the core contracts (relating to components of service which are thought to be satisfactory) to be agreed, subject to annual monitoring, for three-year periods. In this way, commissioners and providers can put the energy, which might otherwise have been deployed in renegotiating the detail of the total contract, into working together on the development of identified aspects of the child and adolescent mental health service on a planned basis.

210 Commissioners should take into account the following:

- Presently, most of the current contracts for CAMHS are minor integral elements of larger contracts for mental or child health services. Commissioners should move towards discreet and/or better developed contracts for CAMHS.

- Commissioners may (and with their increasing sizes of population of responsibility are likely to) hold contracts with a variety of providers for CAMHS. In this case, it is essential that contracts with different providers enable continuity of care (eg there should be protocols for transfer, discharge, shared care, joint audit etc).

- Commissioners should co-ordinate contracting arrangements to facilitate an effective range of service provision offering equality of access and value for money.

- Commissioners should ensure that contracts with the non-statutory sector offer some degree of permanence (ie three to five years rather than annual negotiation) to maximise their effectiveness. *(See Suicide Prevention - The Challenge Confronted - for models for contracting with the voluntary sector.)*

- In difficult or complex cases, individuals may all too easily bounce backwards and forwards between agencies and providers. Contracts should move towards an individual focus, recognising the shared and specific responsibilities of each agency for the client/patient/pupil.

- The finished consultant episode (FCE) is inadequate as a contract currency for CAMHS as is one which measures only episodes of face-to-face contact. In the absence of national guidance, local contracts should also recognise the activity undertaken by CAMHS in work with families, and in role support of other professional groups such as the education support services, social workers or health visitors.

- Many specialist CAMHS operate a system of self-referrals or encourage patients and families to revisit their service in the early stages of potential relapse which reaps rewards in terms of early intervention. Contracts should avoid the assumption of all referrals being made from primary level health services.

- The requirements for research and training should be considered when specifying services.

DEVELOPING THE KNOWLEDGE BASE

211 Commissioners require sufficient knowledge of the role, work and management of child and adolescent mental health services to ensure their effectiveness in directing local resources for service, research and development, continuing professional education and general training in the field.

212 Therefore, commissioners require a knowledge of:

- Reviews of current practice

- Local needs assessment projects

- Other CAMHS

- The work of local providers (Langlands 1994), users, carers and advocates

- National and local research initiatives and intentions and the Regional and National R and D Strategy

- The needs of staff for training and continuing professional development and the impact of training on staffing levels

- Their legal obligations and best practice in relation to:

  - consent to treatment in respect of the requirements of the *Mental Health Act 1983* and its *Code of Practice* and the *Children Act 1989;*

  - restriction of liberty, under the *Children Act 1989* and the *Mental Health Act 1983;*

  - the *Education Act 1993* and the *Code of Practice for the Identification and Assessment of Special Educational Needs*

  - the *Disabled Persons Representation and Consultation Act 1986,* in particular Sections 5 and 6 which relate to support to be provided by social services departments to school leavers with disabilities and special needs;

  - complaints procedures;

  - after-care;

  - the need for mental health opinions in court; and

  - the availability of legal advice.

213 These matters are elaborated in Annex A and in *Young People, Mental Health and the Law* (NHS Health Advisory Service 1995).

RESPONSIVENESS TO POPULATIONS

214 Commissioners must take direct account of their local populations. This means drawing opinion from them, and providing information to them in relation to the services, available and planned, for children and adolescents with mental health problems.

215 This involves several key tasks.

- Assessment of the nature and extent of CAMHS required to meet needs.

- Consideration of how providers might be encouraged to involve carers, uphold the rights of children and develop acceptable policies on confidentiality.

- Commissioning of advocacy services for children and adolescents.

- Development of supportive networks, including social and leisure activities, aimed at promoting positive mental health among children and adolescents.

PARTNERSHIPS WITH PROVIDERS

216 The responsibility for the development of child and adolescent mental health services is held jointly by purchasers and providers. Evidence from the service visits indicates that the typical absence of a commissioning presence created instability and uncertainty in providers. As commissioning approaches emerge, it is essential that mature relationships develop between purchasers and providers.

217 Such relationships would ensure:

- Congruence between purchasing strategies and provider business plans.

- Agreement on the change management process, if required, (eg. bridging resource, project management responsibilities etc).

- The ability to influence the provider.

- Open communication and sharing of strategic intentions.

- Agreement on data collection and performance monitoring frameworks.

- Efficient handling of Tier 4 referrals from Tiers 1 to 3.

- Agreement on research and development priorities.

- Agreement on the importance of providing training programmes that ensure in-service development of current staff and the training of staff for services in the future.

HEALTHY ALLIANCES

218 The development of an effective commissioning approach requires key agencies, such as health and primary care authorities and local authority social services and education departments to be brought together. Joint commissioning or shared contracting should be directed towards providing effective pathways of

care for young people that include appropriate and timely health, social and educational inputs. A united approach also ensures easier access for parents, carers and guardians to the caring, assessment, diagnostic and therapeutic processes, as they are no longer part of an insular service each of which deals with the problem presenting to it.

219 The benefits of co-ordinating the commissioning approach include:

- Consideration of a plurality of contributions to mental health services.

- Reduction of the potential for financial disputes on placements in very specialised services.

- Easing of access for parents, carers and guardians to the health, welfare, caring and education services at the appropriate level.

- Reduction of duplication or gaps in service provision.

- Development of a jointly owned strategic direction for CAMHS as a whole across agencies.

220 Chapter 12 explores these joint commissioning principles in greater detail. In addition, there are a number of other alliances that commissioners may develop to encourage the *prevention* of mental health problems in young people. Examples include those in Table 13.

Table 13

Examples of Alliances Aimed at Prevention of Mental Health Problems
• Local authority or voluntary sector schemes to provide better leisure and recreational facilities.
• Liaison with the youth service and voluntary action groups to reduce the social isolation of young people.
• Support for education initiatives to reduce bullying or provide counselling within schools.
• Work with primary care workers to identify problems in families at early stages.
• Development of child help and support telephone lines etc.

ORGANISATIONAL FITNESS

221 The ability of commissioners to develop an effective commissioning approach for child and adolescent mental health services will be influenced for the better by:

- The ownership of an effective commissioning strategy by senior officers, including chief officers.

- Appointing dedicated project managers for CAMHS.

- Focused organisational structures that relate to children's services.

- Arranging short-term secondments to gain specialist knowledge or to share inter-agency approaches.

LESSONS FROM THE HAS SERVICE VISITS

222 Opinion derived from the service visits, and other HAS Thematic Reviews highlight the following as good commissioning practice for child and adolescent mental health services (Drinkwater, 1995).

223 Good commissioners:

- Support, build-on, and generalise from successful services.

- Agree explicit aims and objectives with their providers in service specifications.

- Develop mechanisms for regular feedback from patients, carers and their advocates.

- Resist the temptation to impose unnecessary external standards.

- Insist that service providers develop their own explicit standards which are subject to regular review.

- Require service providers to show that they provide regular, team-based, multi-disciplinary training, in addition to uni-disciplinary training.

- Are prepared to accept that effective outcomes result from investment in the development of successful processes, which are the subject of regular review.

CHAPTER 10

The Principles of Providing Child and Adolescent Mental Health Services

INTRODUCTION

224 Good practice in providing services should be guided by the rights and needs of clients, the clinical realities and knowledge of possible health gain from intervention, rather than service demands or idiosyncratic practices. Providing quality services to young people means facing a variety of challenges. These include identifying priorities and balancing the conflicting needs and expectations of patients, families, and professional groups.

225 Child and adolescent mental health service providers should be able to demonstrate ways of responding to and resolving these conflicting demands. The following table presents a framework of values and principles which should guide the deployment of high quality services.

Table 14

The Principles of Providing Child and Adolescent Mental Health Services
• Accessibility
• Multi-disciplinary approaches
• Comprehensiveness
• Integration
• Accountability
• Development and Change

226 There will be continuing debate about the most effective ways of applying these principles in practice. The existence of debate of this kind may well be a positive sign of evolving provision.

ACCESSIBILITY

Community-Orientated Services

227 It is essential that child and adolescent mental health services should promote a user-friendly image through maximum accessibility to patients and to other agencies. Physical, geographical, organisational, inter-disciplinary and professional barriers will all influence the image a service projects to its potential users.

228 One of the basic principles of mental health services is that of providing services as closely as possible to the person's home and within their community. This applies especially to child and adolescent mental health services which have had a long tradition, throughout their history, of being community-orientated. Indeed, the balance between hospital and community provision, and the style of both types of service, are such that much of the resource established both outside and within hospital premises has usually had a strong orientation to *assertive outreach* into the community.

229 Confusion arises because Tier 1 services (traditionally known as primary care services in the NHS) and Tier 2 and 3 services may be provided in community settings. For instance, individual professionals from primary health care teams may work with young people and their families in a variety of community premises and within a young person's home, school or other residential establishment. Similarly, staff from the specialist tiers (Tiers 2, 3 and 4) of the child and adolescent mental health services may also hold clinics in health

centres, work in schools and conduct appointments at the homes of individual clients/patients. They may work with families jointly with workers from other agencies who may occupy a position in their own organisation at a different level, equivalent to a different tier. Specific therapeutic teams from specialised parts of a child and adolescent mental health service may work in a family's home, providing family therapy while other individual specialists or teams may work in a consultative capacity without seeing individual pupils/patients in educational settings. Outreach workers from components of child and adolescent mental health services, offering very specialised outpatient or day and inpatient facilities, may also visit and work with families at home and liaise with the staff of social services departments and with educationalists within the community.

230 In these circumstances, it is all too easy to equate community services with primary care services. Traditionally, in health service provision, there has been an assumption that more specialised services are provided in hospital settings. However, the location of service provision and the degree of specialism employed are not necessarily directly linked.

231 The last two decades have seen an initially slow, but now more rapid, movement of mental health services for adults into the community, with highly specialised services being provided outside hospital environments. Equally, child and adolescent mental health services have offered specialist services outside hospital settings, as well as inside them, over a number of years. Mental health services for adults are moving towards an integrated position in which specialist services provided in the community are integrating with primary level services, and also with the more specialised hospital services, which continue to be required, in order to establish a seamless continuum of care. The same principle should apply to child and adolescent mental health services.

232 Experience has shown that this concept needs to be clearly understood by commissioners and senior provider managers, as well as those who work intimately within services at all levels. Additionally, the integration of primary (first contact) and specialised services into a blend of comprehensive provision requires clarity about the roles of the various levels or components of the community service. Such integration also requires the negotiation and monitoring of more formal protocols and filters across the boundaries between levels of specialism. Without this, there is a risk of role confusion, diffusion and skill dilution with regard to the goals for individual elements of the wider service.

233 The integration of services holds much promise for the improved accessibility and comprehensiveness of response. The tiered model of service, presented in this document, is offered as a template around which these complexities may be considered and the clarity of service functioning may be negotiated. In this way, local people can move smoothly to the service they require in a truly comprehensive, community-orientated mental health services for children and adolescents.

Children, Young People and Families

234 Children, young people and families must all feel that a service has enabled them to present their own perspective on the problems that they bring, and

that they have been listened to. This is crucial where, for example, the referred child, young person or family is from a minority ethnic or cultural background. Such communication is also a potent test of a service's accessibility.

Key considerations for children, young people and families are:

Referral

235 Parents may instigate the referral of their children for help, or adolescents may seek help for themselves. Referral systems should be clear and informative. They should leave no confusion in the mind of the referrer as to the process, or of the progress of a patient within the system. There should be a clear statement of the timing of service responses and when contacts can be expected. Information for service users should be clear and informative.

Assessment

236 Clear statements are required on how long this is likely to take, who will be involved, where it will happen, and what is its main purpose. This is crucial where, for example, a systemic family therapy model is used in preference to work orientated primarily towards individuals.

Intervention

237 Information is required about the projected number and length of appointments, their overall pattern and purpose, the venue, and the choice of intervention methods. Although, it can be difficult to be either clear or precise about therapeutic process and content, it is better to address this openly rather than to leave patients/clients/families mystified, or feeling that they are the subjects of some arcane process.

Agencies and Services

238 The service must be open to all agencies in contact with children and families. Key considerations for agencies are:

Information

239 Sufficient publicity material must be available to agencies so that they can make an informed judgment about the range and accessibility of services.

Consultation and liaison

240 The policy of a service, about formal and informal consultation and liaison, should be clear, and the functions of these services protected. The need for these effective interventions was a concern heard recurrently in the service visits.

Public Awareness

241 One of the functions of good practice is that services should directly and indirectly raise public and professional awareness of child and family mental health issues and of the service provision available to meet them. This may mean the positive promotion of mental health as an integral feature of child and adolescent development in all aspects of education, including the use of the media (Mental Illness Key Area Handbook, 1994).

MULTI-DISCIPLINARY APPROACHES

242   *"A satisfactory child and adolescent mental health service requires a wide range of
assessment and treatment provision and this is only possible when contributions are
available from the full range of relevant professionals"* (Cox and Wolkind, 1990).

243   Although the structure, role and functioning of multi-disciplinary teams have
been changing in recent years, the basic philosophy, underlying the practice of
professionals, from the same and different disciplines working together, remains
the same.   Effective child and adolescent mental health services rely for their
success on the individual and professional skills of individual professionals (at
Tier 2), and on the pooling of those skills when required for more complex
psychosocial assessments and interventions (at Tiers 3 and 4).

244   Traditionally, child guidance clinics were organised on the basis of bringing
together, in one setting or service, the skills and knowledge of a number of
professionals.   In this way, the capabilities of a psychiatrist, an educational
psychologist and a psychiatric social worker could contribute to understanding
and managing each case. In the sixties, seventies and early eighties, these teams
expanded to include clinical psychologists, child psychotherapists, community
psychiatric nurses, occupational therapists and family therapists.   In more recent
years, the educational psychologists and social workers have been withdrawn
from clinical team membership by employing authorities in many areas.   As a
result, the remaining team membership has tended to become more health
service orientated.

245   In parallel, the professional autonomy of team members has been increasingly
recognised, and in many services team members work independently.   In ideal
situations, each professional discipline has remained in close contact with the
other members of the professionals in the service overall, so that the children,
young people and families with whom they work have ready access to all
appropriate skills.   But experience, cited earlier in this review, shows that this
has been difficult to sustain and negotiate.   In addition, the enormous increase in
the number of referrals to child and adolescent mental health services in most
parts of the UK has meant that professional staff have had to be more
discriminating in their use of time and the models of intervention employed.   As
a result, they have taken a greater share of individual responsibility for the work
undertaken.   This does not mean that joint work by professionals from different
disciplines no longer occurs. It can, and does, and co-exists alongside work by
individual specialists.   Even when individual professionals work alone, multi-
disciplinary approaches are required for case discussion and supervision by
colleagues from other disciplines.   In this way, workers can retain access to
specialists from other disciplines even though they may not be working directly
with them on individual cases.

246   In essence, concepts of multi-disciplinary working have altered, though it should
be recognised that the principles of integration and co-ordination, in bringing a
necessary range of skills to bear in helping families to resolve complex
problems, have not.   A variety of models of service organisation has emerged as
a result.   In some places, close multi-disciplinary team working has continued,
whereas in others, aspects of service, such as child psychiatry and child
psychology services are organised and/or managed separately.   As services have
developed and because resources vary, it is the case that some CAMHS have

continued to be organised on the basis of all the professions being members of core multi-disciplinary teams, whereas others have separated with some of their activities becoming parts of, often loosely, networked services. Often these movements have been poorly planned and co-ordinated. The position of the HAS is that there is no one best model of modern organisation of CAMHS. In reality, different contexts require different mixtures of service components. The key, longer-term concepts are those of flexibility and of recognised and negotiated networks of service, with the needs of children, young people and their families being paramount (ie services should be child-centred).

247 It is not the purpose of this review to be dogmatic about any one style of approach to service organisation and management. What is important is that the principles lying behind good practice, which emerge from the evidence presented earlier in this review, are recognised. Central in these is the need for co-ordinated approaches to service provision. Each in the range of models available has its advantages and disadvantages but, whichever model is chosen, its properties should be recognised. Commissioners and all relevant providers should work to achieve child-centred, integrated service delivery. This is no mean task and, once achieved, its maintenance requires continuing attention. If close multi-disciplinary team working is the chosen model, there will be issues to be solved relating to leadership and the allocation of responsibilities for decision-making. If the model is of a more segregated kind, the need for vigilance and active steps to co-ordinate the roles, responsibilities and care across professional groups and between service components must be recognised and communication practised in order to create a looser but, nonetheless effective, network of care.

248 The provision of training is an integral part of specialist level service functioning. This means that not only may trainees of the disciplines represented in the teams and across a service be present in the service but trainees may also be taken-on from professions or disciplines which would usually operate outside Tiers 2, 3 and 4 of child and adolescent mental health services. They might include trainees in paediatrics, school medical officers, educational welfare officers, generic social workers, health visitors or school nurses. It is important to the training of all professionals who work with children that they are exposed to, and understand, the roles and functions of the different professionals in a multi-disciplinary child and adolescent mental health service.

249 Whatever style of team or network structure, organisation, management and functioning is employed, key features of effective multi-disciplinary approaches to work are:

• An agreed joint statement of aims and objectives.

• A clearly understood and effective managerial structure.

• A central base which promotes cohesion and continuity in multi-disciplinary working.

• Maintenance of competent practice among professionals by addressing issues concerned with:
  - training and supervision;
  - referral practices and procedures; and
  - personal time and resource management.

- Working co-operatively rather than competitively, and recognising the need for further specialist skills development in self and others to maintain compatibility and complementarity of approaches.

- Monitoring and support via regular focused meetings.

- Appointing a professional to act as co-ordinator and convenor.

- Acknowledging and addressing leadership issues and tensions within the service generally and specifically in multi-disciplinary teams.

- Ensuring that all involved are clear about when cases are dealt with by co-ordinated networks of professionals and when they are being dealt with by specific multi-disciplinary teams.

- Ensuring within all elements of the service that prime responsibility for each child, young person or family is clear. In the case of teams, this requires the explicit allocation of responsibility to designated key workers.

250 An important matter is to understand something of the theory and practical realities of team work and team functioning. In general terms, teams can be effective in providing:

- A broad range of ideas, approaches and stimulation in understanding and resolving problems.

- Support to, and reality testing for, individual professionals.

- A focused and fertile forum for reviews of service goals, objectives and performance.

- Potent circumstances for learning new skills.

251 Nonetheless, teams have limitations and experience shows that they may not be the best forum for:

- Accepting the legal responsibilities for decision-making in difficult circumstances.

- Resolving problems of managerial and clinical leadership.

252 A mature position would be to use teams for the activities for which they are best suited and to ensure that tasks which are better taken on by individuals are appropriately, fairly and overtly allocated according to explicit reasoning.

253 Additionally, the complexity of multi-disciplinary working across the various tiers of service, gives rise to a number of models of intra-service management. Whatever model is adopted, decision-making at case level should concern the provision of clinical services based on multi-disciplinary discussion of the issues and, in this sense, the group of professionals which should be involved with any individual or family should consider itself a team. Within this broad remit, each team or service will need clear definitions of the different levels of responsibility in regard to:

- Overall leadership.

- Professional supervision.

- Clinical decision-making by the key workers allocated to individual cases.

- Legal case accountability.

- Procedures for planned and emergency referrals to the service,
including admission and discharge procedures for day patient and
inpatient units.

254 Multi-disciplinary work extends to multi-agency work, and it is important that
providers in health, education and social services and the voluntary sector
recognise each other's roles and contributions so that the possibilities for
complementary or joint work is always borne in mind.

COMPREHENSIVENESS
Children, Young People and Families

255 Evidence from the service visits illustrates the fact that different services will
have different views on the breadth and definition of problems suitable for
referral to the specialist components (Tier 2, 3 or 4) of a child and adolescent
mental health service. The tiered model of service predicts that, as integration
with other agencies increases, professionals who work with children and
adolescents are likely to deal with a greater range of general medical, social and
educational needs of children and the impact of life events upon them.

256 It is essential that no child is excluded from the comprehensive child and
adolescent mental health service because of the nature of their problem, (eg.
learning disability, drug and alcohol abuse), their sex or ethnic background.

Age Range

257 The upper and lower ends of the age range cannot be rigidly fixed.   The
important consideration for both purchasers and providers is that, whatever
age range is selected, there should be services provided which are appropriate
for children, adolescents and for older adolescents and young adults which
ensure the delivery of seamless and effective patient/client-centred services.

258 Parry-Jones (1995) makes a case for increasing the prominence of services for
adolescents. His reasons include:

- The increasing social value attached to adolescence and youth by
society.

- The recent increase in the status of adolescent medicine.

- The need to exercise the optimum treatment of those adolescents who
suffer major psychiatric disorders and illnesses.

- The poor overlap between adolescent and adult services in many areas.

- The need to invest in prevention and mental health promotion. This is
illustrated by studies which have shown linkages between mental
disorders in adolescence and later adulthood.

- The need to improve education, training and research with reference to
this phase of development.

259 Undoubtedly, there is increasing societal interest in a wide range of problems
which beset young people and young adults and increasing awareness of what
can go wrong. This is evidenced by the interest of the Audit Commission in
services for children and adolescents and its most recent concern with troubled
and troublesome youth.

260 Parry-Jones' call for increased interest in services for adolescents resonates with the separate designation of service components for children and adolescents in *Mental Illness Services - A Strategy for Wales* (Welsh Office 1989). In England, the Chief Medical Officer drew attention to the health of adolescents in his annual report for 1993.

261 Earlier in this document, it was proposed that services should be provided for children, adolescents and young adults in an age range of approximately 10 to 25 years. This ideal is supported by the HAS and reiterated here. Its enactment in full would call for significant changes to current patterns of service provision and shifting of investment in most existing services in England and Wales. Nonetheless, such a move would help to enact the principle of providing enhanced mental health services for older adolescents and young adults with less disruption. Whatever approach is taken, it is important that mental health services for the 16 to 25 age range are specifically commissioned and provided. Commissioners are in an ideal place to move services in this direction.

262 It is good practice to keep children out of hospital wherever possible, and adolescents should not be accommodated on the adult wards of general mental hospitals simply because of the nature of their disturbance, difficulties in handling them or the lack of a local adolescent psychiatric and other services. Evidence shows that the debate over youth mental health services becomes most critical where some form of residential placement is required. The upper and lower age limits should, therefore, always be flexible and the interfaces carefully organised so that individual clients do not fall through the gaps.

263 However, whatever the age spectrum provided for by each service, there needs to be close liaison with other agencies involved regarding service planning and development and the management of individual children and adolescents. This includes obstetric, community health, hospital and neonatal paediatric services at the younger end and adult mental health and general medical services at the older.

The Work of Child and Adolescent Mental Health Services

264 The work done by child and adolescent mental health services can be broadly divided into six main categories which consist of:

- Direct work with children, adolescents and their families.

- Consultation and liaison.

- Service management, advisory and administrative tasks.

- The generation of advice to local agencies on policies relating to child care and mental health issues.

- Audit, service review and research activities.

- Training and continuing professional development.

Each of these will have an important place and part to play in a comprehensive child and adolescent mental health service.

265 Each child and adolescent mental health service should be able to provide, or provide access to, a number of functions.

- Assessment services which includes testing, diagnostic and investigatory services.

- Specialist reporting services, including those for the courts.

- Advice and short-term interventions, including the recognition and containment of concern and anxiety about children's welfare, education and health.

- Management and treatment of a range of differing styles, including those for individuals, groups, parents, and families.

- Management and treatment of different types, including counselling, dynamic psychotherapy, psycho-analytic psychotherapy, play therapies, behavioural and cognitive therapies, social skills training and activity-based and creative therapies, prescription of medication (including psychotropic drugs), and marital therapies for parents.

- The ability to advise families and other agencies on alterations in the life circumstances of children and adolescents and their families, including, for example, recommendations as to appropriate schooling.

- Referral to other sources of expertise, investigation, diagnosis and management.

- Collaborative work, including advice to agencies, involvement in case conferences and statutory proceedings.

- Liaison and consultation services.

- Training and continuing professional development.

- Research.

266 Assessment and intervention should take place in a range of different places including community clinics, health centres, hospital clinics, day and inpatient units and resource centres, social services department facilities, school and other education facilities, and family homes and alternatives to home.

Care Packages

267 Increasingly, the thinking of local authority purchasers is towards defining managed packages of care orientated to the assessed needs of children, adolescents and their families. Specialist CAMHS staff are also beginning to focus on the development of care packages geared to each individual's particular problems and exploring integrated care pathways (ICPs). Written care packages can: provide enhanced mechanisms for sharing information; encourage and enable informed debate; provide mechanisms for improved purchaser-provider communication; support evaluation and audit; and stimulate good practice (Bailey, 1995). These clinically-driven approaches are likely to prove helpful in shaping specialist services. They could also help children, adolescents, their families and referring agencies to make better choices about the delivery of care.

Training and Continuing Professional Development

268 Detailed consideration of training and continuing professional development lie outwith the scope of this report and within the province of advice from professional organisations. However, the HAS supports the view that commissioners and providers must recognise the importance of training and continuing professional development in their approach to strategy.

Selected Service Components

269 Much of this review has considered the present position with regard to service components relating to direct work, service management and service audit. It is not the intention to consider each of the service components in detail in this document. Instead, certain service components and matters in providing them have been selected for more detailed consideration in the sections that follow.

Consultation and Liaison Services

270 This section provides explanatory notes about the consultation, liaison and policy advisory roles which have been mentioned at various points in this report. These three tasks have in common the possibility of specialist child and adolescent mental health professionals working with other health service staff and with other agencies but in ways which may involve limited contact with individual identified patients and their families or sharing responsibility for them.

Policy advice to agencies

271 All child and adolescent mental health services staff should have an understanding of children's emotional development and needs, both when these proceed normally and when problems and disorders occur. These staff are, therefore, in a potentially powerful position to offer advice to a wide range of health and other agencies in their generation of policy relating to the management of children and young people. This is a legitimate role for child and adolescent mental health services and it should occupy a recognised and negotiated part of the total services, and be reflected in contracts with purchasing authorities.

Liaison

272 Liaison services refer to circumstances in which a member or members of the specialist components of a child and adolescent mental health service work alongside other child care professionals to provide a psychological and/or psychiatric perspective. In practical terms, this may involve the joint management of individual cases, or describe the circumstance in which the mental health professional has limited contact with the index patient, but offers advice to another professional who has the primary role. Work of this kind is illustrated by the input offered to paediatric services, general medical services and accident and emergency departments in respect of children and young people, who are considered to have engaged in episodes of deliberate self-harm by the physicians who have admitted them to their care. In these circumstances, it is usual for the young person to be seen and interviewed by a specialist mental health service member while the young person remains in the overall care of the admitting physician. Subsequently, young people in this circumstance, and their families, may be offered follow-up care by the specialist components of the child and adolescent mental health services. Work of this kind may also be practised in relationship to children with chronic physical

conditions, pupils presenting problems in school or young people in the care of local authorities. The service visits showed that such liaison services are highly valued and that they are another aspect of the role of child and adolescent mental health services which must be considered when priorities are set and they should, again, be recognised in service contracts. (See also British Paediatrics Association, 1994c.)

Consultation

273   Consultation can take many forms. It may imply a circumstance when a child or young person and/or the family is seen briefly by a specialist mental health service staff member or by a team from the service to offer another professional opinion. This is similar to a traditional second opinion. This exercise may also describe a circumstance in which a specialised (Tier 3) or very specialised component (Tier 4) of an overall service is asked for a brief intervention aimed at resolving a block in therapeutic progress experienced by other workers operating in Tier 2 or Tier 3. This form of consultation may also be a variant of liaison work, described earlier, in which the specialist mental health professional may be involved in advising another professional after only brief contact with the index patient or client. As an example, a growing area of consultation involves a specialist professional in seeing an abused child with a view to advising on his or her needs and future management or with a view to providing an assessment for use in legal proceedings. Services of this kind are usually provided from Tiers 3 and 4.

274   Frequently, the term *consultation* is used to describe an altogether different exercise, but with similar aims, in which the patient is NOT seen by the consultant. Rather, the consultant, who may come from a variety of disciplines, will establish a setting in which the client of this exercise, who is a fellow professional, presents a case or series of cases to the consultant who views them through the eyes of the presenter. Consultations of this type may take a number of forms and can be conducted in a group format. However, they have in common a rigour and a set of skills which focus on a particular task or problem; they educate the participants and enable them to share in, and contribute to, the solution or management of the problems they present (Steinberg and Yule, 1985 and Steinberg, 1989).

275   It is not uncommon for Tier 1 workers to seek consultation with those at Tier 2 in child and adolescent mental health services. This may be illustrated by the circumstance of a health visitor seeking advice about a young child's behaviour problem from a staff member of a Tier 2 component of a child and adolescent mental health service. The purpose of this consultation would be that of enabling the health visitor to gain confidence and skills, based on those acquired in her training and experience, through which she could better understand and tackle the problem with which she has been presented. As another example, it is not unusual for consultant psychiatrists and psychologists to receive referrals from general practitioners of adolescents whose behaviour is problematic, when the adolescent is already known to the social and/or education services. Experience shows that this information is often not known or disclosed in letters of referral. In this circumstance, an intervention which brings together the work of the professionals who are already involved may well be far more effective than a psychiatric or psychological assessment.

276 These assumptions also apply when an individual specialist mental health professional seeks consultation with another member of a child and adolescent mental health service who has a particular set of skills. Similarly, complexities of interaction in an organisation which deals with young people, such as a residential home or a school for children with special needs, may require consultant input from a team of people drawn from a child and adolescent mental health service. This team might work together with the organisation seeking advice (Tier 3) to aid the understanding and management of the children in its care. Similarly, the very specialised knowledge of Tier 4 staff could be applied to aiding specialist mental health workers operating in other tiers of the service in managing complex cases within their own resources.

277 The benefits of this kind of indirect consultation are three-fold. First, a young person may have been deflected from a referral to a specialist mental health service (or to a more specialised and expensive tier of it). Second, the problem may well have been resolved. Third, as a result, the experience and ability of the professionals to help future children and adolescents may well have been increased.

278 In this way consultation, as a training and development process, represents progressively reciprocated specialism as one moves through the tiers of service provision. This is summarised graphically in Figure 14. However, the specific skills required of 'consultants' must be recognised and training in them must be deliberately included in continuing professional development programmes.

Figure 14

The Inverted Cone of Provision

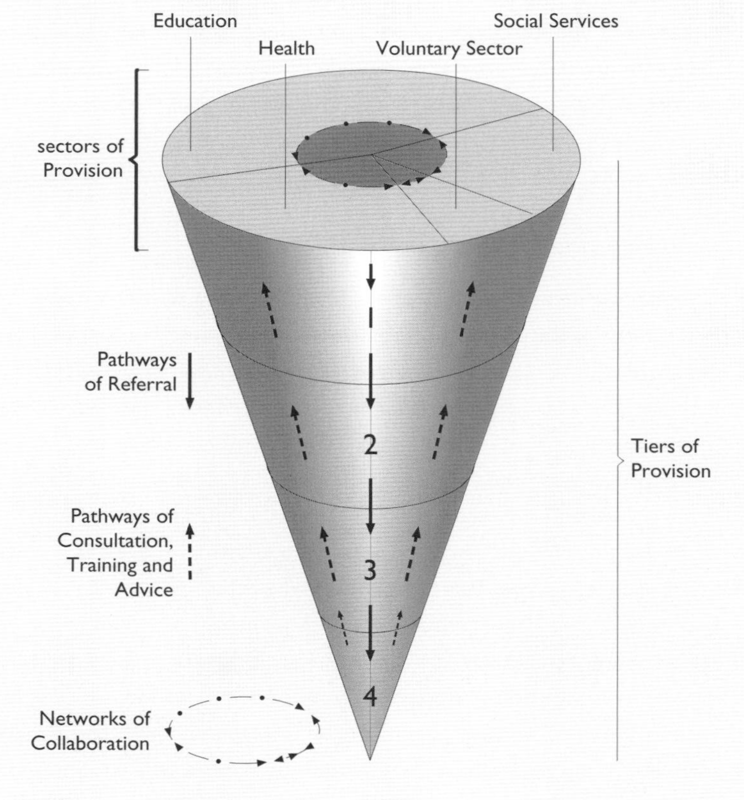

279 Consultation is widely regarded as an integral part of child and adolescent mental health services. It has, in common with liaison and policy advice, complexity of description and particular challenges for contracting, monitoring and audit of effectiveness. Nonetheless, its value and importance should be recognised by purchasers and providers alike and contracts should recognise that this is an important component of work offered by mature child and adolescent mental health services. Additionally, the Children Act 1989 and the Education Act 1993 require the NHS to make available resources to support the local authority in its work with children. This, evidently, has implications for child and adolescent mental health services, and involves their being involved in both direct work with the clients of local authority departments and in consultation with the staff of those departments.

The Staff of Specialist Child and Adolescent Mental Health Services

280 The barest minimum of professional staffing required for a child and adolescent mental health service is that of a child and adolescent psychiatrist, a clinical psychologist specialising in child and adolescent work, a child and adolescent mental health trained nurse and full administrative and secretarial support. It is a sound principle that no professional should work in an unsupported way and, in instances where staffing is minimal, close team work is essential. The core team will be considerably enhanced by the skill of a social worker, a psychotherapist, an occupational therapist, an educational psychologist, as well as specialist therapists such as family, creative and speech and language therapists.

281 This section will not consider each of the professions in turn or in detail. Instead certain of the professions have been described where this is seen as adding significantly to the understanding of commissioning, purchasing and provider managers.

Psychology and Child Psychotherapy

282 Psychologists working with children are primarily of two types - educational and clinical. Experience from the service visits indicates that there is frequently confusion over the training, roles and work of these two disciplines, even within the health services. Additionally, many purchasers expressed uncertainty about the role and work of child psychotherapists. For this reason, a very brief account of the work of each is included here.

Educational psychologists

283 Educational psychologists are generally employed by the education departments of local authorities to assess and provide intervention with children in school who have special educational needs. They have considerable skills in working with children and many also take a consultative approach to working with the staff of the schools they serve. Nonetheless, the demands for assessment, arising from the provisions of the Education Act 1981, have changed the working patterns of many educational psychologists. This heavy statutory workload has reduced the availability of educational psychologists to child and adolescent mental health services, to which they make a highly valued contribution.

284 It is recommended that health authorities and education departments should

come together to consider the future roles of educational psychologists, by adopting joint approaches to commissioning child and adolescent mental health services. Contributions from educational psychologists to child and adolescent mental health services might be made in return for specific aspects of that service providing support to the education authority.

Clinical psychologists

285 Clinical psychologists are widely employed by the NHS and are considered as core members of an integrated child and adolescent mental health service. They are skilful and entrepreneurial professionals with attributes that can be harnessed within a multi-disciplinary context to ensure imaginative and innovative service delivery. In some child and adolescent mental health services, they work intimately within multi-disciplinary teams. In others, they work more independently of other components of a widely defined child and adolescent mental health service. The HAS service visits indicated that, where this is the case, clinical psychologists and other service components and staff often appeared to be inadequately integrated. Usually this resulted from poor planning and managerial direction or from communication problems or disagreements about roles.

286 In some situations, because of poor integration at all levels, there appeared to be competition between those services organised around the child and adolescent psychiatry and those organised around the clinical psychology professions. It is not the intention of this review to espouse any one model of service organisation. However, it is important that, where child and adolescent mental health and clinical psychology services are separate, their differing roles and work are understood. Their work should be negotiated and subject to clinical audit to ensure that there is a comprehensive child and adolescent mental health service, to which all relevant professions can contribute. This would ensure there is neither duplication nor gaps in service, whether the different professions work within the same or in separate teams.

Child Psychotherapists

287 Child psychotherapists receive a four year post-graduate training in communication with children and adolescents which enables them to understand the feelings and thoughts of young people and thereby cope more effectively with their emotional and behavioural problems. The work of child psychotherapists is informed by a psychoanalytic theory and a knowledge of child development. They approach their work with a particular understanding of the inner experience of children and adolescents and how this influences every-day relationships.

288 Mostly, child psychotherapists help children on an individual basis, though many work with parents and families and with groups of children too. They usually see a child once weekly; some children will only need a few sessions, combined with family work; many, however, need to continue seeing the psychotherapist over an extended period of time.

289 Child psychotherapists deal with a wide variety of children's problems, both moderate and severe in nature. Mainly, they practice in multi-disciplinary teams and are based in child and adolescent mental health departments and child and family consultation centres. They also work in health centres and GP surgeries, student health and adolescent services.

The Skills of Professions Who Work in Mental Health Services

290 The range of professions which undertake work with children and adolescents who have mental health problems and disorders bring different skills to the multi-disciplinary pool which should be consolidated by each worker's individual training, interests, and experience. It is important to stress that few skills can be the sole prerogative of one discipline. In a mature service, the key worker for each client/patient should be chosen because his or her skills and experience are appropriate to the needs of the client/patient. The criterion for selection should not be the worker's discipline of origin. Irrespective of which tier of service is involved, there are some basic attributes that all members of a multi-disciplinary service or team should possess and these include:

- Empathetic interviewing and counselling skills.

- A working knowledge of child development.

- Up-to-date working knowledge of child and family problems and disorders.

- Understanding of the particular impact of major events on children's lives eg. abuse, bereavement etc.

- An awareness of how the professional's own life experiences informs their approach to others.

- Familiarity with manifestations of serious or potentially serious psychiatric disorders.

291 Further skills required by those who work at Tiers 2, 3 and 4 include:

- Special interview techniques suitable for eliciting information from all age groups eg. play therapy skills.

- A knowledge of family, group and systems dynamics and how these affect individuals in them.

- Sufficient knowledge and ability to apply appropriate psychologically-based therapies and psychiatric treatments.

292 It is important to recognise that disciplines other than psychiatry, psychology, social work and child psychotherapy offer specific training in child and adolescent mental health work. This is particularly relevant for nurses and occupational therapists within child and adolescent mental health services who tend to be drawn from the adult mental health and/or paediatric fields. The skills learned in that work are not always transferable or sufficient for work with younger age groups.

Nurses

293 Providers of child and adolescent mental health services should ensure that nursing staff appointed to senior posts in this field are able to demonstrate, through specific experience and training, the understanding and skills required for working with children and their families. With the implementation of the requirements of the UKCC for the Post-Registration Education and Preparation for Practice (PREP) of nurses, in 1995, all nursing staff will have the responsibility to demonstrate that they have an up-to-date knowledge of their specialist field of work.

294 There is a specialist child and adolescent mental health nursing qualification (ENB603) but the service visits suggest that there is difficulty in gaining access to such courses, which are currently available in only six centres. Problems with funding places on these courses were also reported. It is important to recognise the need for nursing staff to have access to appropriate training courses.

Occupational Therapists

295 The broad undergraduate training of occupational therapists, which includes mental health modules, gives them an understanding of psychologically-based approaches and an ability to translate them into practical strategies. They are able to analyse a child and family's function or dysfunction in areas of daily living, such as emotional and physical development, interaction, social skills and organisational skills. They are trained to devise therapeutic activity for children, parents and families, bearing in mind their needs and also roles within systems (family, school, social). There is also an emphasis in occupational therapy training on group work. This can be offered in community, outpatient, day patient and inpatient settings. Within individual and group treatments, occupational therapists have the ability to analyse, select and apply occupations as specific therapeutic media to treat people who are experiencing dysfunction in daily living tasks, interactions and occupational roles, such as play, social activities, art etc.

Approaches to the Assessment, Treatment and Therapeutic Interventions

296 It is not appropriate for a comprehensive child and adolescent mental health service to be governed by single approaches applied across all problems, clients and situations. The team/service should contain within it the potential for working with a sufficient range of:

- Individual and group psychotherapies

- Marital and family therapies

- Approaches which are based on activities

- Psychopharmacological treatments

- Approaches which focus on liaison and consultation activities

Where a specialist team cannot provide any one of these approaches, it should be able to provide ready access to appropriate services that can offer it in a suitable context.

Facilities

297 A fully comprehensive network of child and adolescent mental health services, which provides intervention at Tiers 1, 2, 3 and 4, includes:

- A readily accessible range of services provided locally at the Tier 1 level eg. in general practice, health centres, and schools.

- Specialist child and adolescent mental health services, providing a community network of locally responsive outpatient, home and school-based interventions offered by staff operating at the Tier 2 level.

- Facilities which offer more specialised outpatient services as well as therapeutic day units. These facilities should provide for work at the

Tier 2 and 3 level of specialisation and will often provide training for the staff of the service as well as training for external professionals and students.

- An integrated range of community and hospital-based sites for service provision. The hospital sites should provide access to a full range of modern investigative and diagnostic services.

- Access to Tier 4 services in the form of very specialised clinics and inpatient units (eg. for adolescents requiring inpatient care).

- All service sites should be supported by adequate receptionist, secretarial and administrative services.

Inpatient and Day Patient Units

298 These services are provided at Tiers 3 and 4.

Day units

299 Usually day units will be provided at the Tier 3 level of specialisation. The purpose of a day unit is to provide more intensive input than is possible from the community resources of a child and adolescent mental health service. Its use may also avoid the need for referral of children or young people to more specialised Tier 4 services, which may lie at a significant distance from the homes of children referred.

300 Day units may operate on the basis of weekly or sessional attendance. In the latter case, it is not uncommon for each half day to be geared to a specific therapeutic activity. Children, young people and families attend for those sessions which are part of their planned programme, decided on the basis of assessment of their needs. In the health service, such units are usually run by highly trained multi-disciplinary teams and should have a sophisticated and developed ethos for caring for children. They can be highly effective. In some Trusts, former inpatient units have been converted to day units as part of a well thought out and imaginative plan to offer a wide range of programmes tailored to the needs of individual children and adolescents, but with the added value of responding to serious disorders while maintaining the children's connections with their family and local community. On this basis, young people may attend on a sessional basis and maintain part-time attendance at school. Such a facility may also be used for weaning a child into and out of an inpatient unit, again as part of a planned programme, where there are intimate connections between a day unit and an inpatient facility.

301 It is important for commissioners as well as the staff of, and referrers to day units to be clear about:

- The aims and operational policies of the day unit.

- The place of day units in the overall spectrum of child and adolescent mental health services and, particularly, their relationship to other very specialised services offered by the NHS and by the education, social services and voluntary sectors.

- The working relationships of day unit staff with staff of child and adolescent mental health services at Tiers 1, 2 and 3. This should ensure that day attendance is a planned and evaluated episode in a more complete package of care and is not regarded as an aim or problem solution in itself.

- The relationships of the day unit with other agencies and sectors of child care. It is highly unlikely that children attending NHS child and adolescent mental health day units only have health-related problems. There are strong grounds for day units being jointly commissioned as they may well need to meet the educational and social needs of their attendees alongside their health needs.

- Outreach. Day units may function as resource centres and it is important that their operational policies consider their ability to employ staff working in specialised ways (Tier 3) to enrich other community aspects of a child and adolescent mental health service (Tiers 1 and 2), rather than providing care and intervention based solely on expecting families to attend the unit as a routine aspect of policy.

302 The interfaces between health service day units and family resource centres run by social services departments and day special schools, or educational units for children with emotional and behavioural difficulties, need to be fully understood to prevent duplication of services and poorly planned, disintegrated care.

Inpatient units

303 In this report, inpatient units in the health service are considered to be highly specialised, Tier 4, services. Relative to the significantly large numbers of children and young people who are appropriately referred to the specialist tiers (2 and 3) of a comprehensive child and adolescent mental health service, there are few who will require inpatient care. However, there are children and young people who, despite the existence of a fully comprehensive system of community-orientated mental health services, may require an intensity of treatment which can only be provided on an inpatient basis.

304 There is no absolute statement which can be made about the kinds of conditions which may require a child or young person to be considered for inpatient care. Nevertheless, some conditions are of such severity, produce behaviour or emotion of such types or intensity, or generate disability to the children and/or their carers of such degrees, that admission is essential. In general terms, the conditions which may give rise to consideration of inpatient care and treatment include: psychotic conditions such as acute psychosis, mania and possible schizophrenia (which are relatively rare in young people but of rising incidence over the period of adolescence); severe depressive disorder; life-threatening or intractable eating disorders; severe psychosomatic conditions; severe neurotic disorders (such as incapacitating obsessive-compulsive disorder and intractable phobias); and a variety of mixed conditions which may involve neurological conditions (eg epilepsy) or endocrine conditions (eg diabetes mellitus) in association with severe emotional disorder.

305 Consideration of admission should be based on a multi-focal assessment, which should take into account not only the severity, nature and complexity of the disorders and their impact on the life of the child or young person and his or her family, but also the abilities of the community network to cope adequately with helping the young person in distress. It would be foolhardy to persist with the use of community resources which are offering little traction on problems on a doctrinaire basis when inpatient or day patient treatment might accelerate recovery.

306   Additionally, day and inpatient units may undertake a variety of complex assessment and rehabilitative tasks for children and families with disorders of these kinds and for those with a wider range of complex relational and interactional problems. Examples include the assessment of children and adolescents with neuropsychiatric disorders, pervasive developmental disorders and those whose management is complicated by the co-existence of serious physical and mental health disorders.

The strategic roles of day patient and inpatient units

307   Inpatient and day patient facilities should not only be used to bring effective therapeutic leverage to bear on severe and otherwise intractable problems, but admission to them should also be considered as a strategic manoeuvre within more comprehensive therapeutic programmes. Some children and adolescents (for instance those with severe habit disorders) may need a period of preparation before they can benefit fully from a relatively short, but incisive, admission to a day patient or inpatient facility. The staff of inpatient units, as day units, will have been trained to a high level of skill in dealing with the most severe disorders. These skills can be used as an enriching source in consultation with staff in other tiers of a child and adolescent mental health service, as well as in training.

The resource centre concept

308   Appropriately and strategically used, day and inpatient units can act as resource centres offering a variety of styles of intervention to a wide surrounding area. In this circumstance, the distinctions between day care, residential inpatient care and assertive community outreach and consultative services become blurred. This should imply no lack, or blurring of objectives - but the reverse. Services of this type can provide highly focused sets of interventions which are picked, as if from a menu of highly specialised services, to meet the well assessed, carefully considered and monitored needs of individual patients. Thus, there will be many routes through resource centres of this kind in which each patient could well receive a different combination of very specialised interventions. Additionally, the residential position of individuals as outpatients, day patients or inpatients may be varied strategically over time in the pursuit of therapeutic goals. (Figures 15a and b).

Figure 15a

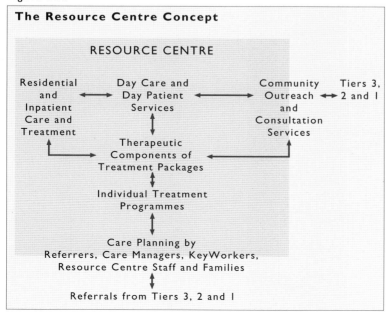

Figure 15b

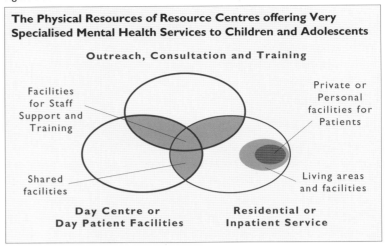

309   Services organised in this way can be highly flexible and responsive to changing need, and, to user and carer opinion. The numbers of young people using them can be increased compared to traditional in and day patient regimes. Thus, they are clinically appropriate, cost-effective and child/adolescent-centred. But, they do require careful setting-up and regular review alongside well planned monitoring of each child or adolescent. Also, the demands on staff can be high and this accentuates their needs for training and support. It should also be remembered that resource centres present significant demands to the contracting process which cannot be simply built on ECRs, patient bed days or day attendances.

Other highly specialised services

310   In addition to the very specialised services covered so far, there are other highly specialised services which may be provided on a supra-regional or national basis. These include medium secure facilities which provide adolescent forensic mental health services; and those providing for the mental health disorders of young people with sensory handicaps. It is essential to have a contractual basis to sustain these facilities and to ensure that they are available to each district. The NHS Health Advisory Service has proposed a mechanism for the provision of Tier 4 adolescent forensic psychiatric/mental health services built on the existence of a small number of medium secure inpatient units across England and Wales, with a greater number of Forensic Adolescent Psychiatry/Mental Health Community Teams (FACTS) serving England and Wales. These would provide assertive outreach as well as consultation and liaison services (NHS Health Advisory Service, MHAC, SSI, 1994). Possible contractual mechanisms for these and other very specialised services are considered in chapter 13.

Access to inpatient units

311   All health service commissioners should ensure that there is access to health inpatient facilities for adolescents. They may not be an intimate part of the comprehensive child and adolescent mental health service in a locality, but, if this is the case, there should be clear and explicit contractual and clinical arrangements relating to access. An important principle is that no young person under the age of 16 should be admitted to an adult psychiatric ward, unless there are major extenuating circumstances. This, in itself, requires the provision of appropriately orientated inpatient resources specifically for adolescents.

312 In recent years, many mental health professionals have become concerned about: the closure of adolescent inpatient units; the resulting reduction in this resource; and consequent loss of highly specialised skills associated with the staff of these units (Parry-Jones, 1995).

313 The clear view of the HAS is that ready access to NHS inpatient units for adolescents should be sustained. This calls for retention of inpatient capacity in all areas and development of it in other areas. Commissioners should also be aware that there are practical difficulties in coping with the whole range of mental health problems of adolescence in a single facility (eg. dealing with drug-using sixteen year-olds in the same setting as phobic eleven year olds may well be considered inappropriate). There is a need to ensure that a commissioning approach is applied to these Tier 4 facilities which is able to consider their size, roles, range of therapeutic capability and their financial security, against an assessment of need and management of their performance.

314 Inpatient facilities for younger children have reduced markedly in recent years, partly in recognition that children of this age rarely have mental illnesses or pure psychiatric disorders or mental health problems, and partly because separation of younger children from their parents is undertaken with the greatest caution unless there is evidence of physical, sexual or emotional abuse. The latter group of young people, regrettably large, requires longer-term solutions to be found to their assessment and therapeutic needs. Nonetheless, inpatient facilities for younger children, when used strategically and appropriately in the context of a wider therapeutic programme, do undertake valuable and effective work. These units will provide social and educational inputs and should, ideally, be resourced by the three main statutory agencies. Again, the interface between these facilities and education and social services establishments needs to be clearly understood to prevent duplication or gaps in the service.

INTEGRATION

315 The integration of provision for children and adolescents, requires each agency to be explicit about the kinds of service, interventions and facilities that they provide so that care of individual clients and patients can be programmed in ways which draw, if necessary, on the resources of a variety of organisations. Each agency and service component should be able to provide a menu of the types of work which it is able to offer. This would enable key workers to focus their advice to children and families through the provision of well informed and co-ordinated care packages.

316 Services which do not act in concert risk further disruption to the sense of personal identity of the children who use them. Such services may, unwittingly, reflect and reinforce conflicts that already exist within families. Examples of the effects of a breakdown in relationships between services are well documented in reports from child abuse inquiries. Families may, all too easily, fall through loose and fragmented networks with calamitous consequences. Also, there may be unnecessary duplication of services resulting in inefficient distribution and delivery of scarce resources. Child and adolescent mental health services should, therefore, have the notion of networking at their core, in order to ensure that all services are as fully integrated as possible across agencies and offer a continuum of care, rather than handing on clients at key points in their lives.

317 Figure 14, reproduced again here, provides a visual conception of an idealised integrated service. In this, the contributions of the main sectors of care, and the needs for services of a range of capabilities and specialisations are drawn together with the facilities for reciprocal consultation, training, support and advice in a three dimensional model. Each sector could be conceived as providing Tier 1, 2, 3 and 4 services.

Figure 14

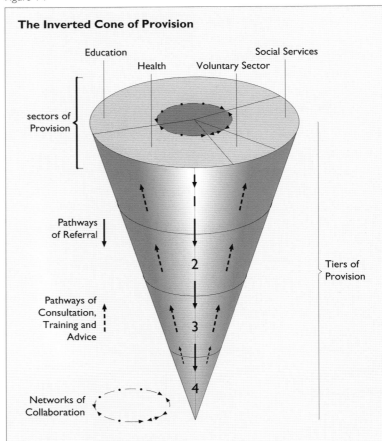

The Inverted Cone of Provision

Figure 16 also demonstrates this approach. What these figures cannot show at all well is the balance of responsibilities and contributions of each sector. This is because the relative contributions of each sector at each Tier will vary with responsibility and role, the nature and disposition of local services, the problems presented by young people and their families and their views and opinions on the care they desire. Also, the pathways of individuals and their families through the various service tiers and sectors of provision are, inevitably, likely to be complicated. Viewed in this way, the model is certainly idealised, though it does convey something of the potential relationships in local networks of provision.

Figure 16

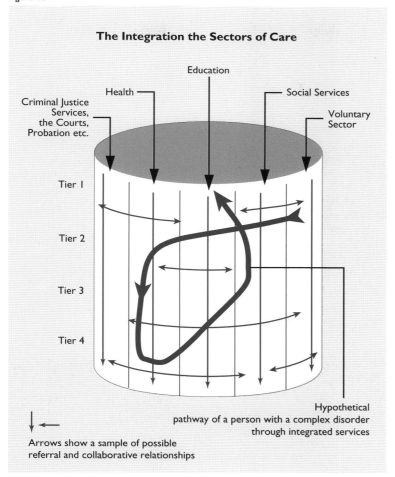

The Integration the Sectors of Care

Education

Health

Social Services

Criminal Justice
Services,
the Courts,
Probation etc.

Voluntary
Sector

Tier 1

Tier 2

Tier 3

Tier 4

Hypothetical
pathway of a person with a complex disorder
through integrated services

Arrows show a sample of possible
referral and collaborative relationships

Figure 16 illustrates just a small number of the many possible relationships in potentially complex inter-agency networks. The pathway of a hypothetical patient/client through the tiers of care provided by a number of sectors shows the value of a patient/client orientated approach to the integration and provision of services and the potential role for key workers.

This hypothethical pathway could, for instance, describe the integrated care pathway of a female adolescent who complained of misery to a voluntary sector counselling agency. This agency referred the young woman for further assessment by the social services department which consulted with her school before enabling her and her family to enlist the help of her GP. This resulted in the young woman's referral to a specialist child and adolescent mental health service which, later, provided a period of inpatient treatment in an adolescent unit as she was considered to be suffering severe depression. On recovery, the adolescent was referred by the teacher on the staff of the adolescent unit for specialist educational advice to help her to make-up her lost academic development. She and her family received continuing support and family counselling from the social services department during her re-integration into her local comprehensive school. Here, this young woman was monitored and supported by the school nurse and school doctor.

ACCOUNTABILITY

318 Good practice entails accountability in each of five broad areas:

Professional

319 The issues to be considered here include:

Codes of Professional Practice

320 Each discipline within CAMHS will have its own code of good practice.

Personal Development

321 Individual staff within each team/service have responsibility for their pre- and post-qualifying training and for keeping up to date with developments. The service has an overall responsibility for ensuring adequate access to training and continuing education.

Legal Responsibility

322 Most professions now have authoritative statements on professional codes of practice. Some areas of work place specific requirements on team members eg. under the terms of *Working Together Under The Children Act 1989* (1992) or *The Mental Health Act 1983* and its *Code of Practice* (1993).

Services

323 Significant items here are:

- Clinical audit, quality assurance and outcome measurement.

- Contract monitoring and compliance.

- Fulfilment of individual worker's contracts of employment.

- Compliance with local unit and agency procedures and protocols.

- The responsibility of the service for members of its staff (through support, supervision and good communications).

Other Agencies

324 Child and adolescent mental health services should be accountable to other agencies:

- As potential referrers, to keep them aware of the services offered and of the progress of individual clients that they have referred. This demands clear information on services for referrers.

- As colleagues, requiring an input from the staff of the child and adolescent mental health service in collaborative case work.

Children, Young People and Families

325 There are many areas in which good practice aims to meet the expectations and needs of children and families in a sensitive way (eg. the 21 key questions outlined in *With Health in Mind*, 1992). These include:

- Effectiveness in responding rapidly to the patients' need.

- The general and specific requirements of confidentiality.

- A duty to keep the children and families, who are using services, informed and involved in their own treatment programmes.

- Duties of advocacy as well as direct treatment.

- Informal and formal complaints procedures which act speedily upon the concerns of children and families.

Legal Issues

326 Providers must understand their legal obligations and accountability in relation to:

- Consent to treatment in respect of the *Mental Health Act 1983 and its Code of Practice and the Children Act 1989*.

- Restriction of liberty under the *Children Act 1989 and the Mental Health Act 1983*.

- *The Education Act 1993* and the *Code of Practice for the Identification and Assessment of Special Educational Needs*.

- *The Disabled Persons Representation and Consultation Act 1986*, in particular Sections 5 and 6 which relate to support to be provided by social services departments to school leavers with disabilities and special needs.

- Complaints procedures.

- After-care.

- The need for mental health opinions in court.

- The availability of legal advice.

These matters are elaborated in Annex A and in *Young People, Mental Health and the Law* (NHS Health Advisory Service 1995).

TRAINING, DEVELOPMENT AND CHANGE

327 Continuing effectiveness in practice requires child and adolescent mental health services, and individual staff within them, to remain sensitive to their own developmental and training needs. The staff network should be one that recognises the continuities in training between service staff members and can audit these sufficiently to allow a skill base to be established. This will enable a team or a whole service to explore its skill-mix, to identify areas for development at individual and service levels, and to increase awareness of, and responsiveness to, wider social change and the genesis of new problem areas.

328 Specialist child and adolescent mental health services can offer formal and informal training opportunities to professionals who work in parallel services and specialist services acknowledged outside, through reciprocal arrangements or joint training initiatives (as in joint consultancy teams for child protection). Liaison and networking across individual tiers of service, between the different tiers and with other child-oriented agencies, increases the accessibility of other professionals. Shared training initiatives also increase the accessibility of ideas across boundaries.

329 There is also a need for providers to be aware of their future staff requirements, and to think ahead to ensure that sufficient resources are

allocated to make certain that requirements for trained staff can be met in the future.

330 Training in child and adolescent mental health is required at pre-qualification level for student nurses, undergraduate medical students, post-graduate trainee clinical psychologists, occupational therapists, social workers and teachers. Following initial qualification, post-graduate training in psychiatry, psychology, psychotherapy, nursing and occupational therapy is required by health trainees of varying grades of experience, as well as for educational psychologists, specialist teachers and social workers employed by the non-health agencies.

331 Individual disciplines have their own organisations, colleges and other bodies which set training goals and standards and which monitor training and the achievement of those standards within their own profession. Universities have academic departments which have important pre-and post-qualification responsibilities. The HAS is mindful of the important, leading roles played by all these organisations. This review, therefore, emphasises the importance of training, continuing professional development and of academic departments but leaves detailed consideration of these matters to these bodies.

PART C

*Commissioning Child
and Adolescent
Mental Health
Services*

Action Points

Commissioners should utilise the guidance provided on assessing need; health gain; outcome measurement; joint commissioning and commissioning very specialised services to achieve the action steps of:

- Developing a multi-agency approach to commissioning CAMHS.

- Assessing need locally and auditing current services.

- Developing a strategic approach to planning a comprehensive CAMHS network.

- Consolidating and securing existing services through developing a discrete contracting framework for CAMHS.

CHAPTER II

*Needs Assessment,
Health Gain
and Outcomes*

332   The need for services that can respond effectively to particular sets of problems among a sector of the population, such as children and young people, is now seen as a function of the level and types of the problems in that group (Rutter, 1994) and the overall burden it places upon society, as well as the capability of current services to make an impact. Matters of significance relating to the definitions, epidemiology and nature of problems and disorders are considered in chapter 5 and this should be read in conjunction with this chapter.

333   The term *needs assessment* focuses upon those needs for which there are known to be effective interventions (NHSME, 1991). This is the basis for purchasing services, upon which improvements in health can subsequently be measured. It also allows priorities to be set, based not only on the most significant needs but also on the services which are most effective.   The relationship between these two is key in making commissioning decisions. For instance, very effective interventions may be available for conditions which are rare, whereas only interventions which are less effective may be available for conditions which are common. Making sure that these latter services are available may result in greater benefit overall than purchasing highly effective therapy for the few. It is the task of commissioning agencies to find a balance between these positions which is appropriate to the profile of their local communities.

THE ELEMENTS OF NEEDS ASSESSMENT

334   There are three main elements of needs assessment (NHSME, 1991):

- Epidemiological and expert professional evidence about the level and types of mental health problems in the population of children and adolescents, and about factors that are known to increase risks.

- The treatment and management strategies available and their known efficacy and cost-effectiveness, based on research evidence and on expert opinion. The performance of existing local services must be assessed in these terms.

- The views of local people, both users of services and the general public, on what services they regard as important and on their accessibility and acceptability. Direct consultation with the public, particularly with people who have used the services and their carers, is necessary but general practitioners, relevant non-statutory organisations and the Community Health Councils, amongst others, can act as valid representatives of user and carer views.

An Epidemiological Overview

335   The numbers of children who might be expected to have different conditions in a typical district will depend on the size and characteristics of the particular population; these vary widely and typical numbers may be misleading. It should be borne in mind that the numbers estimated for single types of problem may be misleading because, in a number of instances, several problems are likely to occur in the same children.

336   A recent ambitious project estimated the numbers for one DHA - Hounslow and Spelthorne - according to the sorts of epidemiological criteria that have just been outlined (Light and Bailey, 1993). An important point can be illustrated using this data.   It was estimated that 8,342 (14%) children in the district would

be suffering some degree of physical abuse or neglect - being kicked, punched, beaten, burned, or injured and that 60 children (0.1%) were likely to have been very severely abused; these would certainly have received medical treatment and could be identified through NHS records. About 200 Hounslow children are on the local authority Child Protection Register in any one year - the sort of figure found for many districts. All data, such as this, which relates to degrees of severity and to differing perceptions of demand, should be taken into account in assessing need. Different estimates of need by different agencies should be brought together to develop joint commissioning of appropriate services.

337   There is now some consistent evidence to indicate that many forms of child and mental health problems are becoming more frequent. It is documented that, since the second world war, there has been a considerable rise in the rate of juvenile delinquency (Rutter, 1991). Suicide rates in young people are also continuing to increase - at a time when, in the population as a whole, they have been falling (NHS Health Advisory Service, 1994e). Rates of depressive disorder in young people seem to be rising too, although some of this may be due to better recognition of the condition. Alcohol problems in young people are worsening as is substance misuse more generally. It is probably true also that anorexia nervosa and other serious eating disorders are becoming more prevalent in young people.

338   A variety of individual features may explain why one person is likely to commit a crime, become depressed or attempt suicide. But the overall rise in rates in these conditions is a function of social, political and economic factors which are unrelated to individual personal characteristics. It is by no means clear which social factors are responsible for the worsening rates, but the increase in rates of divorce and of unemployment may well be related because both are associated with psychopathology at an individual level. Further research is needed, and is indeed being undertaken into these questions, but again it emphasises the need for joint commissioning, particularly in promoting child and adolescent mental health, and for prevention, because the causes are much wider than those that traditionally lie within the expertise of the NHS. Joint commissioning is therefore an imperative with other agencies such as the social services, education and housing departments, voluntary bodies, and the law enforcement agencies.

Effectiveness of Services - Treatment Efficacy and Health Gain

339   The effectiveness of treatment approaches should be considered in relation to the goals that are set for intervention and for child and adolescent mental health as a whole. These may include the promotion of normal development and fostering autonomy, as well as the reduction of symptoms, and enhancing long-term personal and interpersonal functioning.

340   Some earlier studies in the USA have indicated that, left untreated, symptoms or problems in adolescents deriving from common emotional disorders continue, sometimes for long periods and into adulthood, whereas mental health interventions offered to comparable groups of young people have resulted in their having fewer problems several years later. Despite the existence of an enlarging number of studies, approaches to prevention and management have been insufficiently scientifically researched so far. There is, though, growing evidence of efficacy across the range of therapeutic approaches - psychodynamic, behavioural, cognitive, educational, and environmental manipulation (Graham,

1992). Gradually, for example, substantial evidence is suggesting that certain types of treatment for certain types of order are ineffective or contra-indicated, such as the application of individual psychotherapy to the treatment of autism, or medication in the treatment of conduct disorders. Conversely, substantial evidence indicates that other types of treatment are most appropriate, for example the use of medication in the more severe forms of the hyperkinetic disorder syndromes and Tourette's Syndrome, and the combination of individual and family psychotherapy in anorexia nervosa. Currently, the demonstration of benefits applies primarily to shorter-term treatments.

341 It is also now recognised that lasting therapeutic benefits are often likely to depend on altering the children's life patterns and circumstances, as well as on helping them to develop better ways of dealing with these. Family therapy and behaviour modification methods are effective in this area. At the core of the various cognitive therapies, approaches have focused on social problem-solving, self-concepts and concepts of coping. In tandem with such therapies, there is a demand for an investment in steps to help improve parenting and family relationships, to increase the quality of schooling and to upgrade residential facilities for young people.

342 The basis upon which the management of individual patients problems and disorders can be most effective, depends on accurate assessment, diagnosis and investigation of the increasingly complex and serious mental health problems in children and families (Nicol, 1990). Effective interventions for this burden of ill-health and distress depend primarily upon the types of mental health disorder. The following summary is based on contributions to the document *With Health in Mind* (Kurtz, 1992) and is a brief overview which is intended to provide an introductory summary for those people who are unfamiliar with the child and adolescent mental health arena. It is not a comprehensive or detailed review of treatments for child and adolescent mental health problems which is beyond the remit of this report. For a more comprehensive account of treatment efficacy, health gain and outcome targets, see Wallace et al, 1995.

- *Psychotic disorders*
  Acute psychoses and schizophrenia respond to medication and appropriate psychiatric and nursing care.

- *Pervasive developmental disorders*
  A composite home-based intervention programme has been shown to be effective in autism and other pervasive disorders in younger children. At an older age, this can be reinforced and supplemented by educational programmes provided through schools. The home-based programme should consist of behavioural approaches to the different aspects of disability, language, social handicap and behaviour problems. Treatment for the family is also needed, which takes into account the home environment.

- *Hyperkinetic disorders*
  Here, behaviour modification and treatment with cerebral stimulants have both been found to be effective. Again, it is the composite approach that is important, with flexible use of all types of treatment together with support for the family.

- *Eating disorders*

  Family therapy has been shown to be more effective than individual therapy in younger (under 19) sufferers of anorexia nervosa when the condition is of less than three years chronicity. These young people may also need an inpatient programme, which should be intensive and carried out early in the course of the disorder. Adequate staff is needed so that these young people are not left in limbo for many months before help and treatment can be given. There is a significant death rate in untreated cases.

- *Conduct disorders*

  With milder disorders, the group therapy approach for both younger and older children and behavioural approaches has been shown to have an effect. Generally, conduct disorders are regarded as particularly challenging by the many health and welfare agencies. Research conducted by health service inpatient units on the management of children and adolescents with severe conduct disorders suggests that their problems and disorders respond rather less well than do those arising from emotional disorders (Offord and Bennett, 1994). Nevertheless, longer duration of intervention through multi-modal therapies employing a range of techniques together and/or sequentially have been shown to be more successful. Cognitive problem-orientated skills training may be effective (Kazdin, Siegel and Bass, 1992). Conduct disorders in older children and young people may respond well to residential educational approaches. The programme has to be set up with great skill and care but, if it is, the results are encouraging. In younger children, family intervention approaches have again been shown to be of great help and these should be offered from a properly staffed child and adolescent mental health service. Further research into the effective management of children and adolescents with conduct disorders is required.

- *Neurotic Disorders*

  The range of disorders for which there is effective management is extending all the time. Milder problems and disorders in younger and older children respond well to individual psychotherapy, group therapy, and behavioural approaches. Obsessive compulsive disorder also responds relatively well to behavioural approaches and certain types of antidepressant medication. This is important, as it is now understood how entrenched these symptoms can become later on. Sleep disorders in young children and enuresis respond to behavioural approaches. Family therapy can make a contribution to disorders with a psychosomatic component such as recurrent abdominal pain.

- *Physical child abuse*

  Physical abuse has been shown to respond, in some cases, to family approaches and attempts to improve the quality of family interaction, thus reducing the chance of re-abuse. Clinical trials of family therapy are underway. Children's mental health workers can make major contributions to treatment planning in cases of child abuse.

- *Depressive disorder*

  Depressive disorder in children is commonly missed at primary care level and is often misunderstood by parents. It requires specialist expertise in communicating with, and understanding, children. Depression is eminently treatable with family support and cognitive therapies, although the benefits of medication have yet to be proven. Severe cases require day care or inpatient management.

The recent publication *So Young So Sad So Listen* (Graham and Hughes, 1995) provides a wealth of information applicable to young people, families and a wide range of professionals. It includes Action Sheets for parents and teachers who might be concerned lest their children might be depressed.

- *The impact of psychodynamic therapies*
  Psychodynamic therapies have been less researched, but this is largely because thoughts and feelings are so much more difficult to measure than behaviour. There is some evidence that tailored programmes of psychodynamic therapy are as effective as other approaches and preferable in many situations.

- *Liaison and consultation services*
  The advice, support and consultation offered by child and adolescent mental health services to parents and other agencies such as schools, educational welfare and psychology services and local authority social services are varied and difficult to quantify but are highly valued, especially when problem removal is unlikely but difficult, anxiety-provoking situations are involved.

343 Recently, considerable attention has been directed towards the longer-term impact of child and adolescent mental health disorders. Some of these can, if not effectively treated, continue into, or result in, health problems and disorders later in adult life. The linkage between child and adolescent mental disorders and disorders later on in life in the same individuals was considered by the Welsh Health Planning Forum in its *Protocol for Investment in Health Gain - Mental Health* and summarised diagrammatically. Figure 17 reproduces that diagram here.

Figure 17

Examples of Disorders in Childhood and Adolescence which can Result in Mental Distress and Illness in Adulthood

Disorder	Possible Onset in	Possible Consequences For	
		Adolescence	Adulthood
Sexual Abuse	Childhood ▶	• depression ▶ • suicidal behaviour • neurotic disorders	• depression • suicidal behaviour • anxiety states • neurotic disorders
Emotional disorders	Childhood ▶	• school refusal ▶ • depression	• depression • anxiety states
Conduct disorders	Childhood ▶	• delinquency ▶	• antisocial personality disorder • increased risk of offending
Eating disorders	Childhood ▶	• associated with increased mortality ▶	• eating disorders
Manic depressive disorders (bipolar affective disorders)	Adolescence ▶	• associated with increased mortality ▶	• manic depressive disorders (bipolar affective disorders)
Psychotic disorders eg. schizophrenia	Adolescence ▶		• psychotic disorders eg. schizophrenia

Recognition of Problems and Assessment

344   Effective management cannot be offered unless treatable problems in children are identified. It is known that many mental health problems go unrecognised. In one study, mental health problems were perceived to be the main reason for visiting the general practitioner in only 2% of children but were found in 23% (Garralda and Bailey, 1989). Mental health problems were recorded as the main reason for attending general paediatric outpatient clinics in 5 to 10% of children but were found to be present in 28%.

345   Another interesting project demonstrates how perceptions of need differ, even within the medical profession (Evans and Brown, 1993). In South West Hertfordshire, it was shown that 27 of 232 children who were 8 to 14 years old and attending their general practitoner, had psychiatric disorder, assessed according to the Rutter parental questionnaire. The general practitioners, however, felt that a much lower proportion of children attending their surgeries needed specialist mental health services but were unsure about a specific number. Only six of the children assessed as having a psychiatric disorder, according to the Rutter questionnaire, had attended the child and family clinic. The parents of 28 of the children overall, thought that their children would benefit from specialist mental health services but the children with high scores on the Rutter questionnaire and those whose parents who thought they needed services tended to be in different groups, with only 10 children in both groups. Four of these had had contact with the clinic. The other six children clearly had unmet needs. Another 17, with high Rutter scores, were assessed as likely to benefit from services, although their parents were not convinced of this. These findings are illustrated by Figure 18.

Figure 18

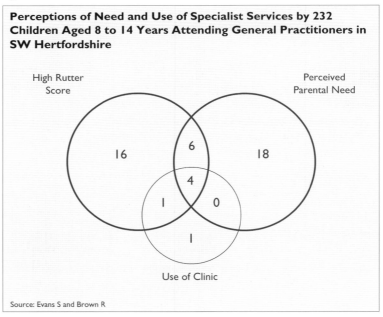

Perceptions of Need and Use of Specialist Services by 232 Children Aged 8 to 14 Years Attending General Practitioners in SW Hertfordshire

High Rutter Score

Perceived Parental Need

16   6   18

4

1   0

1

Use of Clinic

Source: Evans S and Brown R

346   Evidently, there are many children with mental health disorders who would benefit from services but are not in contact with them. The needs perceived by parents with concerns about their child differ from those defined by a GP or by a child and adolescent mental health specialist.

347 This research also highlights another feature of needs assessment - which is that of the importance of distinguishing between need which expresses demand and/or expectation and that which reflects experience of service use. Patient/clients approach services with certain positive and negative expectations of them. These may be framed by the transmitted experiences of others or reflect powerful, but less tangible influences such as guilt, anxiety and denial. As patients/clients and their carers use services, their expectations are replaced by opinion formed by their experience. These opinions may also be influenced by situational and idiosyncratic factors. Nonetheless, expectations and experience both influence the ways in which potential service users and carers will express their needs and the call for, and demands on services.

348 One of the tasks which faces commissioners is that of being aware of and, by their actions, balancing the triangles of tension (Figure 19, from Muth, 1994 and Williams, 1994). These capture the essence of the commissioning role.

Figure 19

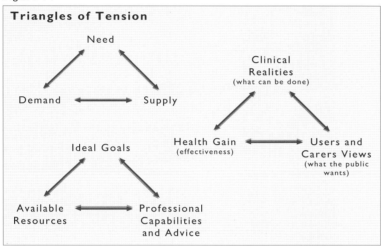

349 The findings of Evans and Brown also emphasise the tasks facing providers, including the need to maximise the opportunities for assessment of all children who may be able to benefit from help from the services. Assessment, investigation and diagnosis are the bases for effective management of disorders. Assessment must be skilled. Consultation and training by specialists for paediatricians, GPs, community nurses, social workers and teachers is a service which is likely to improve effectiveness in bringing more children to notice and in obtaining appropriate treatment for them. Extending services beyond the clinic by facilitating other professionals in schools and primary care will enable services to reach these children, indirectly, and make available advice from agencies which are seen by parents as appropriate. This may be the only way to support children and families when parents find specialist services unacceptable. Statutory duties, under the Children Act 1989, also increase opportunities to bring people with expertise in mental health to work with children suffering neglect and abuse (Home Office, Department of Health, Department of Education and Science, Welsh Office, 1991).

350 Effective services include preventive approaches for all children. A good example is the personal and social education curriculum in schools. This aims to promote self-esteem and to better enable young people to make healthy choices about many matters including, for example, the use of alcohol. Preventive programmes,

eg Headstart, aimed at children known to be at risk (such as economically disadvantaged three to four year olds), are shown to have a lasting influence on scholastic achievement and emotional adjustment (Farran, 1991).

Information Sources

351   A variety of the types and sources of information can be used to assess needs. They include national statistics, other routinely collected data, special studies and local statistics relating to children and young people. These are illustrated by Figure 20.

Figure 20

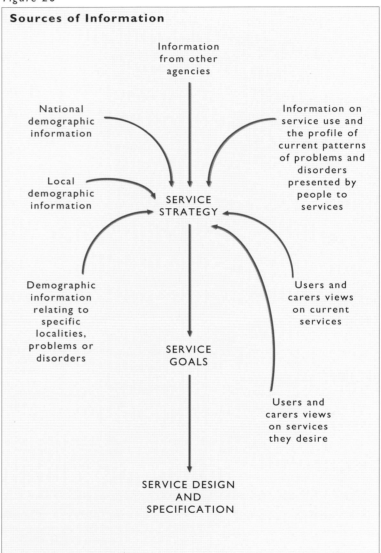

352   The data from nearly all sources needs to be interpreted with care but should include information about the size of the population and how it is distributed within geographical and administrative areas. Much of this data is published through the Office of Population Censuses and Surveys (OPCS) and will include trends as well as current population sizes, numbers of children in different age groups, the sex distribution and so on. Socio-economic data can be linked so that groups of children living in areas with poor housing, in temporary accommodation or where there is high unemployment can be identified. Indices

of deprivation, such as Jarman indices, can be applied and, combined with knowledge of the risk factors and will map areas where there are greater risks of mental health problems in children. Mortality data is of limited use in identifying needs for mental health services but the number, rates, and characteristics of deaths due to suicide and of accidents related to the use of alcohol or drugs must be monitored. Accidents are the most common cause of death in adolescence, with suicide the second most common cause, and two-thirds of adolescents who commit suicide are thought to have been intoxicated at the time (NHS Health Advisory Service, 1994). The lifetime incidence of deliberate self-harm in adolescents has been estimated as around 3%.

353 Information about disorder depends primarily on the use of services and so does not truly reflect needs, but must be examined to assess the appropriateness and uptake of services. Other useful indicators include the child disability register kept by each local authority, which is likely to be more useful if it is compiled jointly with the community paediatric department. The Child Protection Register is another indicator. Children and young people in care, children and adolescents living in bed and breakfast accommodation, children receiving special schooling, as well as young people who miss a lot of school or are in trouble with the police, are all likely to require child and adolescent mental health services. School-based surveys of behaviour are now quite frequently carried out at regular intervals and will indicate the levels and trends in the school populations of behaviours, such as drug-taking, and can indicate the need for particular types of intervention, some of which may best be school-based, whereas others might involve the larger community. Additionally, the police and probation services are able to offer local information on matters relevant to risk factors for disorder.

354 Readers will find a wealth of more detailed information extracted from national and international surveys and research on the prevalence and incidence of mild, moderate and severe problems and disorders in a text by Wallace et al. (1995) and that on mild psychological problems by Hall and Hill in *Health Care Needs Assessment* (Stephens and Raftery, 1994).

355 Because the sources of information, as well as the service providers, are scattered in different parts of the system, the process may seem daunting and only too easy to ignore. But the problems will not go away if they are not measured or estimated, and the problems *are* daunting. There is fresh evidence in the *Report of the Youth Council* that *a person under the age of 25 telephones the Samaritans every four minutes.*

356 Services are becoming better equipped to offer effective help. The reforms to the NHS force all to face the existence of health and social care problems and to commission and purchase what is needed. A start must be made on estimating local needs for mental health services for children and young people, locating the groups at high risk, identifying the most worrying unmet need, making the necessary alliances with colleagues in other relevant disciplines and agencies, and genuinely sharing resources. There will be a variety of ways of developing services. If, locally, primary care is strong, effective prevention and care for people with mental health problems and disorders can build upon this and other types of services can be structured accordingly. In other local situations, greater attention may need to be given to knowledge and skill resource among the specialists - in child and adolescent psychiatry, clinical and educational psychology, nursing, social

work, psychotherapy and occupational therapy. In all cases, greater expertise in this field must be developed more widely so that the large range of professionals and lay people who can, and do, offer help, do so more effectively.

A Framework for Outcomes

357 Every service should develop a systematic approach to collecting information. It is recommended that this should be conducted jointly by both commissioners and providers so that the information collected reflects the requirements of both and involves single approaches to families using the services and other agencies. The information collected should include a simple but appropriate approach to collecting outcome data.

358 An essential part of the assessment of needs is the monitoring of outcomes and then redefining the original needs assessment in the light of evidence of service efficacy and effectiveness, also in the light of the changing local circumstances (Jenkins, 1990). Needs assessment should therefore be a circular, ongoing task realistically linked to service performance and influenced by the changing pattern of professional capacity and capability.

359 Annex B, *A Suggested Framework for Outcomes in Child and Adolescent Mental Health Services*, by Berger, Hill and Walk is reprinted from a longer publication from the Association for Child Psychology and Psychiatry which details a proposed core data-set for child and adolescent psychology and psychiatry services. Annex B explores the complexities involved in collecting outcome data in mental health services and presents a simple and actionable approach. Readers may also wish to consult and consider the full data-set as it contains information and an approach to gathering information which could well prove useful to commissioners and service providers alike.

Acknowledgement

360 This chapter is based on work done by Dr Z Kurtz and a version of its contents was first presented by her at the conference jointly run by NAHAT and Action for Sick Children (ASC) to launch the ASC Quality Review of child and adolescent mental health services entitled *With Health in Mind*. The HAS is grateful to Dr Kurtz for preparing this paper and acknowledges the important role taken by Action for Sick Children in preparing *With Health in Mind*, a document which has proved influential in promoting the position of child and adolescent mental health services with many of the responsible authorities.

CHAPTER 12

BACKGROUND

361 Great emphasis is placed throughout this document on the development of a joint approach to commissioning. This is partly a consequence of evidence derived from the service visits, which revealed that agencies with a commissioning responsibility were usually operating unilaterally, producing services which were thought to be less effective than they could be. It is also a result of the view, synthesised from all sectors of this thematic review, that enormous benefits are to be gained for service users if commissioners work together.

362 *Joint commissioning* is a term that is now widely used but may have very different local interpretations (Heginbotham, 1994). It can be applied to a number of activities which, when performed jointly by the agencies involved, contribute to the overall process whereby health-related strategy is turned into effective care for service users and carers. Activities described as joint commissioning may fall into one or more of the categories listed in Table 15. A comprehensive approach to joint commissioning would involve all of these activities.

Table 15

Joint Commissioning Activities
• Joint assessment of population needs
• Joint assessment of individual needs
• Joint assessment of the needs for research and development
• Joint assessment of the training needs of the staff
• Joint agreement of strategy
• Joint service planning
• Joint care planning/care management/care programming
• Joint purchasing - eg. of new projects, sharing resource on existing projects and/or individual care packages
• Joint evaluation/monitoring

363 The pursuit of a joint commissioning approach may ultimately be aimed at all service areas or may be selectively applied to particular activities or client groups.

364 There has been a rapid increase in both the understanding and the misunderstanding of approaches to joint commissioning since the NHS and Community Care Act (1990) required health and local authorities to work much more closely in establishing community-based services. Clear lessons can be drawn from this experience. However, for child and adolescent mental health services, there is an added complexity, that of incorporating the responsibilities of those involved in the education of children and adolescents, essentially making joint commissioning a tripartite activity.

Joint Commissioning Interests

Health Care	Social Care	Education
DHAs	SSDs.	Education Authorities
FHSAs		Schools
GP Fundholders		

365 Added to this are the necessary commissioning interests of users, carers and families and the more indirect but important involvement of the police authorities, criminal justice system and the Family Proceedings Courts.

366 Experience from the visits highlighted the fact that, while there were examples of reasonable dyadic relationships occurring between health and social services or social services and education, no examples of the three main sectors commissioning services in a co-ordinated manner were found. A small local study commissioned by the Association of Directors of Social Services in the Yorkshire region (Brown 1992) revealed that there was no systematic process governing access to specialised health, social or education services for the most difficult and disturbed adolescents, leaving them bouncing between agencies over several years.

The Realities of Joint Commissioning

367 There are considerable difficulties in establishing a joint commissioning approach that involves such a large number of interests.

368 The service visits indicate that the baseline of collaborative work between the three sectors is thin and each may have its own definition and approach to commissioning. These differences may be manifest in:

- The degree of devolvement of budgets

- The relative autonomy of budget-holders

- Assessment criteria and priorities for purchasing

- Purchasing mechanisms and procedures

MODELS OF JOINT COMMISSIONING

369 In moving towards a joint approach, there may be benefits in considering a variety of models which different localities might adapt to local needs and relationships. The emphasis in all these models is on practicality and the basic activities which contribute to a joint commissioning approach. Individual models are not mutually exclusive and it is possible in some areas for all or a combination of the models to operate simultaneously.

Model I - The Strategic Approach

370 The main elements of the approach are the joint assessment of population and of agency needs, the audit of existing service budgets, compilations of a joint resource inventory and development of a joint strategy. An approach of this kind would encompass all the interested parties or stakeholders and its achievement may take a substantial length of time. In brief, the approach operates mainly at the level of service planning.

Model II - The Locality Approach

371 The main focus is on purchasing care for individuals. This approach is based on the devolution of purchasing responsibility to a locality level which involves GP fundholders and/or locality purchasing forums (health sector), locally managed schools (LMS) (education sector) and local authority social services

commissioning managers (social services sector). In this model, the primary task of the three statutory agencies is to agree, and to commission care packages for individuals, co-ordinating the components to be delivered by each sector.

372   There are complications to be overcome which include the differing stances of local and health authorities. Social services departments are responsible for purchasing packages of care while health authorities contract for sectors of care (Unsworth, 1994); there may be difficulties if individual schools do not have direct control over budgets for special needs education. Nonetheless, it may be possible for local mechanisms to be developed which bridge the gaps between health authorities and social services departments and which enable schools to authorise use of budgets held by education authorities.

373   The approach operates mainly at the level of individual care planning. It is important that it be established within a framework of agreed purchasing aims and objectives at a strategic level.

Model III - The Specialised Services Approach

374   This approach focuses on establishing a joint financial basis for use or development of specialised services. It is in this area that authorities have the greatest difficulty in agreeing on the relative responsibilities for care of, arguably, the most difficult group of children and adolescents.

375   The approach requires the three main statutory sectors to devise a mechanism for handling placements in specialised services that affords a minimum of disruption to the care of the individuals concerned. This may be achieved through jointly funding a local service or agreeing a standard percentage split of costs for placements outside the district of residence. (The complexity and multi-faceted nature of the problems faced by these few individuals would usually warrant a split of costs.)

Model IV - The Service Alignment Approach

376   This approach is probably the most commonly seen joint approach within child and adolescent mental health services. Its focus is on the deployment of unilaterally commissioning resources in a co-ordinated manner. For example, a social services department may arrange to place a number of social workers in a multi-disciplinary health service-based child and adolescent mental health service or team, in return for a number of sessions from the consultant psychiatrist or clinical psychologist at residential care establishments, or in supporting the work of the local authority in assessing very vulnerable people.

377   The vehicle by which this joint approach operates is the local service agreement, although some arrangements may still be handled on an informal basis.

378   A variant of this approach might see one commissioner purchasing services from providers who are more usually associated with another sector. For example, a local school might buy in the services of a school nurse from an NHS trust in order to offer counselling to young parents of school-age children or adolescents with minor psychological concerns.

379 All of the approaches listed above are rooted in examples of existing practice found in the service visits made by the HAS, although few have been applied to child and adolescent mental health services. They are potential routes by which an overall, jointly agreed approach to child and adolescent mental health services might be developed.

CHAPTER 13

Commissioning Very
Specialised Services

BACKGROUND

380 Developments in the purchaser-provider system are taking place rapidly. The system is also becoming complex, with an increasing range of health service purchasers and purchasing approaches. Despite the reduced numbers of health authorities and their functional integration with FHSAs in many areas, the growing number of GPFHs and closer commissioning approaches with social service departments present demands to all purchasers. These include harmonising their strategies, ensuring the appropriate regulation and management of the market and mounting consistent and co-ordinated quality strategies. Some purchasers have moved towards tackling these tasks for smaller communities through locality purchasing.

381 However, there are a number of instances in which there is a requirement for the provision of services of a very highly specialised nature to small numbers of potential users. These services were recognised by the NHS Executive as presenting problems in the purchaser-provider system and its guidance, *Contracting for Specialised Services, EL(93)68*, endeavoured to comprehend, and respond to, the need for the development of appropriate commissioning models.

382 Until recently, many such specialised services have been purchased on an ECR basis, leaving nearly all the risk with their providers. This can result in the knock-on risk of the loss of service, and of the associated staff expertise, in the circumstance of a single trust not being able to predict demand and its income and, thereby, sustain such a service. Alternatively, some very specialised services are commissioned by single purchasers (occasionally consortia of purchasers) which absorb all the responsibility through block contracting, despite their weighted capitation not reflecting the real and wider population using such services.

383 This background summary applies in full measure to a further tranche of services which do not easily fall within the perspective of one region. There are a number of health services which, because of their super-specialisation, the facilities required and the number of potential users are not most economically or effectively provided within each region. This is despite the fact that national and semi-national services cannot provide local and truly community-orientated responses to need.

384 Specialised services are often associated with academic centres, which thereby acquire high levels of expertise in specific areas. These services draw in people with complex problems from surrounding areas, and their costs should reflect some of the research costs incurred by the academic centres supporting them.

385 Moreover, these highly specialised centres are important sources of training for professionals who wish to work at very specialised levels of provision, as well as for those who are training to work in other tiers. However, it is important to recognise that research and training are not the sole responsibility of specialist units but require to be co-ordinated across all levels of service, and all agencies in one region. For, if time and academic support are not allocated to those working in non-specialist services and to research into effective interventions at the Tier 1 and Tier 2 and 3 levels, then the majority of children, young people and their families may not benefit.

386 All highly specialised services, ie, those at Tier 4, should be commissioned in such a manner that they are sustained and integrated into an acknowledged network of service running from primary levels of response in each locality, through secondary levels and into tertiary and higher echelons of specialisation. A network of this kind should enable co-ordinated packages of care to be delivered for each patient/user and their carers. These should draw on all the appropriate levels of specialisation such that locally provided community aspects of care can be delivered in conjunction with very specialised services provided from bases at a distance, as well as with very specialised responses from aggregated national and semi-national services. Such a system would also facilitate a cascade of education, training, advice, consultation, liaison and staff support to be offered. Figure 14 in chapter 10 summaries this situation diagrammatically.

DEFINING VERY SPECIALISED (TIER 4) SERVICES FOR CHILDREN AND ADOLESCENTS

387 It is clear from the service visits that children and adolescents with a wide range of mental health and associated conditions require certain very specialised services and it would appear that these requirements are infrequent and/or sporadic in the populations of the size of smaller health districts. These occur with such infrequency that:

- Provision of services of these levels of specialisation in every locality would not be cost-effective

- The degree of specialist skill required to respond to the problem would be unlikely to be available as standard in every locality

- The nature of the problem may be uncommon on the basis of its complexity, risk and persistence, such that local services were not able to provide an effective response.

388 Because the present position of services is historically determined, each locality will have a differing definition of those services that fall outside of its locally contracted and provided child and adolescent mental health services. This situation will be influenced by a number of the factors summarised in Table 16.

Table 16

Factors in Purchasing Tier 4 Services
• The local incidence and prevalence of the conditions in question.
• The experience and competence of the locally contracted and provided services.
• The value placed by the purchaser on the need to provide services close to the homes of the service users and their families.
• The cost of the very specialised services under consideration.

389 The types of disorder and clinical condition for which very specialised services may be required are described in chapters 7 and 10.

390 In circumstances which require commissioners to purchase very specialised services that operate on a supra-district, regional or national basis, it is important to ensure that commissioners retain a strong influence on the quality

of provision of care to the individuals concerned. This may be difficult if each commissioner's relationship with the provider is on an ECR basis. Reciprocally, it may be difficult for providers who have contractual relationships with a number of purchasers.

391 To ensure that a commissioning approach is applied to these services, commissioners must work together in the full awareness of the Tier 4 services for children and young people which are also provided by the education and social services. This approach should incorporate all the stages of needs assessment, contracting and performance management and is seen as mutually beneficial to both purchasers and providers (Table 17).

Table 17

The Benefits of a Commissioned Approach to Very Specialised Services	
Purchaser benefits	Provider benefits
• Quality control • Influence on continuity of care • Access to information • Influence on costs • Influence on providers to disseminate skills through training and research	• Financial security • Ability to undertake financial and service planning • Support for investment in training and research

MODELS FOR COMMISSIONING TIER FOUR SERVICES

392 Following a recent review of one such service with a national catchment, the HAS presented three possible models. These are to establish:

- A number of district health authority consortia, each of which would contract for a proportion of the service.

- An underwriting mechanism administered by a single, or by a number of DHA consortia or the NHS Executive itself. This would guarantee a level of income for each service, calculated on the basis of fixed and semi-fixed costs. Should the underwriting procedure be triggered in two consecutive years, a review of need would be undertaken to assess the requirement for the level of service offered.

- A lead commissioning authority for each such service that would contract on behalf of the country's or a group of commissioners. The authority would be responsible for setting up and implementing an appropriate commissioning strategy. This would be based on assessment of need and involve quality assurance, monitoring of contracts and outcomes and performance management.

393 Establishing any of these models requires constructive dialogue between commissioners and there may be a facilitative role for NHS Executive Regional Offices in this process. Experience of collaborative commissioning models to date suggests a number of success criteria (Table 18).

Table 18

Success Criteria
• A high level of trust in partner authorities
• Transparency in the contracting process
• Good information on service use and costs
• Adopting a medium to long-term view on value for money
• Basing decisions on a robust needs assessment exercise

CHAPTER 14

A Commissioning
Action Plan

394 Commissioning child and adolescent mental health services, is a significant challenge for many purchasers. Not only have they received little previous attention from purchasers, but it is also clear that they represent only one element of an increasingly demanding purchasing agenda.

395 This chapter sets out a set of steps, or building blocks, by which purchasers might begin to address the challenge or by which more advanced purchasers can assess and review their progress. It is recognised that, in many cases, the relationship between these activities is not linear and that purchasers will often need to respond dynamically and opportunistically as the context changes within which child and adolescent mental health services are purchased. Such changes may, for example, occur in the commissioning positions of partner agencies, or in legislation with respect to the care of children, or in the patterns of substance-misusing behaviour by young people.

396 The five action steps listed below (Table 19) are those that purchasers might employ in moving towards more effective commissioning of child and adolescent mental health services. The timescale by which they would be achieved will depend on the position in each district. It is strongly recommended that each step is taken jointly by all agencies with a commissioning or funding role.

Table 19

Action Steps	
1	Agree a multi-agency approach to CAMHS
2	Service mapping and audit
3	Assessment of need
4	Service planning and development of a strategic approach
5	Consolidation and review by use of mature contracts

1. DEVELOPING A MULTI-AGENCY APPROACH TO CHILD AND ADOLESCENT MENTAL HEALTH SERVICES

Activity

397 An exercise designed to ensure that all the key agencies with a role in the commissioning of CAMHS are linked to facilitate effective joint working.

Key Questions

- Do we have a dialogue with all funding or commissioning agencies?

- Is this dialogue occurring at the right level of seniority in each organisation?

- Are the chief officers aware of, and supportive of this dialogue?

- Are we utilising any joint resource for the benefit of the patients, clients or users of CAMHS?

- Is there a forum which includes all partner agencies in addition to any bilateral meetings?

- Has agreement been reached on who might lead or co-ordinate joint activity on CAMHS?

- Do the current relationships provide a strong enough base to facilitate joint approaches to service audit, planning, contracting and evaluation?

2.   SERVICE MAPPING AND AUDIT

Activity

398   An exercise designed to create an inventory of the nature and extent of all child and adolescent mental health service provision within the district. This should include statutory and non-statutory providers and the provision purchased or funded by partner agencies.

Key Questions

- What do we currently purchase?

- How much does it cost?

- What is purchased by others?

- Are there gaps and overlaps?

- Are these services financially and professionally secure?

- Do we have useful information from these services?

- How does the provision in total compare to our assessment of need and identified goals?

3.   ASSESSMENT OF NEED

Activity

399   A pragmatic exercise designed to estimate the level of provision required to satisfy the needs of the population for help with child and adolescent mental health problems and disorders.

Key Questions

- Do we have a common language between agencies which facilitates the identification of need?

- How are different conditions, behaviours or problems prioritised by the range of agencies?

- Can we identify problems on a scale that is relevant for commissioning purposes?

- What is our position on out-of-district services? Is this shared?

- Have patients, clients, users and carers been fully involved in the assessment of need?

4. SERVICE PLANNING AND DEVELOPMENT OF A STRATEGIC APPROACH

Activity

400 An activity, which may be continuous, which is designed to agree the development of child and adolescent mental health services within a strategic framework. This may not necessarily be explicit but must be understood by all purchasers.

Key Questions

- Do we have an agreed understanding of the short-term actions required by each agency and an agreed sense of the long-term direction?

- Are our plans capable of responding flexibly to changes?

- Do our investment plans enable us to respond flexibly to change?

- Can we evaluate and assess any progress made?

- Which parts of our strategic approach might usefully be published and shared with providers, and other agencies (eg. the Courts of Law through Courts Users' Committees)?

- How does the strategic approach fit with the 'Children's Action Plans' approach and the Education Act 1993 Code of Practice?

5. CONSOLIDATION AND REVIEW BY USE OF MATURE CONTRACTS

Activity

401 An exercise designed to review the current CAMHS contracting position and to produce a contracting framework to secure changes in the network of service provision negotiated through the wider commissioning process. In this approach, contracts are not the goal of commissioning, but are used as a confirmatory mechanism.

Key Questions

- Do we have appropriate and discreet contracts for child and adolescent mental health services that allow us to influence practice?

- Are the services we desire contractually and actually secure?

- Do our contracts reflect and facilitate good practice in child and adolescent mental health services (eg. family work, consultation to primary care staff, self-referrals)?

- Have we secured, through contacts, our desired level of out-of-district services, including day and inpatient provision?

- Do we have any form of contractual insurance, through collaborative contracting, for excessive morbidity leading to a rise in out-of-district placements?

Action Points

Providers should use the guidance set out in this part to:

- Assess the competence and suitability of their current managerial arrangements.

- Review their relationships with providers in other tiers of the network of services.

- Consider how closely their current service relates to the tasks and expectations set out for each tier.

CHAPTER 15

Key Leadership and Managment Issues

402   Managing change and the evolution of new systems are major tasks facing commissioning authorities, GPFHs and their provider trusts. Their effectiveness and success is linked very closely to their managerial structures. Investment in good management is a prerequisite of effective service development but, for many commissioning authorities and trusts, managerial development must, of necessity, run concurrently with service development.

THE HEALTH TRUSTS – LEADERSHIP AND MANAGEMENT

403   Within current trust structures, it is not uncommon for managers to be appointed from among the senior clinical staff who carry managerial and supervisory responsibilities in their professional, clinical practice. In the short-term, it is likely that the managerial knowledge and skill required by these clinician managers will be provided through in-service training and local staff development programmes. In the long term, some of these managers will wish to consolidate and 'legitimise' their managerial status by taking more formal managerial training. This may yield considerable benefit, particularly through externally validated programmes, such as the MBA.

404   The experience of the HAS, drawn from its many service visits, is that:

– Clear vision and inspirational leadership;

– Effective communications; and

– Sound management

are matters which have a strong influence on the capacity and quality of service delivery. Experience, drawn from the service visits, indicates that this is just as much the case for child and adolescent mental health services as it is across the broad spectrum of mental health services.

405   The view of the HAS is that the roles and identities of leaders and managers should be clearly specified in each service. The tasks, boundaries, responsibilities, and reporting structure for staff taking on these duties need to be defined, and training and support should be provided. The opportunities and challenges presented by the involvement of clinicians in director, leader and manager roles have been considered by the HAS (NHS Health Advisory Service, 1994d).

406   There is insufficient space in this text to consider the general properties of leadership and management in the health and welfare services. Nonetheless, it is evident, from the HAS service visits, that these tasks are of signal significance in child and adolescent mental health services. There is a common tendency to consider leadership and management as component tasks of one another. While leadership is to be distinguished from management, it is a vital component in the repertoire of all managers, clinical directors and lead clinicians.

407   It is the function of leaders to have the vision to identify the direction in which services should travel or develop. They should ensure that the staff of services want to go on the journey, do so with enthusiasm and commitment and are able to use their skills to good effect. The role of managers is to ensure that the staff are fully equipped for the journey and that the whole range of relevant factors is taken into account when planning the route.

408 Just as management style varies between individuals and with differing tasks, there is no one model of leadership. Leadership is, however, not synonymous with imposing opinions or solutions, but is centrally concerned with inspiring others and enabling them to give of their best and, thereby, to achieve their potential.

409 Importantly, the core tasks in managing child and adolescent mental health services are as for all services and include:

- Awareness of the environment in which these services are planned and operate.

- Strategic leadership.

- Strategic planning and management.

- Service organisational management.

- Awareness of the importance of the CAMHS as an organisation and of its culture

- Change management.

- Service operational management.

- Staff motivation and the management of people (human resources).

- Individual and organisational performance monitoring and management.

- Organisational development.

410 Each requires its own skills and techniques. The development of the capacity to undertake all of these tasks of general management within CAMHS will benefit child and adolescent mental health services and fuel their forward movement. Generally, the service visits indicated that many of these management skills were missing from this important sector of mental health services.

411 Again, based on evidence from the service visits, the key requirements for the effective operational management of a child and adolescent mental health service were identified as:

- A cohesive and coherent strategic plan based on sound leadership and managerial principles.

- Clear service specifications and supporting information.

- A sensitive, appropriate and clear approach to the philosophy of management practice which is in tune with the nature, work, setting and goals of the service.

- A clear and credible operational management structure.

- An effective hierarchy with an identified leader for both strategic planning and operational management.

- A clear grasp of the work of the services and of the professional constraints.

- A view about the gaps in provision of the present service.

- A view of the opportunities for service development and as to how, where and in what way the capacity of the current service is developing.

412 In addition, managers from all backgrounds should be aware of the points of growth in management thinking and technique. Good examples are those of the growing influence of risk assessment and risk management and of total quality management practice.

Child and Adolescent Mental Health Services

The Organisational Management Position

413 Provided that clear structure and effective management functions are in place, and relationships with other aspects of the child health and mental health services are also clear, whether a child and adolescent mental health service is placed and managed within a child health or mental health provider unit may be, relatively, less important. The management position of the specialist health service elements and tiers of the service is best decided on a local basis and will be heavily influenced by the nature, size and composition of the local trusts. In some cases, the health service specialist child and adolescent mental health service components are appropriately managed in an 'acute' trust alongside the child health services, while in others, the service will be part of a mental health and/or community trust.

414 In the case of larger, generic trusts, similar decisions will relate to whether the child and adolescent mental health service and its patients are best served by being managed within a child health, mental health or community directorate (British Paediatric Association, 1994c). In smaller trusts, it may well be most appropriate for the child and adolescent mental health service to form a separate directorate.

415 Whatever model of service management positioning is enacted, the reasons for its choice should be positive, overt and to the maximum benefit of the service and its patients. The structure should recognise the identity and nature of the service and support the full involvement of the clinical professionals in negotiating contracts with purchasers, as well as in service leadership and management.

The Organisational Management Structure and Processes

Some key issues in organising leading and managing services

416 At several points in this review, the diverse range of current organisational management structures in the specialised tiers of child and adolescent mental health services has been dwelt upon. Several matters should be uppermost in the considerations of those who lead and manage these services.

417 First, the broad variants of approach to the organisation of service delivery should be recognised. These include services in which the staff members endeavour to work within close multi-disciplinary teams which share the professional work and the responsibilities according to rules which are negotiated by, and within, the teams. In other instances, certain professionals, professional groups or elements of service work separately from others. A recurring style found in the service visits was that of a separation between child psychology and child psychiatric services. Increasingly, the services visited also reported separation of professionals employed by local authorities and those employed by the health service, where they had previously worked within combined services.

418 Another matter of central significance, in choosing a managerial structure and management processes, is the need to recognise that the structure must be capable of achieving high quality integration between sectors of care, between service components and between individual members of staff. This review recognises the history of community-orientation of most services and of the multi-disciplinary nature of the care which children and adolescents with mental health problems and disorders require. The review also supports the importance of multi-focal approaches to service delivery involving health, education and social services alongside the services provided by the courts, the probation service and the voluntary sector.

419 Within the health service contribution, services should be provided from community-based sites but the specialised investigative and therapeutic resources of hospital facilities are also necessary. Therefore, the health service component should include both community and hospital service bases. Work done in these varied ways requires co-ordination and this poses challenges to managers.

420 Furthermore, the diverse nature and siting of many child and adolescent service brings other key challenges, particularly those involving the continued professional development of staff and their support. The HAS endorses the opinion that members of professional staff working within child and adolescent mental health services should not work in isolation. Therefore, systems of communication are required, particularly in dispersed services, which enable staff to benefit from mutual collaboration and effective supervision. Opportunities for discussion of individual cases and opinions on service management and development are essential. Training events, both uni-disciplinary and multi-disciplinary, can achieve a variety of functions within this continuing requirement for effective professional communication.

421 Leaders and managers of services also need to be aware of the need for the premises used by CAMHS to be appropriate to the age, level of development and culture of the children, adolescents and families who attend. This calls for attention, to the adequate, for example, layout, decoration and use of rooms and the provision of play materials. The ethnic range of the community served is another matter which must be taken into account. Access to translation and the services of interpreters for an appropriate range of languages should be available. Services should also have adequate receptionist, supporting and secretarial services available to them at each site.

Models of management

422 All of these issues present challenges in managing the integrated approach to child and mental health services espoused by this review. While the reviewers do not recommend one particular model of organisational management structure, they are clear in recognising the need to co-ordinate service delivery. Different tasks emerge from different structural models and so the organisational structure which is adopted must be clear. This will enable both the internal and the external issues which arise for a specialist service to be negotiated more readily. Whatever model is adopted, managers and clinicians will face the continuing need for liaison with service partners from partner agencies which contribute to the totality of child and adolescent mental health service provision.

423   The complexity of multi-disciplinary working in teams, across various tiers of service, also gives rise to a variety of possible tensions in allocating and exercising leadership and the role of co-ordinating service delivery. These must all be recognised if they are to be resolved. (Chapter 10 considers multi-disciplinary approaches in some depth.)

424   The managerial model utilised at service level will need to address certain important issues if some of the consequences of poor managerial structure, described in chapter 7, are to be avoided. Some of these issues are particular to the managerial role and some to the individual postholder. The service manager's role must be clear to staff, as must the hierarchy and their respective positions in it. The manager must ensure that staff are clear about their part in the management process, particularly about monitoring and reviewing targets set for individuals and for the service. The planning process must be clear so that staff know how to influence it. The process must inform staff and provide them with sufficient feedback and maintain their motivation for service development.

425   Managing a service which involves staff from a range of professional backgrounds, at different stages in their career development, raises issues for the service manager. In general, service management may be greatly facilitated where the manager is an experienced clinician with formal management training. In all other circumstances, general managers must have clear professional advice available to them. Again, it must be clear whether it is the general manager or the clinician who takes responsibility. In the former case, the relationship will be one between a service manager and a lead clinician and, in the latter, between a clinical director and business manager.

426   Examples of issues which managers of child and adolescent mental health services must tackle include:

- Those who have had little previous experience of child and adolescent mental health services in particular, and children's services in general, should be able to recognise and respond to a possible credibility gap with professionals.

- The need to balance knowledge of professional issues in service delivery with the need to retain objectivity.

- The importance of consulting with staff who have de facto and/or designated clinical leadership roles. Managers should learn to handle those staff who have direct and indirect influence, by virtue of their status or personality.

427   These issues will be less apparent where there is a lead clinician or clinical director with clear management responsibility. In this circumstance, the management support provided to the professional leader is crucial (NHS Health Advisory Service, 1994d) if he or she is to succeed as a professional, as a leader and as a manager.

SUCCESSFUL SERVICE MANAGEMENT

428   Evidence derived from good practice identified in the service visits suggests that the following matters are particularly important in effective service management:

- Having a written strategic plan and business plan.

- Having accessible and intelligible service information.

- Identification of a manager with responsibility for business planning.

- Good communication with other statutory agencies.

- Good communication with service users.

429   Finally, opinion derived from the service visits suggests ways in which services might move forwards. It is recommended that the managerial structure and management processes and practice should aid the movement of services from being built on principles which are described here as standard, to achieving those which are listed as good practice (Drinkwater, 1995).

Issue	Standard Practice	Good Practice
Perspective	professional	a balance of patient, carer and professional
Aims and objectives	assumed	specified
Focus	throughput of people, or cases	effective processes and systems
Quality	appeals to professional standards	incorporates internally generated continuous quality improvements alongside professional standards
Training	profession specific	a balance of team-based and profession specific training

CHAPTER 16

THE PRESENT SITUATION

430   In this review, the phrase primary care is used to describe agencies that offer first-line services to the public and with whom they make direct contact. Workers in primary care settings therefore hold a unique position in the spectrum of health education and social care. Health visitors and GPs engage with families and young children in order to monitor their development and their problems. Teachers see all children and are ideally situated to note the early occurrence of mental health problems. School nurses and school medical officers engage with children and young adolescents and are able to monitor development and identify problems or concerns within the school setting. Social workers in child care teams engage with families in the community and provide a range of interventions to help restore families to more effective and rewarding styles of functioning; and to avoid the deterioration which may result in, or from, family breakdown. Family aides, carers, and support workers, from both the statutory and voluntary sectors, offer various types of assistance in home settings and family centres which help to prevent family breakdown.

431   All of these primary care workers regularly encounter early manifestations of difficulty, problems and disorder in children. Some of these are complex and serious and require immediate referral to Tier 2 or 3 (specialist) level of the child and adolescent mental health services. The bulk of more minor problems is, and should be, handled within the primary care sector through discussion, and counselling. Often, this work is undertaken by individual professionals, who work alone or in loosely identified teams, and who receive little recognition for what they do in respect of the mental health of children and adolescents. The HAS service visits identified some areas in which small groups of primary care professionals formed their own support and discussion groups. Less frequently, primary care workers have been able to obtain regular support and consultation from specialists such as psychiatrists, clinical psychologists or social workers with special experience. Partly as a result of this, some primary care workers have taken forward their own professional development through in-service training programmes, short courses focusing on childhood mental health problems, and more formal basic and intermediate level counselling programmes.

DEVELOPING TIER ONE SERVICES

432   The provision of mental health services by these primary care workers (Tier 1) are clearly important. The HAS believes it would be wrong to neglect the achievements made, often invisibly, at this level of direct contact. The visits made by the HAS indicated the potential for developing the role of Tier 1 services. Additionally, the demands on Tier 2 and 3 services are recognised and there is a need to ensure that these are used to their best advantage. There is a parallel case for developments, to Tiers 2, 3 and 4 – the specialist services – and the HAS believes that much could be achieved by increasing the impact of Tier 2 services in particular. However, the service visits also showed the pressures which primary care services are under and it was evident that, if the potential of Tier 1 provision is to be realised, the focus should be on providing support to workers within its services. Staff who undertake these Tier 1 roles would be helped by the recognition of their work related to mental health in their job descriptions and would be supported by greater access to more

specialist workers. Such an approach is already evident in some areas, in an informal way, but in other areas it would be new.

A Primary Child and Adolescent Mental Health Worker

433 Faced with existing waiting lists and demands to see young people with more serious problems, a recommendation of greater support from the more specialised CAMHS to those less evident components in Tier 1 might appear merely to increase the volume or shift the nature of the demands on Tier 2 and 3 providers. For this reason, the HAS recommends that local services should develop the roles and appointments of primary mental health workers.

434 The primary mental health worker envisaged here would be a professional tasked with supporting and enabling existing Tier 1 professionals and improving the links between the primary and specialist tiers of service. Professionals undertaking these duties would need to be integrated with a specialist community child and adolescent mental health service (Tiers 2 and 3) and receive regular and effective supervision.

435 The concept of a primary mental health worker which is presented here arose, independently, from the work of the HAS when conducting its service visits and through subsequent deliberations of the project's core working group. A similar concept was put forward by Hall and Hill in 1994. While recognising that there are differences, Hall and Hill's proposed child mental health worker would have a role broadly similar to that of the primary mental health worker proposed for consideration here. Readers may well wish to consider pages 542 and 543 in Volume 2 of Health Care Needs Assessment (Stevens and Raftery) in taking their thinking forward.

436 The primary mental health worker's role would include:

- Consolidating the skills of existing primary care workers.
- Helping primary care workers to develop new skills and build their confidence.
- Supporting the education of primary care workers in child and adolescent mental health matters.
- Aiding recognition of child and adolescent mental health disorders and the referral of cases to the more specialist tiers, when appropriate.
- Assessing and treating some individuals with mental health problems who are considered appropriate for management in Tier 1 level services.

437 The role of primary mental health worker could be exercised in a variety of ways:

- A conceptual approach in which the duties are identified but spread across a number of the staff of Tier 2 specialist child and adolescent mental health services.
- Initiatives undertaken by the specialist child and adolescent mental health services might cumulatively, achieve the aims of the primary mental health worker identified here.

- The tasks of the primary mental health worker are undertaken by the specialist (Tier 2) service though allocated to individual professionals on an overt, rotating basis

- Individuals are appointed to specific primary mental health worker posts which are established to deliver the kinds of services identified in this report.

438   The role of primary mental health worker, as envisaged, might be open to a wide range of professionals. At present, the mental health professionals who appear most suited to the role of primary mental health worker are community psychiatric nurses, health visitors, mental health trained social workers, basic grade psychologists or senior registrars and clinical assistants in child and adolescent psychiatry and senior occupational therapists. Such a post could provide a valuable training experience to many of these professional disciplines. Specific in-service training for the role would be essential for the professionals appointed.

Balancing the Work of Child and Adolescent Mental Health Services

439   Chapter eight considers the challenges of operating an effective service. One of these concerns the management, the roles and distribution of resources between Tiers 1, 2, 3 and 4. All commissioners, purchasers and providers are encouraged to review these matters so that the balance of services, as between the primary, direct-contact and more specialised services, is appropriately directed. This report calls for the development of Tier 1 services. But it would be unfortunate if this development were to take place in an unmanaged way. The benefits of greater availability and more accessible services for young people with problems and minor disorders, and more rapid transit of those with more serious disorders to appropriately specialised tiers, must be balanced with the risk of greatly expanding the range of problems brought to specialist tiers and of diverting resources away from children and adolescents with serious problems and disorders. This is an important matter for local service strategy, and in service delivery. Recent interest in the development of protocols for referral and of care packages has much to offer in practical responses to this challenge.

THE PURPOSE OF TIER ONE CAMHS

440   Augmented and supported in the manner described in this chapter, Tier 1 (primary) level staff might be able to take on a wider range of activities. The aims of mental health services in Tier 1 might become those of:

- Working to prevent more serious mental health problems in adolescence and early adult life, by early intervention.

- Enabling families, particularly those with young children, to function in a manner that is sensitive and responsive to both positive and negative behavioural cues.

- Enabling families to address difficulties at as early a stage as possible.

- Enabling families to resolve parenting difficulties effectively.

- Enabling children, young people and families to feel that they are effective partners in the intervention process.

- Providing expertise through staff who have mental health responsibilities legitimately incorporated in their work.

THE EXPECTATIONS OF CHILDREN, YOUNG PEOPLE AND FAMILIES AT TIER ONE

441   Visits to services and contact with children, adolescents and families suggest that their expectations of services include:

- The availability of advice at an early stage, without the necessity for formal referral to more specialised services.

- To have their views heard and respected, and their agreement sought at appropriate stages in the process of assessment, care and treatment.

- To have the reason for referral to Tiers 2 to 4 child and adolescent mental health services explained in clear and appropriate terms, and their agreement requested.

- To have guaranteed confidentiality within relevant legal restraints.

- To participate in interventions which are open, visible, and clear.

- To receive feedback and the opportunity to comment.

- To be treated in a manner which affirms the rights and responsibilities of parents.

- To receive interventions from workers who are sensitive to issues of discrimination, and the variety of forms they can take.

TASKS IN TIER ONE CHILD AND ADOLESCENT MENTAL HEALTH SERVICES

442   Within the primary care setting, the tasks embodied in the roles of professionals, including health visitors, social workers, school nurses, family aides, teachers, and GPs contribute to the full panoply of mental health services for children, adolescents and their parents.   These people will perform the tasks listed below to varying degrees.   The responsibility of the primary mental health worker, recommended in this review, would be that of supporting these professionals in their tasks and enabling appropriate access to more specialised services in Tiers 2 to 4.

Core Tasks

443   - Accessing families through routine developmental screening.

- Identifying those aspects of development which are likely to generate difficulties in parental handling, eg. eating, sleeping and temperament.

Tasks for Staff Working in Tier One of Comprehensive Mental Health Services and of Primary Mental Health Workers

444   - Identifying the contribution of social and environmental factors to difficulties in development.

- Being sufficiently informed about normal development, so that difficulties which exceed the 'normal' parameters can be identified.

- Engaging with parents and children in their homes, to establish trust and a climate for intervention.

- Sustaining relationships with children, young people and families over time, and terminating them appropriately.

- Employing basic skills in analysing and assessing difficulties, and in making preliminary formulations about the nature and causes of problems.

- Utilising supervision and professional support to clarify developmental issues, and the possible causes of problems and disorders.

- Employing basic level interviewing skills to enable parents and children to communicate their distress in safe, trusting, and confidential relationships.

- Identifying serious or potentially serious psychiatric disorders in children and adolescents.

- Discharging duties in accordance with the priorities agreed with commissioners and within an agreed time scale.

- Having sufficient skill and flexibility to work with individuals or small groups, in clinical or non-clinical settings.

- Being aware of the complexity of difficult behaviour in children; the various ways in which this may manifest itself; and the need to be open-minded about possible explanations.

- Being alert to the possibility of difficult behaviour in children masking an abusive, or potentially abusive, situation.

- Awareness of the statutory and legal framework within which children, families, and staff function.

- Liaison with other workers in primary care to ensure that a comprehensive appraisal of the family's situation can be made.

- Providing access to Tier 2-4 child and adolescent mental health services, and ensuring a smooth transition of care and responsibility on referral.

- Identifying and working with those children and young people who may avoid referral to the statutory agencies, eg substance misusers.

- Co-ordination of the inputs from other agencies, having knowledge of the systems, responsibilities and constraints, statutory or otherwise, on those agencies (notably education and social services).

CASE VIGNETTE 1 - TIER ONE

445   Joanne, aged three, began to have disturbed nights about a week after beginning attendance at a local day nursery. This coincided with her mother's return to full-time employment. Joanne became difficult to settle at night and, having fallen asleep, would awaken at regular intervals during the night. Her parents began to feel stressed and irritable because of lack of sleep, and this seemed to make Joanne's behaviour worse.

446   After discussion, the family GP considered that Joanne should be referred to the health visitor who, with support and advice from the primary mental health worker was able to draw up, in conjunction with her parents, a simple behavioural programme to help her. The health visitor was also able to discuss with Joanne's parents more constructive and consistent ways of handling her.

Two Tier Provision –
Inventions Offered by
the Individual Staff of
Specialist Child and
Adolescent Mental
Health Services

TIER TWO PROVISION – INTERVENTIONS OFFERED BY THE INDIVIDUAL
STAFF OF SPECIALIST CHILD AND ADOLESCENT MENTAL HEALTH SERVICES

CHAPTER 17

447 The tasks of Tier 1 are described in the previous chapter, as is the role of a primary mental health worker. One of these tasks is to improve the filtering mechanism operating between Tier 1 and higher tiers. Local criteria for passing through that gateway will influence the tasks of mental health professionals at Tiers 2, 3 and 4. The Tier 2 level involves services (whether organised around multi-disciplinary teams or through networks of separate service components or disciplines) in using their professional skills individually.

THE PRESENT SITUATION

448 At present, the tasks of Tier 2 are provided in the health service by individuals from a variety of multi-disciplinary contexts. Traditionally, these individuals have formed multi-disciplinary teams consisting of psychiatrists, psychologists, community psychiatric nurses, occupational therapists, psychotherapists and social workers who together have the training and experience to perform the tasks identified later in this chapter. In more recent times, there have been moves towards greater separation of components of services. This has reflected developments in the professions in addition to pressures which have been less positive. As a result, many differing patterns of service have emerged which were described previously (Williams, 1992, Williams and Skeldon, 1992 and Williams and Farrar, 1994). They have been illuminated by the surveys and service visits which have contributed to this review. (The history of and principles underlying multi-disciplinary approaches are considered in some detail in chapter 10.)

THE PURPOSE OF TIER TWO CHILD AND ADOLESCENT MENTAL HEALTH SERVICES

449 • To enable families to function in a less distressed manner.

• To enable children and young people to overcome their mental health problems.

• To diagnose and treat disorders of mental health.

• To increase the skill level of all those working with children, young people and families.

• To enable children and young people to benefit from their home, community and education.

• To enable children, young people and their families to cope more effectively with their life experiences.

THE EXPECTATIONS OF CHILDREN, YOUNG PEOPLE AND FAMILIES AT TIER TWO

450 The visits conducted by the HAS suggest that children, young people and their families who come into contact with specialist services at Tiers 2 and 3 might, in addition to those matters identified for Tier 1, expect:

• Confidentiality.

• Some choice about therapists and treatment methods.

• To understand what is happening to them and to agree to it.

• To feel that the service is enabling them, as partners, to improve the problem with which they have been presented.

TIER TWO PROVISION

INTERVENTIONS OFFERED BY
THE INDIVIDUAL STAFF OF
SPECIALIST CHILD AND
ADOLESCENT MENTAL
HEALTH SERVICES

- Mutual commitment to an improvement in the mental health problem or disorder.

- Cultural sensitivity

- Access to competency in specialist skills.

TASKS IN TIER TWO

451
- Assessment, treatment and management of children, adolescents and their families whose mental health problems and disorders cannot be managed in Tier 1 because of their:
  - complexity;
  - risk;
  - persistence;
  - interference with social functioning and normal development; and
  - the need for specialised skills in assessment and intervention;

- Support and advice to primary mental health care workers.

- Provision of support, advice and education to and consultation with professionals working with children and young people with the intention of normalising children's experiences, avoiding crises and preventing family breakdown. Examples of professionals who may benefit from, and be enabled by, such input are, GPs, health visitors, school teachers, field social workers, school nurses, community medical officers, residential social workers and specialist foster parents.

- Acting as gatekeepers for access to Tier 3 and 4 interventions. This requires knowledge of the availability and appropriateness of such care, and relationships which ease the passage of children and young people into it.

- Working as part of a multi-disciplinary team or of a service to ensure that the full range of professional services and therapeutic skills are available in Tier 2 to children, young people and their families.

- Provision of specialist assessments and reports for statutory agencies, and for social services case conferences, the courts, statements of educational need etc.

- Provision of a perspective on child and adolescent mental health problems and disorders which derives from education and training. This should be based on a holistic approach and practitioners should be capable of using systemic, interactional and developmental concepts in coming to opinions about young people's functioning in their environment.

- Offering specialist treatments and interventions, eg. family therapy, individual psychotherapy, behaviour therapy, and cognitive therapy.

- Provision of new perspectives on a child's mental health problems which lead to care and treatment strategies being redesigned where and when appropriate.

- Working closely with other agencies which provide services to children and young people to ensure that those professionals and agencies understand clearly what is happening to these young people.

- Working to clear priorities which have been agreed with the service commissioners, including agreed timescales for seeing identified priority groups (eg. one target might reasonably be that young people who have taken overdoses should be seen within one working day).

- Agreeing clear criteria with commissioners, for referral to Tier 4 services.

CASE VIGNETTE 2 - TIER TWO

452   Amanda, a 15 year-old girl, was referred by her GP to the child and adolescent mental health service because she had been steadily losing weight for the previous year and her menstrual periods had ceased four months before. Amanda was then at 80% of the weight she should have been for her age and height.   It was agreed that a child and adolescent psychiatrist would see Amanda and her family so that her physical and mental state could be assessed and monitored alongside considerations of the need for undertaking family therapy.

CHAPTER 18

Tier Three Provision – Services Offered by Teams of Staff from Specialist Child and Adolescent Mental Health Services

453 The work of Tier 3 of a comprehensive child and adolescent mental health service requires identified multi-disciplinary teams to address particularly complex problems. At this level, teams also offer mutually supportive training, and training for those in Tiers 1 and 2. In practice, it is often unusual for the whole of a multi-disciplinary child and adolescent mental health service to meet other than for the purposes of supervision, audit and teaching. Complex assessment and therapeutic activities are performed by identified teams of those professionals with particular skills, eg. in family therapy or the management of substance misuse. Other teams may meet together for supervision of therapeutic activity such as cognitive or psychodynamic psychotherapy, or specific meetings may be arranged to discuss the need for and co-ordination of the other professional activity involved in the management of children, young people and/or their families.

454 Essentially, therefore, the tasks of Tier 3 are undertaken in the health service by specialist teams formed for a specific task, eg. risk assessment teams, family therapy teams, day unit teams, substance misuse teams.

THE PURPOSE OF TIER THREE CHILD AND ADOLESCENT MENTAL HEALTH SERVICES

455 These include the purposes of Tier 2 child and adolescent mental health services, with the addition that team working provides a valuable opportunity for teaching and training. These are integral parts of service and team functioning.

THE EXPECTATIONS OF CHILDREN, YOUNG PEOPLE AND FAMILIES AT TIER THREE

456 These are similar to those of Tiers 1 and 2. It must be recognised that children, young people and families are more likely to feel intimidated by a team of professionals, hence extra time and effort must be spent in engaging each child, young person and/or family.

TASKS IN TIER THREE

457 In addition to those of Tier 2, the tasks of Tier 3 services are:

- The assessment, treatment and management of children, adolescents and their families whose mental health problems and disorders cannot be managed in Tier 2 because of their complexity, risk, persistence and interference with social functioning and normal development and the consequent need for specialist skills.

- To act as gatekeepers, with clearly agreed criteria, for entry to Tier 4 services; to have knowledge of the availability and appropriateness of such care; and to have relationships which ease the passage of children and young people into such care.

- To work within a larger multi-disciplinary team or network of service components to ensure that the full range of teams at Tier 3 is available to children, young people, their families and other agencies working with them.

- To ensure a smooth transition of individual cases or families to Tiers 2 and 1 services before completion of the involvement of Tier 3 services.

TIER THREE PROVISION

SERVICES OFFERED BY
TEAMS OF STAFF FROM
SPECIALIST CHILD AND
ADOLESCENT MENTAL
HEALTH SERVICES

- To provide specialist assessments and reports for those who have
  referred cases for team-based interventions.

CASE VIGNETTE 3 - TIER ONE → TIER TWO → TIER THREE

458   Michael was a 4½ year-old boy, approaching transfer to a primary school
reception class. His parents found him difficult to manage and he was aggressive
with the other youngsters at play school. He was referred to the child and
adolescent mental health service by his GP.

459   A primary mental health worker, in this case a community psychiatric nurse,
visited the child and parents at home with the intention of undertaking brief
parent-child behaviour modification to help the parents in their management of
Michael. However, after two visits it became clear that Michael seemed
insensitive to social cues and had rather odd speech. He did not respond to
simple behaviour modification measures.

460   Following discussions in the child and adolescent mental health service it was
decided that a team approach was appropriate. Michael and his family were
assessed by a psychiatrist and a psychologist. He was found to have a number
of developmental delays and his mother was becoming quite markedly
depressed. It was considered necessary to contact the education authority,
with Michael's parents' consent, to ensure that the school chosen for him was
appropriate to his abilities. One member of the specialist team continued to
support Michael's parents and a clinical psychologist from the team arranged a
more structured behavioural management programme. It was also agreed with
Michael's parents that the head teacher and the educational psychologist for the
school chosen for him be informed by the team of his problems and of the
intervention programme.

CASE VIGNETTE 4 - TIER THREE

461   Paul was a 13 year-old boy whose biological mother had not been able to care
for him and, consequently, he had spent much of his early life in foster homes
along with his two older brothers. At the age of two he had been placed in a
long-term foster home with his brothers, but the difficulties of their behaviour
led to the two younger boys leaving the family after six years. At the age of
eight, Paul was placed in a foster home with a view to adoption. There were
problems with his behaviour from the beginning of that placement. He stole
money regularly, was defiant, disobedient and disruptive and failed to make
progress in school. His behaviour improved somewhat after his adoption. After
renewing regular contact with his older brother, his behaviour again
deteriorated to the point that his adoptive father assaulted him and he was
removed from this family and accommodated by the local authority in a foster
home.

462   A referral was received by the child and adolescent community mental health
service requesting an assessment of Paul's needs and recommendations about a
future placement. In order to assist, it was necessary for the clinical
psychologist, who took on the case, as key worker, to understand the effects of
Paul's early life on his present development and relationships, to involve a family
therapy team to work with the adoptive parents to help them to cope with this
emotionally damaged, behaviourally difficult boy. Liaison was required with Paul's
social worker from the local authority social services department and its legal

advisers to determine and agree the most helpful psychological, family and social interventions. This role was undertaken by the social worker attached to the specialist service from the local authority.

CHAPTER 19

Tier Four Provision –
Very Specialised
Interventions and
Care

463 The tasks of professionals at Tiers 1, 2 and 3 are described in previous chapters. Close working relationships between staff at Tiers 2, 3 and 4 are essential to ensure ease of referral, access and return of patients/pupils/clients to their original services, and to ensure that Tier 4 is seen as part of the continuum of care for clients and families.

THE PURPOSE OF SERVICES WORKING IN TIER FOUR

464 The fundamental purpose is to work with both clients\pupils\patients and the agencies from their own district so that interventions are provided within a continuum of care. This should ensure that children and young people can return to less intensive and more local forms of care and treatment as soon as this is reasonable, but at a point when the risk of compromising treatment efficacy is considered to be minimal. The nature of Tier 4 services is described in chapters 7, 8, 10 and 13.

EXPECTATIONS OF CHILDREN, YOUNG PEOPLE AND THEIR FAMILIES AT TIER FOUR

465 In addition to those identified at Tiers 1, 2 and 3, these include:

- Clear understanding of access, ie. travel arrangements and visiting arrangements, if, for example, the service is an inpatient unit.
- Good standards of accommodation.
- Clear understanding of the responsibilities placed on staff when they are acting 'in loco parentis'.
- An understanding of the complex legal issues which may pertain to such young people.

EXPECTATIONS OF AGENCIES REFERRING YOUNG PEOPLE AND THEIR FAMILIES TO VERY SPECIALISED SERVICES

466 These include:

- Ease of access and information on referral mechanisms to Tier 4.
- Clear criteria for referral.
- A philosophy in which care responsibilities are shared; for example, with regard to updates on progress and agreement on discharge arrangements.
- Understanding of the legal implications in respect of the provisions of the Mental Health Act 1983, the Children Act 1989, and the Education Act 1993.

467 Clear understandings need to be reached between referring agencies in Tiers 2 and 3 and the accepting agency in Tier 4 to ensure continuity of care and matters such as shared responsibility and discharge arrangements. There are also issues to be negotiated concerning boundaries of professional responsibility and activity in a dual-service situation, ie. when personnel in Tier 4 services are working with a child and his or her family alongside staff from Tier 3 who are continuing to play a part in the overall management treatment plan for that family. This demands close working relationships and communication between staff in Tiers 4, 3 and 2 at all stages.

468 It is imperative that access to very specialised services in Tier 4 is not seen as providing opportunities to bypass Tiers 2 and 3. It is recommended that all responsible authorities should integrate their approach to child and adolescent mental health services in Tiers 1, 2 and 3, and enable Tier 4 services to retain their capacities for intensity and high levels of specialist functioning.

469 Services at Tier 4 are usually staffed on a multi-disciplinary basis. Traditionally, staff consists of psychiatrists, psychologists, psychiatric nurses, an occupational therapist, a psychotherapist and social workers. Added to these personnel, in residential settings, there is also the need for specialist teachers and nursing input in order to offer intensive and highly skilled responses to the needs of potentially very disordered young people.

TASKS IN TIER FOUR

470 • Assessment, treatment and management of children, adolescents and their families whose mental health problems and disorders cannot be managed in Tier 3 because of their complexity, risk, persistence and interference with social functioning and normal development, consequently requiring very specialised skills.

• Provision of interventions that require such a level of skill.

• Provision of specialist interventions, which would not be cost-effective in every locality, service or district because of sporadic demands for them in smaller populations.

• The application of the experience of working with sufficient numbers of patients with relatively rare conditions in order to instigate research into the development of effective treatment and offer staff working in Tiers 1, 2 and 3 training in the management and treatment of those conditions.

• To offer role support to staff working in Tiers 1, 2 and 3, where they are engaged in managing difficult or complex cases that might otherwise have required management in Tier 4. This might apply to extremely dysfunctional families which are unable to travel to specialist sites, or to patients with conditions that, as a result of a process of education and training of staff, are now felt to be appropriately managed in Tiers 2 or 3.

CASE VIGNETTE 5 - TIER FOUR

471   Alastair, aged 14, slowly became disinterested in school, socially withdrawn and isolated. His parents' concern increased when he became uncharacteristically aggressive towards them. Alastair refused to visit his GP and would not speak to her when she visited him at home. Alastair agreed reluctantly to talk to the child and adolescent psychiatrist when she visited him at home. Alastair explained that he could not leave the house because he knew he was under surveillance, and, although he could not explain the significance of this, he said he knew this was true because he had noticed that a lot of the furniture had gone missing from his school. Alastair was suspicious that the psychiatrist had been sent to keep him under surveillance too. The psychiatrist considered that Alastair had a psychotic illness. His parents were frightened and felt totally unable to care for Alastair. A place in an inpatient adolescent unit was found for Alastair, so that he could be cared for and his serious disorder could be treated.

Checklists and
References

CHAPTER 20

1. Have you consulted with:

   - The Director of Social Services? ☐
   - The Director of Education? ☐
   - Voluntary organisations that work with children and young people? ☐
   - The panels of guardians ad litem? ☐
   - User groups? ☐
   - The Court Users Committee? ☐

2. Are you aware of your responsibilities arising from:

   - The Children Act 1989? ☐
   - The Education Act 1993? ☐
   - The Mental Health Act 1983? ☐

3. Do you know what resources are presently deployed in the child and adolescent mental health services? ☐

4. Do you have the information, knowledge and alliances to develop a strategy which:

   - is jointly agreed? ☐
   - is based on needs assessment? ☐
   - has agreed priorities? ☐
   - has a specification? ☐
   - includes a process for achieving necessary change? ☐
   - has evaluation methods built in? ☐
   - can cope with rare, expensive referrals? ☐
   - is reviewable in the light of practice? ☐

5. Does your strategy consider CAMHS in a comprehensive manner? ☐

6. Do you have a provider/s with whom you can work to achieve your strategy? ☐

7. Do you have separate contracts specifically for CAMHS? ☐

8. Are your contracts for defined services rather than being based on FCEs? ☐

9. Do your contracts specify levels of in-service training? ☐

10. Are you confident that the staff of the provider organisations with whom you are in contract are sufficiently knowledgeable about CAMHS issues and provision? ☐

11. Does your strategy and do your contracts cover CAMHS at:

    - Tier 1? ☐
    - Tier 2? ☐
    - Tier 3? ☐
    - Tier 4? ☐

12. Is the CAMHS that is delivered to the populations for which you are responsible, an integrated service in which the various components and providers play acknowledged, co-ordinated roles?

13. Do your providers have mechanisms for avoiding competition between different service components?

14. Do your providers:

    • offer an adequate out-of-hours, emergency service?

    • have a protocol agreed with the acute paediatric and medical services for responding to episodes of deliberate self-harm?

15. Do the clinical staff of the providers advise on and negotiate the contracts for CAMHS with you?

CHAPTER 21

1. Do you have a clear management structure in which CAMHS are integrated? ☐

2. Do you understand your purchaser's CAMHS strategy? ☐

3. Does your purchaser's strategy consider CAMHS in a comprehensive manner? ☐

4. Do you understand your purchaser's CAMHS priorities? ☐

5. Do you understand the way in which your purchaser perceives the contribution of your service to the delivery of comprehensive CAMHS? ☐

6. Do your purchaser's perceptions of the role of your service within the overall provision of CAMHS match your own? ☐

7. Do you have a contact person in the purchasing authority who holds specific responsibility for CAMHS? ☐

8. Do you have a method of delivering CAMHS at the primary service level? ☐

9. Do you have a multi-disciplinary child and adolescent mental health team or network of separate service elements? ☐

10. Are the management and clinical roles of your service clear with respect to elements which are:

    • based on multi-disciplinary teams? ☐

    • integrated into service networks? ☐

11. Is the composition of your service appropriate in respect of:

    • the number and type of the professional disciplines? ☐

    • Staff levels within:

        – service components at Tier 1? ☐

        – service components at Tier 2? ☐

        – service components at Tier 3? ☐

        – service components at Tier 4? ☐

12. Do you have a clear access route to Tier 4 services? ☐

13. Do you have an operational policy for CAMHS? ☐

14. Do you have a business plan for CAMHS? ☐

15. Do you have an adequate information system geared specifically to CAMHS? ☐

16. Do you have clear floors and ceilings for your contractual commitments? ☐

17. Do you have a recognisable and separate budget for your CAMHS? ☐

18. Have you avoided different professional groups or service components competing with each other? ☐

19. Do members of your child and adolescent mental health service have good relationships with:

    • the social services department? ☐

- the education department? ☐

- voluntary agencies? ☐

- the courts, magistrates and guardians ad litem? ☐

- each other? ☐

20. Does your CAMHS provide an out-of-hours emergency service? ☐

21. Does your CAMHS have a clear protocol for dealing with young people who deliberately harm themselves? ☐

22. Do you audit the work done by your CAMHS? ☐

23. Do you have training programmes specifically for staff working in CAMHS? ☐

24. Are secretarial and reception staff working in CAMHS trained for their roles? ☐

The bibliography contains the references to all documents cited in the text. Additional documents and papers, which are not specifically referred to in the text, are also contained. The intention is to provide sources of further information for readers who wish to pursue issues in more depth.

Anderson, J., (1989). *Patient Power in Mental Health - Working for Users?* British Medical Journal, 299, 1477-8.

Audit Commission and Her Majesty's Inspectorate, (1992). *Getting in on the Act: Provision for Pupils with Special Educational Needs: the National Picture.* HMSO.

Audit Commission, (1993). *Children First - A Study of Hospital Services.* HMSO.

Audit Commission, (1994). *Finding a Place: A Review of Mental Health Services for Adults.* HMSO.

Bailey, V., (1995). *Personal Communication.*

Barber, W., Griffiths, M. and Williams, R., (1992). *Behaviour Disorders and Hearing Loss in Pre-School Children.* Update, 1132-1140.

Berger, M., Hill, P., Sein, E., Thompson, M., and Verduyn, C., (1993). *A Proposed Core Data Set for Child and Adolescent Psychology and Psychiatry Services.* Association for Child Psychology and Psychiatry. London.

Black, D., (1990). *The Roles, Responsibilities and Work of a Child and Adolescent Psychiatrist in Child and Adolescent Psychiatry.* In Into the 1990's. Editors: Harris Hendricks, J. and Black, M. Royal College of Psychiatrists, Occasional Paper 8.

Bone, M. and Meltzer, H., (1989). *The Prevalence of Disability Among Children.* OPCS Surveys of Disability in Great Britain. Report 3. HMSO.

Bor, R. and Miller. R., (1991). *Internal Consultation in Health Care Settings.* Karnac Books.

British Paediatric Association, (1994a). *Report of the Working Party on the Needs and Care of Adolescents.*

British Paediatric Association, (1994b). *Community Child Health Services: an Information Base for Purchasers.*

British Paediatric Association, (1994c). *Purchasing Health Services for Children and Young People, Volume 1: Summary. A consultation document.*

Brown, D., (1991). *The Here and Now Children.* Association of Directors of Social Services (Unpublished)

Camden Mental Health Consortium, (1986). *Mental Health Priorities in Camden as We See Them; The Consumer Viewpoint.* Camden Mental Health Consortium.

Campbell, D., Draper, R. and Huffington, C., (1991). *A Systematic Approach to Consultation.* Karnac Books.

Challen, A.H., Davies, A.G., Williams, R.J.W., Haslum, M.N. and Baum, J.D., (1988). *Measuring Psychological Adaptation to Diabetes in Adolescence.* Diabetic Medicine; 5: 734-746.

Challen, A.H., Davies, A.G., Williams, R.J.W. and Baum, J.D., (1992). *Hospital Admissions of Adolescent Patients with Diabetes.* Diabetic Medicine; 9: 850-854.

Chief Medical Officer, (1993). *On the State of the Public Health 1993. The annual report of the Chief Medical Officer of the Department of Health for 1993.* HMSO, London.

Children's Legal Centre, (1994). *The Mental Health Handbook. A guide to the law affecting children and young people.*

Costello, E.J., Burns, B.J., Angold, A. and Leaf, P.J., (1993). *How Can Epidemiology Improve Mental Health Services for Children and Adolescents?* Journal of the American Academy of Child and Adolescent Psychiatry, 32:6, 1106-1114.

Cox, A. and Wolkind, S., (1990). *The Role of the Child and Adolescent Psychiatrist in Child and Adolescent Psychiatry.* In, Into the 1990's. Editors Harris Hendricks, J. and Black, M. Royal College of Psychiatrists, Occasional Paper 8.

Cox, A.D., (1993). *Preventive Aspects of Child Psychiatry.* Archives of Disease in Childhood, 68, 691-701.

Cox, A.D., (1994). *Personal Communication.*

Craig, T., (1992). *Assessing the Effectiveness of Delivery.* In, Creating a Common Profile for Mental Heath. Editors: Griffiths, S., Wylie, I. and Jenkins, R. HSMO.

Culling, J. and Williams, R., (1988). *A Study of the Psychosocial Consequences of Childhood Leukaemia in the Family.* Bristol Medico – Chiurgical Journal.

Delamothe, T., (1992). *Getting Rational Over Rationing.* British Medical Journal, 305: 1240-41.

Department for Education, (1994a). *Code of Practice on the Identification and Assessment of Special Educational Needs.*

Department for Education, (1994b). *Pupils with Problems.*

Department of Health, (1991). *Welfare of Children and Young People in Hospital.* HMSO.

Department of Health, (1992). *Personal Social Services Local Authority Statistics.* HMSO.

Department of Health, (1992). *Choosing with Care,* The Report of the Committee of Inquiry into the Selection, Development and Management of Staff in Children's Homes. HMSO.

Department of Health, (1992). *Committed to Quality: Quality Assurance in Social Services Departments.* HSMO.

Department of Health, (1992). *Concern for Quality.* The First Annual Report of the Chief Inspector of the Social Services Inspectorate for 1991-1992. HMSO.

Department of Health, (1992). *Health of the Nation.* HMSO.

Department of Health, (1993). *Working Together for Better Health.*

Department of Health and Welsh Office, (1993). *Code of Practice; Mental Health Act 1983.* HMSO.

Department of Health, (1993) and (1994). *Health of the Nation - Key Area Handbook: Mental Illness.* BAPS.

Department of Health, (1994). *Mental Illness: Can Children and Young People Have Mental Health Problems?* BAPS: Health Publications Unit.

Department of Health, British Medical Association and Conference of Medical Royal Colleges, (1994). *Child Protection: Medical Responsibilities.*

Department of Health and Department for Education, (1995). *A Handbook on Child and Adolescent Mental Health.* HMSO Manchester Print.

Department of Health, Social Services Inspectorate, (1993). *Evaluating Performance in Child Protection.* HMSO.

Department of Health, Social Services Inspectorate, (1993). *Young People Detained and Remanded: A Study of Local Authority Juvenile Remand Services.*

DeSilva, P., Dodds, P., Rainey, J. and Clayton, J., (1992). *Management and the Multi-disciplinary Team.* In, Management Training for Psychiatrists. Editors: Bhugra, D. and Burns, A. Gaskell, London.

Dodd K.L., (1993). *An Old Problem Solved in Child Care.* British Medical Journal, 306, 873-4.

Donaldson, L.J., (1992). *Maintaining Excellence: The Preservation and Development of Specialised Services.* British Medical Journal, 305, 1280-4.

Drinkwater, C., (1995). *Personal Communication.*

Evans, S. and Brown, R., (1993). *Perception of Need for Child Psychiatric Services Among Parents and GPs.* Health Trends, 25, II.

Farran, D.C., (1991). *Effects of Intervention with Disadvantaged and Disabled Children: A decade review.* In Handbook of Early Intervention. Editors: Meisels, S.J. and Shanhoff, J.P. Cambridge University Press.

Forsythe, M., (1993). *Commissioning Specialist Services.* British Medical Journal, 306: 872-3.

Garmezy, N., (1985). *Stress-Resistant Children - the Search for Protective Factors.* In Recent Advances in Developmental Psychopathology. Editor: J. Stevenson. Pergamon, Oxford.

Garralda, M.E. and Bailey, D., (1989). *Psychiatric Disorders in General Paediatric Referrals.* Archives of Disease in Childhood, 64, 1727-33.

Goldberg, D. P. & Huxley, P. J., (1980). *Mental Illness in the Community: Pathways to Psychiatric Care.* Tavistock Publications, London.

Goodyer, I., Wright, C. and Altham, P.M.E., (1988). *Maternal Adversity and Recent Stressful Life Events in Childhood and Adolescence.* Journal of Child Psychology and Psychiatry, 29, 651-657.

Goodyer, I., Wright. C. and Altham, P., (1990). *Recent Achievements and Adversities in Anxious and Depressed School-Age Children.* Journal of Child Psychology and Psychiatry, 31, 1063-1077.

Graham, P.J., (1986). *Behavioural and Intellectual Development in Childhood Epidemiology.* British Medical Bulletin, 42, 2, 155-62.

Graham, P.J., (1992). *Types of Psychological Treatment: an Overview.* Archives of Disease in Childhood, 67, 237-9.

Graham, P. and Hughes, C., (1995). *So Young So Sad So Listen.* Gaskell and West London Health Promotion Agency, London.

Griffiths, S., Wylie, I. and Jenkins, R., (1992). *Creating a Common Profile for Mental Health.* HMSO.

Gunn, J., Maden, A. and Sinton, M., (1991). *Treatment Needs of Prisoners with Psychiatric Disorders.* British Medical Journal, 303, 338-41.

Hall, D. and Hill, P., (1994). *Community Child Health Services.* In Health Care Needs Assesment. Editors: Stephens, A. and Raftery, J. Radcliffe Medical Press, Oxford.

Heginbotham, C., (1994). *Some Versions of Joint Commissioning.* British Medical Journal, 209: 215-216.

Hill, P., (1994). *Purchasing Psychiatric Care*. Child and Adolescent Psychiatry Specialist Section of the Royal College of Psychiatrists.

Hill, P., (1995). *Personal Communication*

Home Office and Department of Health, (1992). *Memorandum of Good Practice on Video Recorded Interviews with Child Witnesses for Criminal Proceedings*. HMSO.

Home Office, Department of Health, Department of Education and Science and Welsh Office, (1991). *Working Together Under the Children Act 1989*. HMSO.

Hopkins, A., (1990). *Measuring the Quality of Medical Care*. Royal College of Physicians.

Hughes, T., Garralda, M.F. and Tylee, A., (1994). *Child Mental Health Problems: A Booklet on Child Psychiatry for General Practitioners*. St Mary's CAP.

James, A., (1992). *Committed to Quality*. HMSO.

Jenkins, R., (1990). *Towards a System of Outcome Indicators for Mental Health Care*. British Journal of Psychiatry, 157, 500-14.

Jenkins, R., (1992). *Health Targets in Mental Illness*. In Creating a Common Profile for Mental Health. Editors: Griffiths, S, Wylie, I. and Jenkins, R. HMSO.

Jenkins, R., (1992). *Children and Adolescents*. In Creating a Common Profile for Mental Health. Editors: Griffiths, S, Wylie, I & Jenkins, R. HMSO.

Kat, B.J.B., (1992). *On Advising Purchasers. Guidance for Members of the Division of Clinical Psychology of the British Psychological Society*. British Psychological Society.

Kazdin, A., Siegel, T. and Bass, D., (1992). *Cognitive Problem-solving Skills Training and Parent Management Training in the Treatment of Anti-social Behaviour in Children*. Journal of Consulting and Clinical Psychology, 60: 733-747.

Kraemer, S., (1994). *The Case for a Multi-disciplinary Child and Adolescent Mental Health Community Service: The Liaison Model, a Guide for Managers, Purchasers and GPs*. Tavistock Clinic.

Kurtz, Z., (1992a). Editors. *With Health in Mind*. Action for Sick Children /SouthWest Regional Health Authority.

Kurtz, Z., (1992b). *Needs Assessment and Commissioning for Mental Health Care for Children and Young People*. Young Minds Newsletter, 12.

Kurtz, Z., Thornes, R. and Wolkind, S., (1994). *Services for the Mental Health of Children and Young People in England: A National Review*. Report to the Department of Health. South West Thames RHA.

Langlands, A., (1994). Address to the Sir Graham Day Awards Ceremony.

Light, D. and Bailey, V., (1993). *Pound Foolish*. Health Service Journal, 6-18.

Mawhinney, B. & Nichol, D., (1993). *Purchasing for Health: A Framework for Action*. The Health Publications Unit.

McArdle, P., O'Brien, C., and Kolvin, I., (1995). *Hyperactivity: prevalence and relationship with conduct disorders*. Journal of Child Psychology and Psychiatry, 36, 2, 379-304.

Muth, Z., (1994). *Commissioning Comprehensive Community Mental Health Services*. Purchasing for Health. NHS Executive.

National Association of Health Authorities and Trusts, (1992). *Mental Health Services for Children and Young People*. NAHAT Briefing No 23.

NHS Executive, (1994). EL(94)79, *Towards a Primary Care-Led NHS*. Department of Health.

NHS Health Advisory Service, (1986). *Bridges over Troubled Waters: A Report on Services for Disturbed Adolescents.*

NHS Health Advisory Service, (1994a). *Comprehensive Mental Health Services.*

NHS Health Advisory Service, (1994b). *Comprehensive Health Services for Elderly People.*

NHS Health Advisory Service, (1994c). *Drugs and Alcohol, Current Issues in Services for People Who Misuse Substances.*

NHS Health Advisory Service, (1994d). *Clinicians in Management.*

NHS Health Advisory Service, (1994e). *Suicide Prevention: The Challenge Confronted.* HMSO.

NHS Health Advisory Service., (1995a). *Commissioning and Providing Substance Misuse Services for Children and Adolescents.* (In press).

NHS Health Advisory Service, (1995b). *Young People, Mental Health and the Law.* (In press).

NHS Health Advisory Service, Mental Health Act Commission and Department of Health Social Services Inspectorate, (1994). *A Review of the Adolescent Forensic Psychiatry Service, based on the Gardener Unit, Prestwich Hospital, Salford, Manchester.*

NHS Management Executive, (1991). *Assessing Health Care Needs: A DHA project discussion paper.* Department of Health.

NHS Management Executive, (1993). EL(93)68, *Contracting for Specialised Services.* Department of Health.

NHS Management Executive, (1993). *Good Practice and Innovation in Contracting.* Department of Health. Department of Health.

Nicol. A.R., (1990). *Audit in Child and Adolescent Psychiatry.* Archives of Disease in Childhood, 65. 353-6.

Offord, D.R. and Bennett, K.J., (1994). *Conduct Disorder: Long Term Outcomes and Intervention Effectiveness.* Journal of the American Academy of Child and Adolescent Psychiatry, 33:8, 1069-77.

Parry-Jones, W. Ll., (1995). *The Future of Adolescent Psychiatry.* British Journal of Psychiatry, 166, 299-305.

Pearce, J., (1993). *Child Health Surveillance for Psychiatric Disorder: Practical Guidelines.* Archives of Disease in Childhood, 69:394-398.

Peck, E. and Smith, H., (1993). *Contracting in Mental Health Services, A Framework for Action.*

Pfeiffer, S.T. and Strzelecki, S.C., (1990). *Inpatient Psychiatric Treatment of Children and Adolescents: A Review of Outcome Studies.* Journal of the American Academy of Child and Adolescent Psychiatry, 29, 847-53.

Richardson, G., (1994). *Psychiatry - a Contracting Specialty.* Psychiatric Bulletin, 18, 200-2.

Richman, N., (1977). *Behaviour Problems in Preschool Children: Family and Social Factors.* British Journal of Psychiatry, 131, 523-7.

Rutter, M., Maughan, B., Mortimore, P., Ousten, J. with Smith, A., (1979). *Fifteen Thousand Hours. Secondary Schools and their Effects on Children.* Open Books, London, Harvard University Press, Cambridge, Massachusetts.

Rutter, M., (1989). *Isle of Wight Revisited: Twenty Five Years of Child Psychiatric Epidemiology.* Journal of the American Academy of Child and Adolescent Psychiatry, 28. 633-53.

Rutter, M., (1989). Editor: *Studies of Psychosocial Risk: The Power of Longitudinal Data.* Cambridge University Press, Cambridge.

Rutter, M., (1990). *Psychosocial Resilience and Protective Mechanisms.* In Risk and Protective Factors in the Development of Psychopathology. Editors: Rolfe, J., Master, A.S., Ciccheti, D. et al. Cambridge University Press, Cambridge.

Rutter, M., (1991). *Services for Children with Emotional Disorders - Needs, Accomplishments and Future Developments.* Young Minds Newsletter, 9, 1-5.

Rutter, M., (1994). *The Role of Epidemiology in Planning Services.* Address to the Annual Conference of the Child and Adolescent Psychiatry Specialist Section of the Royal College of Psychiatrists.

Rutter, M., Taylor, E. and Hersov, L., (1994). *Child and Adolescent Psychiatry: Modern Approaches.* Blackwell.

Shaw, Spratley, Cartwright and Harwin, (1978). *Responding to Drinking Problems.* Croom Helm, London.

Steinberg, D., (1989). *Interprofessional Consultation.* Blackwell, Oxford.

Steinberg, D. and Yule, W., (1985). *Consultative Work.* In Rutter, M., Hersov, L., and Taylor, E., Editors. Child and Adolescent Psychiatry: Modern Approaches (2nd edition). Blackwell, Oxford.

Stephens, A., and Raftery, J., (1994). Editors: Health Care Needs Assessment, Volume 2. Radcliffe Medical Press, Oxford.

Thornes, R., (1991). *Just for the Day.* National Association for the Welfare of Children in Hospital.

Trowell, J., (1990). *Sustaining Multi-disciplinary Work in Child and Adolescent Psychiatry:* Into the 1990's. Editors: Harris Hendricks, J. and Black, M. Royal College of Psychiatrists, Occasional Paper 8.

Unsworth, E., (1994). *Managing the Internal Market and the Implications for the NHS Drug Advisory Service.* In Drugs and Alcohol - Current Issues in Services for People who Misuse Substances. NHS Health Advisory Service.

Utting, W., (1992). *Children in the Public Care.* HMSO.

Vanstraelen, M. and Cottrell, D., (1994). *Child and Adolescent Mental Health Services: Purchasers' Knowledge and Plans.* British Medical Journal, 309: 259-261.

Wallace, S.A., Crown, J.M., Cox, A.D. and Berger, M., (1995). *Epidemiologically Based Needs Assessment: Child and Adolescent Mental Health.* Department of Health. In press.

Welsh Health Planning Forum, (1993). *Protocol for Investment in Health Gain - Mental Health.* Welsh Office NHS Directorate.

Welsh Office, (1989). *Mental Illness Services - A Strategy for Wales*

West Sussex Steering Group on the Review of Mental Health Services for Children and Young People, (1994). *West Sussex Strategy for Services for Children and Young People with Mental Health Problems.*

Williams, R. , (1992). *The Need to Manage the Market.* In With Health in Mind - Mental Health Care for Children and Young People. Editor: Shelley, P. NAHAT, Birmingham.

Williams, R. and Skeldon, I., (1992). *Mental Health Services for Adolescents.* In Youth Policy in the 1990s. Editors: Coleman, J. and Warren, C. Routledge, London.

Williams, R. and White, R. (1992). Editors: *A Concise Guide to the Childrens Act 1989.* Gaskell, London.

Williams, R. and Farrar, M., (1994). *Commissioning Child and Adolescent Mental Health Services.* In A Slow Train Coming - Bringing the Mental Health Revolution to Scotland. Editor: Dean, C. Greater Glasgow Community and Mental Health Services NHS Trust, Glasgow.

Williams, R., (1994). *Commissioning Services for Vulnerable People,* British Geriatrics Society.

Wolkind, S., (1993). *The 1989 Children Act: A Cynical View from an Ivory Tower.* ACPP Review and Newsletter, 15, No 1.

World Health Organisation, (1992). *The ICD-10 Classification of Mental & Behavioural Disorders.* World Health Organisation, Geneva.

Annexes

Young People, Mental Health and the Law

Author
Mr Richard White

Action Points

Commissioners and **Providers** should:

- Assess their current knowledge of relevant legislation;

- Use the material provided here as the basis for training and education of all staff involved in commissioning and providing CAMHS;

- Discuss an approach to monitoring outcomes and mechanisms for information collection and analysis.

INTRODUCTION

1   This annex addresses some of the legal problems that arise in relation to mental health services for children and adolescents. The intention is that commissioners are made aware of how these legal requirements may impinge on their purchasing strategies and providers become aware of the legal framework in which their mental health professionals work.

2   The issues which this annex addresses are:

   •   Consent to Treatment

      –   General Issues including the Implications of the Children Act 1989 and subsequent Judgements

      –   The Implications of the Mental Health Act 1983 and its Code of Practice

      –   Services for People who Misuse Substances

   •   Restriction of Liberty

      –   The Children Act 1989

      –   The Mental Health Act 1983

   •   Treatment of Children and Young People

   •   Complaints Procedures

   •   After-care

   •   Special Educational Needs

   •   The Need for Mental Health Opinions in Courts and Tribunals

   •   Availability of Legal Advice

3   *The term child or children is used throughout this chapter to include a child, adolescent or children and adolescents. Also, the personal pronoun he or him is used in a number of places in this annex to stand for both genders. This approach has been adopted to reflect the conventional use of personal pronouns in the legislation or judgements referred to in the text.*

CONSENT TO TREATMENT
General Issues
Parental Responsibility

4   The Children Act 1989 introduced the concept of *parental responsibility*, emphasising that the duty to care for a child and to raise him to moral, physical and emotional health is the fundamental task of parenthood. Prior to the Act, case law had established that the older the child the less extensive parental responsibility may become. Lord Denning observed in Hewer v Bryant: "the legal right of a parent ends at the 18th birthday, and even up till then, it is a dwindling right which the courts will hesitate to enforce against the wishes of the child, the older he is. It starts with a right of control and ends with little more than advice."

5   The House of Lords in Gillick v West Norfolk and Wisbech Area Health Authority (1986) AC 112 emphasised that the parental power to control a child

exists not for the benefit of the parent but for the benefit of the child. Lord Scarman said: "Parental rights clearly do exist, and they do not wholly disappear until the age of majority ..... But the common law has never treated such rights as sovereign or beyond review and control. Nor has our law ever treated the child as other than a person with capacities and rights recognised by law. The principle of the law ... is that parental rights are derived from parental duty and exist only so long as they are needed for the protection of the person and property of the child ... parental rights yield to the child's right to make his own decisions when he reaches a sufficient understanding and intelligence to be capable of making up his own mind on the matter requiring decision".

A CHILD'S CONSENT TO MEDICAL TREATMENT

6   Although a doctor may undertake treatment in an emergency if the well-being of the child could suffer by delay, it is normal practice to obtain the consent of a parent as an exercise of their parental responsibility. There may be circumstances, however, in which the child will decide for himself.

The Position of Children Aged 16 or 17

7   Section 8 (1) of the Family Law Reform Act 1969, provides that the consent of a child of 16 years or over "to any surgical, medical or dental treatment which, in the absence of consent, would constitute a trespass to his person, shall be as effective as it would be if he were of full age; and where a minor has by, virtue of this section, given an effective consent to any treatment it shall not be necessary to obtain any consent for it from his parent or guardian".

The Position of Children Under 16

8   In certain circumstances, a child of sufficient age and understanding, who is under the age of 16, can give valid consent. In the Gillick decision it was held that a doctor may lawfully prescribe contraception for a girl under 16 years of age without the consent of her parents. She could have legal capacity to give a valid consent to contraceptive advice and treatment including medical examination. Whether she gave a valid consent in any particular case would depend on the circumstances, including her intellectual capacity to understand advice. There is no absolute parental right requiring the parent's consent to be sought.

9   Speaking of medical treatment generally, Lord Scarman said: "It will be a question of fact whether a child seeking advice has sufficient understanding of what is involved to give a consent valid in law. Until the child achieves the capacity to consent, the parental right to make the decision continues save only in exceptional circumstances. Emergency, parental neglect, abandonment of the child, or inability to find the parents, are examples of exceptional situations justifying the doctor proceeding to treat the child without parental knowledge and consent, but there will arise, no doubt, other exceptional situations in which it will be reasonable for the doctor to proceed without the parent's consent." Applying this to contraceptive advice and treatment, he said: "there is much that has to be understood by a girl under the age of 16 if she is to have legal capacity to consent to such treatment. It is not enough that she should understand the nature of the advice which is being given: she must also have a sufficient maturity to understand what is involved."

10   Lord Fraser established five preconditions which would justify a doctor in prescribing contraceptive treatment:

- That the girl (although under 16 years of age) will understand his advice;

- That he cannot persuade her to inform her parents or to allow him to inform the parents that she is seeking contraceptive advice;

- That she is very likely to begin or to continue having sexual intercourse with or without contraceptive treatment;

- That unless she receives contraceptive advice or treatment her physical or mental health or both are likely to suffer; or

- That her best interests require him to give her contraceptive advice, treatment or both without parental consent.

Refusal of Consent

11   Although the Gillick decision might have been taken to imply that a *'Gillick competent child'* could also veto any proposed treatment, Lord Donaldson MR has since said that this is not so: Re R (A Minor) (Wardship: Medical Treatment) [1992] Fam 11, [1991] 4 All ER 177, CA. According to his Lordship, all that Gillick decided was that a competent child could give a valid consent, not that such a child could withhold consent. This approach was followed in Re W (A Minor) (Medical Treatment) [1993] Fam 64, [1992] 4 All ER 627, CA, in which it was further held that section 8 of the Family Law Reform Act 1969 does not empower 16 or 17 year-olds to veto medical treatment. In most cases, the consent of a parent, if available, will be sufficient and application to the court should not be necessary: Re K, W and H (minors) (Consent to Treatment) [1993] 1 FLR 854.

The Powers of Local Authorities

12   Where a care order is in force, the local authority has parental responsibility and may give consent. The parent retains responsibility, and as a matter of good practice, should still be consulted. If the child is accommodated, the local authority does not automatically have parental responsibility, although the parent may have delegated responsibility to the authority on the child's entry to accommodation. In the absence of any responsibility the local authority could seek a court direction, under section 8 of the Children Act 1989 or through the exercise of the inherent jurisdiction of the High Court.

The Powers of the Courts

13   The court can override both a 16 year-old and a *'Gillick competent' child's* refusal to consent to treatment: Re W (A Minor) (Medical Treatment) [1993] Fam 64, [1992] 4 All ER 627, CA. It is more likely that the court would find that a child refusing essential treatment would not be *'Gillick competent'*.

14   A decision by a parent to consent or refuse to consent to an operation may be overridden by the court. In Re C (A Minor) (Wardship: Medical Treatment) [1990] Fam 26, [1989] 2 All ER 782, CA, it was held that where a ward of court was terminally ill, the court would authorise treatment to relieve the ward's suffering, but would accept the opinions of medical staff looking after the child if they decided that the aim of nursing care should be to ease the ward's

suffering rather than to achieve a short prolongation of life.

15   Where a child has made an informed decision to refuse treatment, but his condition has become life-threatening or seriously injurious, certain statutory provisions, for example where the child is subject to a supervision order, would appear to give the child the right to override a court order for treatment. However, the court may make an appropriate order. In Re J (a Minor) (Medical Treatment) [1992] 2 FLR 165, the Court of Appeal held that treatment of a minor for anorexia could be authorised against her wishes, though the decision as to treatment was one for the doctor.

Consent to Medical or Psychiatric Examination or Assessment

16   The Children Act 1989 provides that the court may direct that a child should undergo a medical or psychiatric examination or other assessment if one of four orders are in force:

— an emergency protection order under section 43;

— a child assessment order under section 44;

— an interim care order under section 38(6);

— a supervision order under section 35.

17   The provisions also state that, notwithstanding the court direction, the child who is of sufficient understanding to make an informed decision can refuse to submit to the examination or assessment. It has been held that the High Court, in the exercise of its inherent jurisdiction can override the child's refusal to consent under section 38(6): South Glamorgan County Council v W and B [1993] 1 FLR 574.

The Implications of the Mental Health Act 1983 and its Code of Practice

18   In some cases, it will be necessary to consider the position of children being treated under the Mental Health Act 1983. The provisions set out above apply, but reference should be made to the *Code of Practice* published pursuant to section 118(4) of the Act.

19   The Code sets out guidance in respect of children and young persons under the age of 18. This contains some statement of the law, as current at the time of writing though this should be treated with caution since it is not up to date nor wholly accurate. The following are relevant extracts:

30.2   Practice for this age group should be guided by the following principles:

a.   young people should be kept as fully informed as possible about their care and treatment; their views and wishes must always be taken into account;

b.   unless statute specifically overrides, young people should generally be regarded as having the right to make their own decisions (and in particular treatment decisions) when they have sufficient 'understanding and intelligence';

c.   any intervention in the life of a young person considered necessary by reason of their mental disorder should be the least restrictive possible and result in the least possible segregation from family, friends, community and school;

d.   all children and young people in hospital should receive appropriate education.

30.4   Whenever the care and treatment of somebody under the age of 16 is being considered, the following questions (among many others) need to be asked:

a.   which persons or bodies have parental responsibility for the child (to make decisions for the child)? It is essential that those responsible for the child or young person's care always request copies of any court orders (wardship, care order, residence order (stating with whom the child should live), evidence of appointment as a guardian, contact order, etc) for reference on the hospital ward in relation to examination, assessment or treatment;

b.   if the child is living with either of the parents who are separated, whether there is a residence order and if so in whose favour;

c.   what is the capacity of the child to make his own decisions in terms of emotional maturity, intellectual capacity and psychological state?

d.   where a parent refuses consent to treatment, how sound are the reasons and on what grounds are they made?

e.   could the needs of the young person be met in a social services or educational placement? To what extent have these authorities exhausted all possible alternative placements?

f.   how viable would be treatment of an under 16 year-old living at home if there was no parental consent and no statutory orders?

Informal Admission to Hospital by Parents or Guardians

20   Relevant paragraphs of the *Code of Practice to the Mental Health Act 1983* advise as follows:

30.5   Children under 16.

        Parents or guardians may arrange for the admission of children under the age of 16 to hospitals as informal patients. Where a doctor concludes, however, that a child under the age of 16 has the capacity to make such a decision for himself, there is no right to admit him to hospital informally or to keep him there on an informal basis against his will: Re R (A Minor) (Wardship Consent to Treatment) [1992] Fam 11, [1991] 4 All ER 177, CA. Where a child is willing to be admitted, but the parents/guardian object, their views should be accorded serious consideration and given due weight. It should be remembered that recourse to law to stop such an admission could be sought.

30.6   Young people aged 16-17.

        Anyone in this age group who is 'capable of expressing his own wishes' can admit or discharge himself as an informal patient to or from hospital, irrespective of the wishes of his parents or guardian: Re W (A

Minor) (Medical Treatment: Court's Jurisdiction) [1993] Fam 64, [1992] 4 All ER 627, CA.

Consent to Medical Treatment

21   The paragraphs below quote from the *Code of Practice to the Mental Health Act 1983:*

30.7   The following guidance applies to young people who are not detained under the Act:

a.   Under 16.

If a child has 'sufficient understanding and intelligence' he can take decisions about his own medical treatment in the same way as an adult: Re R and Re W supra. Otherwise the permission of parents/guardians must be sought (save in emergencies where only the treatment necessary to end the emergency should be given). If parents/guardians do not consent to treatment, consideration should be given to both the use of the child care legislation and the Mental Health Act before coming to a final conclusion as to what action should be taken. Under section 100 of the Children Act 1989, a local authority may also seek leave to ask the High Court to exercise its inherent jurisdiction to make orders with respect to children, if the conditions set out in section 100(4) are met.

b.   The same principles concerning consent apply where the under 16 year old is in the care of a local authority.

Where such a child does not have sufficient 'understanding and intelligence' to take his own treatment decisions, treatment can be authorised by any person or body with parental responsibility. A local authority has parental responsibility for a child in its care, ie under a care order. Wherever possible, parents should be consulted. However, local authorities can, in the exercise of their powers under section 33(3)(b) of the Children Act 1989, limit the extent to which parents exercise their parental responsibility. In the cases of certain pre-Children Act wardships, although the children are deemed to be in care within the meaning of section 31 of the Children Act 1989, court directions may still require treatment decisions to be agreed by the court. Where children are wards of court (and also not deemed to be subject to a care order under section 31 of the Children Act 1989), the consent of the High Court must be sought. In an emergency, consent may be obtained retrospectively (but this should be regarded as wholly exceptional).

c.   Young people aged 16 and 17.

Young people in this age group who have the capacity to make their own treatment decisions can do so in the same way as adults (section 8 Family Law Reform Act 1969). Where such a young person does not have this capacity, the authorization of either parent, guardian or care authority (whichever has the lawful authority in relation to the particular young person) must be obtained. The consent of the High Court must be obtained in the case of wards of court.

d.   Refusal of a minor to consent to treatment.

      No minor of whatever age has power by refusing consent to treatment to override a consent to treatment by anyone who has parental responsibility for the minor, including a local authority with the benefit of a care order or consent by the court. Nevertheless, such a refusal is a very important consideration in making clinical judgements, and for parents and the court in deciding whether themselves to give consent. The importance increases with the age and maturity of the minor. (See Re W (A Minor) (Medical Treatment: Court's Jurisdiction) [1992] 3 WLR 758 at 772 - also known as Re J. See also Re K, W and H (Minors) (Consent to Treatment) [1993] 1 FCR 240) [see above].)

e.   In cases involving emergency protection orders, child assessment orders, interim care orders and full supervision orders under the Children Act 1989, a competent child has a statutory right to refuse to consent to examination, assessment and, in certain circumstances, treatment. Such refusal is not capable of being overridden (see above).

Parents or Guardians Consent

30.8   The fact that a child or young person has been informally admitted by parents/guardian should not lead professionals to assume that they have consented to any treatment regarded as 'necessary'. Consent should be sought for each aspect of the child's care and treatment as it arises. 'Blanket' consent forms must not be used.

Comment

22   This area of the law is neither clear nor uncontentious. For recommendations for change see *Mental Health Handbook: a Guide to the Law Affecting Children and Young People* Children's Legal Centre (1994).

Consent to a Service for People Who Misuse Substances

23   Questions on the provision of drugs, or material in conjunction with the use of drugs and other substances, such as needles or syringes, could come within the Gillick principles. Careful thought would, for example, need to be given in each case as to how the provision and operation of a needle and syringe exchange can be justified as a medical treatment.

24   The five preconditions which emerge from the Gillick decision, could be applied to the provision of a service related to problems of substance misuse:

a.   that the young person (although under 16 years of age) will understand the advice;

b.   that the young person cannot be persuaded to inform his or her parents or to allow them to be informed that he or she is seeking advice or treatment relating to substance misuse;

c.   that the young person is very likely to begin or to continue using substances with or without the advice or treatment;

d.   that, unless the young person receives advice or treatment on the use of substances, his or her physical or mental health or both are likely to suffer; and

e.   that the young person's best interests require the adviser to give advice and/or treatment without parental consent.

25   Valid consent would be ineffective if the prescription of drug or other substance advice or treatment was in itself a criminal offence. It is therefore important for any adviser to ensure that the actions involved in the treatment cannot be construed as a criminal offence; for example where treatment may be interpreted at drug-pushing. If the adviser is to avoid possible prosecution for being an accessory to the unlawful use of drugs, there must be an honest intention to act in the best interests of the young person.

26   The Gillick decision requires that any action should be based on a proper assessment of the circumstances of the case. It refers to assessment by a doctor and clinical judgement, but, when dealing with the mental health of children, a competent assessment may be made by others. An adviser must be able to show the competence to analyse and carry out a reasoned application of the Gillick criteria and must maintain the records to evidence the advice.

RESTRICTION OF LIBERTY

The Statutory Basis – The Children Act 1989

27   The liberty of children may only be restricted in accordance with provisions set out in section 25 of the Children Act 1989, the *Children (Secure Accommodation) Regulations 1991*, and the *Children (Secure Accommodation) No 2 Regulations 1991. The Children Act 1989 Guidance and Regulations, Volume 4, Residential Care (Department of Health 1991*, referred to subsequently as Guidance, Volume 4) supplements the statutory provisions. Secure tracking units are not considered here, since at the time of writing the provisions relating to them had not come into force.

28   Secure accommodation is defined as accommodation provided for the purpose of restricting liberty (section 25(1) of the Children Act 1989). The Guidance recognises that the interpretation of this term is ultimately a matter for the court, but states: "it is important to recognise that any practice or measure which prevents a child from leaving a room or building of his own free will, may be deemed by the court to constitute 'restriction of liberty'." For example, while it is clear that locking a child in a room, or part of a building, to prevent him leaving voluntarily is covered by the statutory definition, other practices which place restrictions on freedom of mobility, for example, creating a human barrier, are not so clear cut Guidance, Volume 4, para 8.10.

29   The use of secure accommodation – by local authorities in respect of children looked after by them and for children accommodated by health authorities, NHS trusts and local education authorities and children accommodated in residential care homes, nursing homes and mental nursing homes – is permitted only where the criteria in section 25 of the Children Act 1989 are fulfilled.

30   Local authorities have a duty under the Children Act 1989 Act to take reasonable steps designed to avoid the need for children within their area to be placed in secure accommodation (schedule 2, para 7). Guidance states: "Restricting the liberty of children is a serious step which must be taken only when there is no appropriate alternative. It must be a last resort in the sense

that all else must first have been comprehensively considered and rejected - never because no other placement was available at the relevant time, because of inadequacies in staffing, because the child is simply being a nuisance or runs away from his accommodation and is not likely to suffer significant harm in doing so, and never as a form of punishment ... Secure placements, once made, should be only for so long as is necessary and unavoidable. Care should be taken to ensure that children are not retained in security simply to complete a pre-determined assessment or treatment programme" (Volume 4, para 8.5).

31 Section 25 provides that secure accommodation may not be used in respect of a child unless it appears:

a. that i. he has a history of absconding and is likely to abscond from any other description of accommodation; and

ii. if he absconds, he is likely to suffer significant harm; or

b. that if he is kept in any other description of accommodation he is likely to injure himself or other persons.

32 A child may only be kept in secure accommodation for as long as the relevant criteria apply. Furthermore, a child under the age of 13 shall not be placed in secure accommodation in any community home without the prior approval of the Secretary of State to the placement of that child and such approval shall be subject to such terms and conditions as he sees fit (reg 4).

33 The maximum period a child may have his liberty restricted without the authority of a court is 72 hours, either consecutively or in aggregate in any period of 28 days (reg 10(1)). There is some relaxation of this restriction to meet difficulties caused by the period expiring late on a Saturday, a Sunday or public holiday (reg 10(3)).

Children to Whom Section 25 of The Act Does Not Apply

34 The restrictions on the use of secure accommodation do not apply to:

a. a child detained under any provision of the Mental Health Act 1983 as the child will be provided for by the mental health legislation;

b. a child detained under section 53 of the *Children and Young Persons Act 1933*, dealing with punishment of certain grave crimes.

35 Children accommodated under the following provisions may not have their liberty restricted in any circumstances:

a. a young person over 16 who is being accommodated under section 20(5) of the Children Act 1989;

b. a child in respect of whom a child assessment order under section 43 of the Children Act 1989 has been made and who is kept away from home pursuant to that order.

Applications To Court

36 Applications to court for authority to use secure accommodation may only be made by or on behalf of a local authority looking after a child or, as extended by No 2 Regulations, where the child is accommodated by a health authority or NHS trust.

37   Application is made to the family proceedings court, except where the matter arises in the context of a case already before a County or High Court in which case application is made to that court, or to the Youth Court where there are criminal proceedings.

38   The criteria applicable to the use of secure accommodation by local authorities is modified in the case of children looked after by them who are: *a* detained children under the *Police and Criminal Evidence Act 1984*, s 38(6); and *b* children remanded to local authority accommodation under the *Children and Young Persons Act 1969*, section 23, but only if:

a.   the child is charged with or has been convicted of a violent or sexual offence, or of an offence punishable, in the case of an adult, with imprisonment for a term of 14 years or more; or

b.   the child has a recent history of absconding while remanded to local authority accommodation, and is charged, with or has been convicted, of an imprisonable offence alleged or found to have been committed while he was so remanded.

39   In these circumstances, secure accommodation may not be used unless it appears that any accommodation, other than that provided for the purpose of restricting liberty, is inappropriate because:

a.   the child is likely to abscond from such other accommodation; or

b.   the child is likely to injure himself or other people if he is kept in any such other accommodation.

Evidence

40   When considering whether to make a secure accommodation order, the court is under a duty to consider whether the relevant criteria for keeping a child in secure accommodation under section 25 are satisfied. The extent to which the welfare principles, under section 1 of the Act have to be taken into account has been a matter for difference of opinion. The Department of Health Guidance states: "It is the role of the court to safeguard the child's welfare from inappropriate or unnecessary use of secure accommodation, both by satisfying itself that those making the application have demonstrated that the statutory criteria in section 25(1) or regulation 6 as appropriate have been met and by having regard to the provisions and principles of section 1 of the Act. The court must therefore be satisfied that the order will positively contribute to the child's welfare and must not make an order unless it considers that doing so would be better for the child than making no order at all" (Guidance, Volume 4, para 5.7).

41   The Court of Appeal has now held that the welfare of the child was a relevant but not the paramount consideration and that the principles of section 1 do not apply: Re M (a Minor) (Secure accommodation order) (1994) Times, 10 November. The role of the court was to decide whether the evidence showed that the authority should be given the power to take such a serious step.

42   An order if made, is permissive; it does not require the child to be kept in secure accommodation. Initially, the maximum period of an authorisation is three months. The court should not automatically make an order for three months but must consider what is necessary in the circumstances of the case:

Re W (A Minor) (Secure Accommodation Order [1993] 1 FLR 692. Authorisation may be renewed for further periods of up to six months at a time (regulations 11 and 12). An order should be for no longer than is necessary and unavoidable and may have a short-term usefulness in breaking a pattern of absconding: W v North Yorkshire County Council [1993] 1 FCR 693.

43   Where an application for a secure accommodation order is made in family proceedings, hearsay evidence is admissible. It is desirable to have a psychiatric report available as evidence: R(J) v Oxfordshire County Council [1992] 3 All ER 660. The court must give reasons for its decision: *Family Proceedings Court (Children Act 1989) Rules 1991,* rule 21.

Accommodating Children and Young People in Secure Accommodation

44   When a child is accommodated by a local authority or health authority, plans should be made for the discharge of the child, when the authority to continue to detain the child expires. There may be occasions when the child cannot immediately be accommodated at home or elsewhere. Although plans should be made sufficiently well in advance to ensure that suitable accommodation is available, it would not seem to be unlawful to permit the child to continue to live on the same premises. Provided the child was advised that he could leave the premises if he so wished, it would appear that he would not come within the provision of being 'kept' within accommodation provided for the purpose of restricting liberty.

Detention Under The Mental Health Act 1983

Assessment - Section 2

45   Any person, including a young person, may be detained under section 2 of the Mental Health Act 1983 for up to 28 days on the grounds that the person is suffering from mental disorder of a nature or degree which warrants the detention of the patient in a hospital for assessment (or for assessment followed by medical treatment) for at least a limited period, and he ought to be so detained in the interests of his own health or safety or with a view to the protection of other persons.

Treatment - Section 3

46   A patient may be detained initially for six months, with renewal for six months and thereafter for a year at a time, on the grounds that:

   a.   the patient is suffering from mental illness, severe mental impairment, psychopathic disorder or mental impairment and his mental disorder is of a nature or degree which makes it appropriate for him to receive medical treatment in a hospital;

   b.   in the case of a psychopathic disorder or mental impairment, such treatment is likely to alleviate or prevent a deterioration of the condition; and

   c.   it is necessary for the health or safety of the patient or for the protection of other persons that he should receive such treatment and it cannot be provided unless he is detained under the section.

Detention of Inpatients

47   An authorized doctor may detain an inpatient under section 5 for up to 72 hours, on the grounds that an application for compulsory admission under section 2 or 3 should be made.

Remand for Report - Section 35

48   The court may remand an accused person to hospital for a report on his mental condition if there is reason to suspect that he is suffering from mental illness, psychopathic disorder, severe mental impairment or mental impairment, and it would be impracticable for the report to be made if he were remanded on bail.

Remand for Treatment

49   An accused person who is on remand, or convicted and awaiting sentence, can be remanded to hospital by a court for treatment under section 36.

Treatment of a Convicted Person

50   An offender may be made the subject of an order authorising guardianship or detention in hospital under section 37.

TREATMENT OF CHILDREN AND YOUNG PEOPLE

51   Questions about the treatment of children and young people include control and restraint, seclusion, destimulation and 'time-out'. There is little statutory or common law basis for regulating these methods of treatment, and it is necessary to look to general principles. Practitioners should certainly be aware that any method of treatment involving restraint or restriction of liberty could be subject to the provisions in section 25 of the Children Act 1989. In respect of any method of treatment, the question of informed consent will arise.

52   *The Children's Homes Regulations 1991* provide for the conduct of homes and for securing the welfare of children in such homes. The regulations also provide for the control and discipline of children in homes. Physical control or restraint of a child must, of its nature, be at least a technical assault. The authority for the assault must arise through the proper restriction of liberty, self-defence or consent. Reference should also be made to Department of Health Guidance, Volume 4, Residential Care and *Permissible Forms of Control (1993)*.

COMPLAINTS PROCEDURES

The Children Act 1989

53   Where a child is being looked after by a local authority, accommodated on behalf of a voluntary organisation or otherwise accommodated in a registered children's home, he or she will be entitled to use the complaints procedure required by section 26 of the Children Act 1989 and established in accordance with the *Representations Procedure (Children) Regulations 1991*.

54   Under section 26 of the Children Act 1989 a local authority must establish and
      publicise its procedure for considering any representations, including complaints,
      made by the following:

      a.   a child whom they are looking after or who is not being looked after
            but is in need;

      b.   a person who qualifies for advice and assistance under section 24
            (having been looked after);

      c.   a parent or other person with parental responsibility;

      d.   any foster parent; or

      e.   such other person as the authority or voluntary organisation consider
            has a sufficient interest in the child's welfare to warrant representations
            being considered by them about the discharge by the authority or
            voluntary organisation of any of their functions under Part III in relation
            to the child.

55   The procedure must ensure that at least one person, who is not a member or
      officer of the authority, takes part in the consideration of the complaint and in
      any discussions held by the authority about the action to be taken in relation to
      the child in the light of the complaint. The authority must have due regard to
      the findings of those considering the representation and must notify the child,
      the person making the representation, and other affected persons, of the
      reasons for its decision and of any action taken or to be taken. Although the
      decision about the child remains with the authority, if they ignore findings or fail
      to give any or any satisfactory reasons, they may be subject to judicial review.

The Hospital Complaints Act 1985

56   Provision is made under the Hospital Complaints Act 1985 for a hospital to
      establish a complaints procedure.

The Mental Health Act 1983

57   The Mental Health Act Code of Practice states:

      30.13   Children and young people in hospital (both as informal and detained
              patients) and their parents or guardians should have ready access to
              existing complaints procedures, which should be drawn to their
              attention on their admission to hospital. The Managers should appoint
              an officer whose responsibility it is to ensure that this is done and to
              assist any complainant.

58   The Mental Health Act Commission also has a power to investigate complaints
      under section 120(1) of the Mental Health Act 1983.

AFTER-CARE

The Children Act 1989

59   Section 24 of the Children Act 1989 provides local authorities with powers and
      duties to prepare young people they are looking after for the time when they
      cease to be so looked after, and the provision of after-care advice and

assistance. They apply to any young person aged under 21 who ceases, after reaching the age of 16, to be looked after by a local authority or accommodated by any health authority, NHS trust or local education authority, or in any residential care home, nursing home or mental nursing home, provided that he or she was accommodated for at least three months.

60   Before a local authority begins to look after a child, or as soon as practicable thereafter, it shall make immediate and long term arrangements for the placement of the child and for promoting his or her welfare: the *Arrangements for Placement of Children (General) Regulations 1991*. Section 23 requires local authorities to provide children with accommodation while they are in their care and to maintain them.

61   These provisions should ensure that a proper admissions policy is in place for every establishment and a care plan for every child. This should contain the criteria for admission, the objectives of the placement, the way in which those objectives will be achieved, outcome expectations and the proposed actions following the placement. That policy should provide a context for after-care, although the extent to which these provisions are implemented in practice is questionable.

The Mental Health Act 1983

62   Section 117 of the Mental Health Act 1983 establishes a duty to provide after-care for certain categories of detained patients. The Mental Health Act Code of Practice, paragraph 27.6, places a duty on the Responsible Medical Officer "to ensure that a discussion takes place to establish a care plan to organise the management of the patient's continuing health and social care needs". Paragraphs 27.7 and 27.8 list who should be involved and emphasise the importance of those who are involved being able to take decisions as far as possible on behalf of their agencies. This guidance is rather weakly worded and a stronger and more enforceable duty should be considered.

SPECIAL EDUCATIONAL NEEDS

63   Under the *Education Act 1993*, local education authorities, and funding authorities for grant-maintained schools, must have regard to the need for securing that special educational provision is made for pupils with special educational needs.

64   A child has special educational needs if he or she has a learning difficulty which calls for special educational provision to be made. A child has a learning difficulty if he or she:

a.   has significantly greater difficulty in learning than the majority of children of the same age; or

b.   has a disability which either prevents or hinders him or her from making use of educational facilities of a kind provided for children of the same age in schools within the area of the local education authority; or

c.   is under five and falls within a or b or would do so if the special educational provision was not made for the child.

65　The Education Act 1993 contains duties to identify, assess and provide for such children with those needs. This may involve a multi-disciplinary assessment in consultation with parents. Mental health professionals may be involved at any stage of the process in advising, assessing or giving evidence.

66　The *Education Act 1993 establishes a Code of Practice* which sets out detailed guidance. It identifies a continuum of need to be dealt with in five stages, extending from action within the school to the making of a statement of special educational needs requiring a specific provision.

67　Parents have a right of appeal to an independent tribunal under sections 169 to 173 against:

- a refusal to make an assessment

- a decision not to make a statement

- the content of a statement

- a refusal to reassess a child with a statement

THE NEED FOR MENTAL HEALTH OPINIONS IN COURTS AND TRIBUNALS

68　Applications to the court for a secure accommodation order and under section 31 for a care or supervision order are likely to require expert evidence to be given. This frequently relates to the mental health of the child or a proposed carer. (For further details of the statutory provisions, see *A Concise Guide to the Children's Act 1989*. Gaskell for the, Royal College of Psychiatrists, 1992).

69　The mental health expert can find that his or her expertise is sought from a number of different sources: the local authority, the guardian ad litem or a member of the child's family. If it is the local authority, the expert he may have been involved before legal proceedings are initiated, but may need to continue involvement thereafter. Otherwise, it is probable that the advice of the expert will be sought specifically for the purpose of the proceedings.

70　In any event, it is important that clear instructions are obtained as to the purpose of the request for advice, what questions are to be considered and what the overall context of the case is. (Further guidance on this aspect of the work can be found in *Child Psychiatry and the Law*, 2nd Edition, Royal College of Psychiatrists, 1993).

71　It is also important to establish the basis for funding. As demonstrated by the fieldwork for the Thematic Review, there is rarely any contractual arrangement for the provision of expert advice for the local authority, in or out of court. It then becomes necessary to establish whether there has to be an extra-contractual referral, which may take time and not be acceptable.

72　If the request for an expert opinion comes from the guardian ad litem for the child, or a solicitor for a member of the family, it is probable that arrangements will have to be made, outside any National Health Service contract. Funding may be provided by the legal aid system, but this can cause delay.

AVAILABILITY OF LEGAL ADVICE

73   The Code of Practice to the Mental Health Act 1983 notes:

30.3   The legal framework governing the admission to hospital and treatment of young people under the age of 18 (and in particular those under the age of 16) is complex and it is the responsibility of all professionals and the relevant local health authorities and NHS trusts to ensure that there is sufficient guidance available to those responsible for the care of children and young people.

74   This should include the provision of legal advice by an appropriate person who is competent to consider both mental health and children's legislation. In some cases, the mental health expert will only be an adviser or witness to action being taken by another agency. In those circumstances, the advice and guidance of their legal advisers may be sufficient. In other cases, the expert may need to have access to legal advice for the purposes of his own agency or if he is unsure about what he is being asked to do, for his or her own professional benefit and protection.

75   It is important that all agencies and individual professionals involved in managing the mental health of children and young people should have ready access to good legal advice. The availability of that expertise and the different professional perspective is an essential benefit to the provision of an appropriate service. Knowledge and understanding of the legal framework should lead to better informed decision-making on policy and individual cases. Ultimately better all-round understanding should enable us to bring about improvements in the legal system itself.

ANNEX B

*A Suggested
Framework for
Outcomes in Child
and Adolescent
Mental Health
Services*

*Authors Dr Michael
Berger, Professor Peter
Hill and Dr David Walk*

INTRODUCTION

76   Increasing attention is being given to health care outcome data. The Department of Health has established two groups to collate and assess information on outcomes - the Expert Advisory Group and the Clinical Outcomes Group - and has published *Assessing the Effects of Health Technologies* (Department of Health, 1992). It has also supported the opening of the UK Clearing House for Information on the Assessment of Health Outcomes at the Nuffield Institute for Health. Purchasing of health care is undoubtedly going to be greatly influenced by the data that will begin to emerge, as well as by considerations of value for money and demonstrable benefits (health gain). These will be assessed within the framework of national priorities identified in *The Health Of The Nation* (Department of Health, 1992) and of priorities set at a local level.

77   Outcome data serves several functions, particularly when linked to the kinds of information provided by the data set. They are important for service management and purchasing decisions, such as local priority setting. Trends and associations in the data can also stimulate more rigorous service and other research.

78   While there are increasingly compelling reasons to collect outcome data, it is important that such data should have ecological validity; that is, indices of outcome and their interpretation should not be isolated from the contexts in which they arise. Thus, services may be under-resourced; patients may have complex and severe disorders; there may be influencing factors outside of the control of the service and treatment may be negated by non-compliance. Judging the outcome of intervention in simplistic terms without regard to such influences can easily lead to erroneous decisions, with deleterious consequences for the community concerned.

79   This paper, taking account of the above, identifies some of the issues in evaluation that service providers in child and adolescent mental health will need to address, with the aim of specifying data sets that could be used in practice to monitor outcomes.

OUTCOMES - SOME DEFINITIONS

80   Outcomes have been defined as:

"...in general,...the results (effects) of processes. They are part of the situation pertaining after a process which can be attributed to that process. ...Health outcomes are the effects on health of any type of process ...Health service outcomes are the effects of health services. Mostly, these will be effects on health, but also include patient's satisfaction with and attitude to services" (Unattributed, 1993, p.10)

81   Desirable outcomes in child and adolescent mental health can be quite diverse, and may be indexed by the reduction of symptoms, an increase in alternative behaviours, the attainment of insight or by the correction of contextual adversity. Some of the changes will relate to family functioning, some to the child or young person and/or to other individuals involved in their care. A helpful list has been published recently by the British Psychological Society (British Psycological Society, 1993), and includes:

- Reduction in severity or frequency of behaviour problems

- Achievement of mutually agreed goals for change

- The acquisition of new skills or strategies

- Improved ability to participate and function in everyday life

- Reduced re-admission rates and duration of stay in instances of chronic illness

- Improved self and parent management of chronic illness and disability

(Adapted from the original, pages 4 and 5).

82 Some of these effects may be apparent at an early stage; others may accrue only after a period of time from the completion of treatment.

83 In addition to these forms of clinical outcome (some of which are more complex than they at first seem), there are the outcomes of service quality and, at a more global level, of service impact. Quality outcomes are concerned with such aspects as the setting, delivery and efficiency of the service, whereas impact evaluation refers to epidemiological change such as will be of direct interest to purchasing agencies. The reduction of successful teenage suicides might be one such indicator, re-admission rates another. Kurtz (1992) lists a number of other possible indicators. Whether or not the effects of local services can be detectable at this level, or even whether our services, given their size, can ever aspire to such an impact, remain questions for the future.

84 Purchasers are also likely to be interested in other types of outcome indicator (such as the uptake of first appointments). However, quality and quantity outcomes would be unlikely to be important if there were no demonstrable clinical change. The challenge to services is to demonstrate that important changes have taken place, and that these are beneficial, the consequence of service contact and not chance occurrences. While we also appreciate the importance - and recognise the complexity - of obtaining epidemiological indicators of outcome for child and adolescent services, this paper is concerned specifically with clinical outcomes at the level of individual clients and their families and carers, following intervention. In particular, it attempts to address the need to take account of important moderating factors in assessing clinical outcome.

OUTCOMES IN MENTAL HEALTH SERVICE INTERVENTIONS

85 Within child and adolescent psychiatry, psychology and related services, there is already a tradition of research into treatment outcomes. While the methodology and results of such studies are of critical importance - for instance in providing models for measurement and in informing decisions about treatment approaches - research studies have limited relevance to the evaluation of *in vivo* intervention. Clinical services do not usually treat homogeneous groups, carefully selected to meet the sorts of criteria necessary in research studies; nor can they rely on a single, coherent and standardised treatment process, as is hoped for in systematic research. For example, response prevention may have been demonstrated to be the treatment of choice for obsessional disorders and certain medications may be shown to

alleviate the hyperkinetic syndrome. But clients with such conditions differ in their individual characteristics, in the nuances of expression of their disorder and in the contexts in which they live and are treated; and parents and other carers may disagree or fail to assist with the interventions proposed. Such factors, unique to each individual case, militate against standardised approaches. Clinicians need to be flexible, influenced by outcome research but practising in a way that may vary greatly from research protocols in order to respond to the variability of each individual case.

86   The range of problems dealt with by a local child and adolescent psychology or psychiatry service is also more heterogeneous than in a clinical trial and individuals often present with several problems, some of them clinical, others social or educational, and these may require services of a diverse nature. (*The Clinical Features List of the Data Set* gives some indication of the range of problems a service may need to address). Any outcome criteria used will have to be able to cope with this heterogeneity in clinical populations and practice.

87   For these reasons, particularly in the medium and long term, there will be little point in simply reassuring purchasers and service managers that the service is using treatments or case management procedures that research has shown to be beneficial. In any event, purchasers are likely to want uncomplicated answers to their questions about value for money - do the interventions work, which are the cheapest and are the clients satisfied? Professionals working in mental health services, however, will want to guard against simplistic questions and answers; parents whose child becomes subject of a Protection Order are unlikely to be happy with a service, and while the child may be safer, he or she may not in the short-term be 'better'. Nevertheless, services do have to recognise and respond to the needs of purchasers.

88   Audit is not an automatic solution to these problems. The end product of medical or clinical audit may well be the recommendation of specific good practice, case management procedures or treatment protocols but, in the absence of better information, these too tend to rely on research findings which again limits the extent of their applicability. Also, successful procedures in one setting may not easily transfer to another, for all sorts of reasons, such as context, training and so on.

89   As a start in approaching these problems, the Data Set has a number of scales dealing with outcomes - for instance, the view of the clinician and his/her judgement of how well the intentions of the referrer have been dealt with. In this paper, some further additional dimensions are suggested, to be considered for inclusion in clinic data sets. Although 'outcome' was not part of the initial brief of the Working Group, it is hoped that the additions (which are being evolved in our Departments at St George's Hospital, London) will prove useful as a starting point in meeting some of the requirements of purchasers and the needs of the services to evaluate what they are doing. At the very least, it is hoped that the framework will provoke constructive discussion culminating in workable solutions. It should be emphasised that, like the Data Set itself, this framework is offered merely as a way of beginning to respond to the questions, and should not be construed as the definitive solution.

APPROACHES TO OUTCOME EVALUATION

90   One typology of health and associated outcome measures (Unattributed, 1993,
p.11) differentiates Quantity of Life, Process Based Outcome Measures, Quality
of Life (with sub-classes Physical, Social, Mental), and Satisfaction With Health
Care. Some of the specific indices include mortality, relapses, measures of
impairment, disability, depression and social adjustment. The typology also
includes measures of handicap and multi-dimensional profiles. It is not
specifically geared to services for children and young people.

91   Approaches to outcome evaluation can sometimes be directly linked to the
assessment framework adopted. For instance, some services (for some or all of
their clients), may systematically formulate a set of treatment or management
goals, explicitly negotiated and agreed with clients, and then assess the
achievement of each at the conclusion of the episode. Such an approach is
helpful but can encourage premature or simplistic formulations and changes of
tack can arise as new information emerges, leading to a need to reconstruct the
targets. This kind of approach also tends to produce multiple outcome data
and, because these are individually based, can generate extensive data sets that
can then be difficult to evaluate.

92   A related approach takes the form of *care plans*. The use of such plans is likely
to become more widespread in this country as a consequence of the
community care legislation. Such plans involve detailed structured assessments
from which follow care proposals with short and long-term goals and the
means whereby the goals are to be achieved. These plans are recorded and
may be monitored by a care or case manager. Service and outcome evaluation
are then based on goal attainment and full and satisfactory implementation of
the recommendations, probably tempered by such phrases as *"within the
resources available"*. Care plans are similar to the *individualised education plans
(IEPs)* used in special educational practice in the United States (Stetson, 1992).

93   Another structured approach with implications for outcome assessment is the
Care Profile (a form of care protocol - *Profiles of Care*, NHSME Resource
Management Unit, 1992). Such profiles model *"the target, or expected, pattern
of interventions needed to provide care to groups of patients with a specific
diagnosis, set of symptoms or procedure to a given level of quality."* (p.3). It is
envisaged that *"Knowledge of the short-and long-term outcomes of the care process
would further enrich the profile information"* (p.4). In this approach, it can be seen
that the types of outcome to be examined are closely linked to the profile.
Although primarily a nursing tool, derivations of this approach aimed at
interdisciplinary care, called *collaborative care plans*, are being developed within
the NHS. One such variant, called the *Anticipated Recovery Plan (Profiles of Care,
p.5)*, is an interdisciplinary approach that *"lists the patient problems, expected
outcomes and tasks or interventions, in specific time frames, needed to meet those
outcomes."*

94   The disadvantage of care planning and protocols is that they can be very time-
consuming and may be less able to deal with the heterogeneity of problems and
the dynamics of practice that present in clinical work in child and adolescent
mental health services. Further, being essentially mechanistic procedures, they
have limited value in the systemic frameworks within which theory and practice
are increasingly being formulated. There is also no clear specification for dealing

with qualitative outcomes of intervention. The advantages of such procedures include systematic frameworks for identifying problems and specifying processes and outcomes, thereby facilitating monitoring and outcome assessment.

95   In addition to these approaches, there are rating scales and other instruments available that could be used for assessing outcome. There are a few global scales for assessing children's behavioural and emotional problems and other instruments for more focused aspects of functioning such as depression or self-image (see McConaughy, 1992). Systematic administration of such scales may not be feasible in routine clinical practice as they take some time to complete and score. Additionally, they have not been validated for the measurement of change over time.

96   The use of care or other profiles or special rating scales and instruments does not exclude the use of global ratings. Even though four or five targets for change may have been dealt with, it is still possible to make overall judgements about outcome, and these may well be useful as summary scores, particularly when aggregated over a series of cases and time period. Global ratings may also allow other, less well defined aspects to be taken into reckoning along with systematic targets.

AN APPROACH TO OUTCOME IN CHILD AND ADOLESCENT MENTAL HEALTH SERVICES

97   The approach proposed here attempts to deal with the heterogeneity of clients and their clinical problems by introducing a set of global ratings that can be used across most if not all cases. Although not as differentiated as some of the other approaches, this procedure has the advantage of a few simple scales that can be quickly completed. This ensures manageability and increases the likelihood of data collection. The scales also provide information that is likely to be accepted by purchasers. Some of the issues that the approach raises are dealt with later.

98   A feature of this framework is the attempt to take account of important moderating factors in clinical outcomes, some of which are outwith the control of the clinician. The framework is built on the assumption that evaluating the work of child and adolescent services needs, in any case, to be linked to a context based on the nature of the problems and the characteristics of the clients and their circumstances. Further, the framework recognises that for each case there may be several stakeholders or parties with an interest in the outcome, and that each of their views should be represented in the evaluation.

99   The Data Set, as it stands, captures some of the important variables, such as individual characteristics and clinical phenomenology, family context, interventions and number of contacts. It also contains two sets of global ratings: a judgement of clinical change; and the clinician's judgement of the extent to which the intervention met the intentions of the referrer. To these have been added global ratings by the patient, carers and referrer. These are described below.

100   We have further extended the Data Set by introducing a set of indices of moderating factors, intended for use in conjunction with the global rating scales. These indices cover characteristics of the problem (complexity, severity) and aspects of manageability of the case (compliance, controllability of external factors).

Problem Characteristics

Complexity

101   The *complexity* of a case differs from the number or severity of the presenting problems or symptoms and reflects the presence or absence of other factors which can influence the ease of treatment and its eventual outcome.   Examples are: the simultaneous involvement of several agencies; a reconstituted family with a multiplicity of carers; an unusual number and variety of clinical problems manifest; or often combinations of these.   While a specific scale might be devised to encompass each, this would be too messy to deal with in practice. Instead, the clinician is asked to make a judgement taking account of these sorts of factors, in arriving at the single rating of complexity as a whole, but not bringing in issues that relate to the other dimensions.   A child with mild learning disabilities who has been sexually abused, leading to the involvement of several agencies, and who is showing disruptive behaviour at home, would be an illustration of a complex case.   A child with nocturnal enuresis as the sole problem would be rated at the low complexity end of the scale.   Chronicity should be taken into account in rating this dimension in some cases (although it would be possible to include chronicity as a separate dimension).

Ratings

1 – Not complex

2 – Low degree of complexity

3 – Moderate complexity

4 – High degree of complexity

5 – Complexity not rated

Severity

102   The effectiveness of intervention can also be influenced by the overall *severity* of the conditions to be dealt with.   A child with autism with life-threatening, self-injurious behaviour would illustrate the severe end of the dimension whereas someone with a few obsessional symptoms or a simple phobia might be coded at the low end of the dimension.

Ratings

1 – Mild

2 – Moderate

3 – Severe

4 – Severity not rated

Case Manageability

Compliance

103   The offer or application of interventions may not necessarily produce desired outcomes; in critical respects clients do not always comply with the course of action suggested.   Thus, psychotherapy requires children to be brought regularly; behavioural treatments may need certain activities to be undertaken as homework; all members may be needed to attend for family therapy.   The clinician may not always be aware of failure, for instance when management procedures need to be implemented at home.   There may be instances of differential compliance, for example where one parent works with the clinician

while the other never attends despite invitation. In all such instances, the clinician must make a judgement of the impact on outcome of the one parent's non-compliance. This dimension is thus introduced because *compliance* over critical aspects of treatment has importance in understanding outcome.

Ratings

1 – Full compliance

2 – Partial compliance

3 – Minimal compliance

4 – Non-compliance

5 – Can't judge compliance

6 – Compliance not rated

Controllability

104 Whereas compliance relates to the client and carer co-operation with treatment, *controllability* refers to the influence of factors external to the client, carers or therapist. Inadequate housing, unavailability of special educational resources, and lack of co-operation from other agencies can have a powerful influence on outcomes. The clinician is asked to judge, overall, the extent to which the outcome was influenced by difficulties or facilitating factors outside of their control. A bi-polar scale is proposed here, although two uni-polar scales might allow more refined data.

Ratings

1 – Facilitative external factors

2 – Some facilitation

3 – Balanced

4 – Some hindrance

5 – Counter-productive external factors

6 – Can't judge

7 – External factors not rated

Outcomes

Clinical Change

105 This is an overall judgement of outcome, the question being whether or not it was felt that the child, adolescent or carers were helped by the service, and the extent of improvement.

Ratings

1 – Problem(s) resolved

2 – Problem(s) largely resolved

3 – Problem(s) partly resolved

4 – Problem(s) the same

5 – Problem(s) worse

6 – Assessment/opinion only

7 – Other

Outcome in Relation to Referrer's Aims

106 The clinician's view of whether or not he or she had met the needs and

requirements (explicit or implicit) of the referrer. These may or may not be identical with the rating of clinical change.

Ratings

1 – Referral aims achieved

2 – Referral aims partly achieved

3 – Referral aims not achieved

4 – Not applicable (eg. in cases of self or parent referral)

Outcome, as Perceived by the Patient

107 This is a judgement by the patient of the extent, if any, of benefit of the contact with the service. At the present time, there is no specific procedure for this rating but it is likely that it will take a form similar to that listed below. In some instances, data may not be available because the child is too young or too handicapped to respond.

Ratings

1 – Very helpful

2 – Helpful

3 – Some help

4 – Made no difference

5 – Worse

6 – Not applicable (eg. young child)

Outcome, as Perceived by Carer/s

108 Similar to that for the patient - in the sense that they are asked to judge the impact or otherwise of the service, not just on the patient, but on their role and relationship with the patient, that is, the overall situation.

Ratings

1 – Very helpful

2 – Helpful

3 – Some help

4 – Made no difference

5 – Worse

Referrer's View

109 This is a judgement by the referrer about the consequences of the referral, whether or not it was, overall, of value or otherwise. As not all referrers will still be in contact with those referred, this rating may not always be available.

Ratings

1 – Very helpful

2 – Helpful

3 – Some help

4 – Made no difference

191

COMMENTARY

110 Each dimension of the framework is rated separately, although it is recognised that some may not be independent. The framework is also simplified in that it evaluates overall or global characteristics rather than dealing with each of the major problems presented by clients. In this sense, it is a superordinate set, an aggregation of lower level components that would in combination go to make up the global concept and rating.

111 The full schema may not apply to all clients and activities. For instance, brief consultations may require a modified form of the framework, as may referrals for reports and second opinions. In reviewing service performance, it may be appropriate to analyse these separately from clinical treatment activities as even a satisfactory assessment may not be expected to affect all the suggested measures of outcome.

112 There are several important issues raised by these dimensions. While we have attempted to make the process of rating as uncomplicated as it can realistically be, the dimensions are undoubtedly simplistic. In-depth outcome studies would need to sub-divide several of the scales. For instance, the carer might be asked to judge whether or not the patient had improved, as well as how far they themselves had been helped to understand and manage the child or young person. On the other hand, there may well be instances where the carer's judgement could itself be of dubious value, for instance where a parent becomes accused of abuse as a result of contact with the service.

113 The ratings on each of the dimensions would need to be made at different times. For instance, severity and complexity should be rated when the professionals are sufficiently familiar with the clients and their problems, but not later. Rating at the end of the episode could lead to biased data - unsuccessful interventions being given ratings of greater severity and complexity. The use of audit procedures and systematic training of staff should however help to reduce some of these effects. In our experience, clinicians' ratings are in close agreement with ratings provided by referrers and parents; a little less so with their child patients. They are not necessarily more optimistic than any of these.

114 The outcome ratings are also problematic - the effects of interventions are generally accepted as dynamic, with evolving effects over time, so that initial positive or negative views may be modified if later changes also come to be associated with the clinical interventions (the so-called sleeper effects). Further, the impact of interventions could have ramifications spreading out in unanticipated directions and areas (ripple effects).

115 Many potentially relevant aspects are not dealt with. For example the clients' perceptions of the service setting, the way services are delivered, the characteristics of the professionals and the credibility of their clinical practice, and so on might be studied.

CONCLUSION

116 In conclusion, while we do not wish to overstate the complexity of treatment outcome evaluations in child and adolescent mental health services, it is also important that purchasing agencies and service managers do not underestimate this complexity. Whatever other customer satisfaction studies and outcome

evaluations are required or requested by the purchasers, it is important that mental health services take their own steps to identify and collect data that will enable them to present a balanced reflection of their efforts and the effects of their work.

REFERENCES

British Psychological Society, (1993). *Purchasing Clinical Psychology Services: Services for Children, Young People and Their Families.* Briefing Paper No 1. Leicester.

Department of Health, (1992). *Assessing the Effects of Health Technologies.*

Department of Health, (1992). *The Health of the Nation: A Summary of the Strategy for Health in England.*

Kurtz, Z., (1992). Editor: *With Health in Mind: Mental Health Care for Children and Young People.* Action For Sick Children/South West Thames Regional Health Authority. London.

McConaughy, S.H., (1992). *Objective Assessment of Children's Behavioural and Emotional Problems.* In Handbook of Clinical Child Psychology, pp. 163-180. Editors: Walker, G.E. and Roberts M.C. 2nd edn. John Wiley, New York.

Stetson, E.G., (1992). *Clinical Child Psychology and Educational Assessment.* In *Handbook of Clinical Child Psychology,* pp. 101-132. Editors: Walker, G.E. and roberts M.C. 2nd edn. John Wiley. New York.

Unattributed, (1993). *Issues in Outcome Measurement. Outcomes Briefing;* pp. 9-13. UK Clearing House for Information on the Assessment of Health Outcomes, Nuffield Institute for Health, Leeds.

Resource Management Unit, (1992). *Step by Step Guide to Producing and Using Profiles of Care,* NHSME, Leeds.

ACKNOWLEDGEMENT

The NHS Health Advisory Service is grateful to the authors of this document and to the Association for Child Psychology and Psychiatry for their agreement to the reproduction of their work in this report.

This Annex is reprinted from:

Berger, M., Hill, P., Sein, E., Thompson, M., and Verduyn, C., (1993). *A Proposed Core Data Set for Child and Adolescent Psychology and Psychiatry Services.* Association for Child Psychology and Psychiatry, London.

It is reproduced with the permission of the authors and the Association for Child Psychology and Psychiatry and is copyright of the Association for Child Psychology and Psychiatry, 1993.

Mr Paul Bates

Mr Paul Bates is currently Divisional Manager for Special Needs within South Tees Community and Mental Health NHS Trust. Paul Bates' clinical background is in mental health nursing. He completed his registered mental nurse training in Newcastle, and then qualified in child and adolescent mental health nursing at the Fleming Nuffield Unit, in Newcastle. After a short period working with children and teenagers in a social services department, Paul Bates was a charge nurse for Burnley, Pendle and Rossendale Health Authority, and was then the Senior Nurse in Child, Adolescent and Family Mental Health in York Health Services for seven years.

Dr Stuart Cumella

Dr Stuart Cumella is Senior Research Fellow and Director of the Centre for Research and Information in Mental Disability (CRIMD) at the University of Birmingham. His academic background is in economics, politics, and social administration, and he has worked as a qualified social worker, a researcher in central government and with the Medical Research Council, and as a manager in the NHS. Stuart Cumella's current research interests are the impact of the internal markets for health and social care on mental health services, the development of outcome measures for learning disability services, primary care and social work, and the development of techniques for analysing the clinical process in community mental health services.

Mr Michael Farrar

Mr Mike Farrar is the Mental Health Strategy Manager for the Northern and Yorkshire Regional Health Authority. He is currently seconded to the Performance Management Directorate, in the National Health Service Executive in Leeds. He is a social sciences graduate from the University of Nottingham and has pursued a varied career in both the public and private sector undertaking managerial, research and development, and strategic planning roles. He has focused on services for people with mental health or addiction problems and has been based predominantly in the north of England. He was also a member of the NHS Health Advisory Service/Mental Health Act Commission/Department of Health Social Services Inspectorate Team which reviewed Adolescent Forensic Psychiatry Services in 1993-94 and is an author of the NHS Health Advisory Service Report on services provided at Ashworth Hospital.

Dr Michael Kerfoot

Dr Michael Kerfoot is a Senior Lecturer and Co-Director of the Mental Health Social Work Research and Staff Development Unit in the Department of Psychiatry of the University of Manchester. He has 16 years' experience of working in child and adolescent mental health services in Liverpool, Newcastle, and Manchester. His main research interest has been in adolescent suicidal behaviour. He has published widely in this field, both nationally and internationally, and has been a regular contributor to conferences in the UK and abroad. He has twice been a visiting Research Associate at the Los Angeles Suicide Prevention Centre, and is an Honorary Consultant to the Samaritans.

Dr Zarrina Kurtz

Dr Zarrina Kurtz is a paediatric epidemiologist and Consultant in Public Health Medicine at South Thames Regional Health Authority and an honorary senior lecturer at St George's Hospital Medical School. Formerly a paediatrician and medical adviser to the Inner London Education Authority, she is honorary adviser in child health to the National Children's Bureau. The main focus of Dr Kurtz' research and policy development is on children and young people with chronic disorders and the respective roles of the health, social and education services. She acted as the representative for purchasing on the multi-disciplinary group that produced the Quality Review of Services for the Mental Health of Children and Young People, With Health in Mind, for Action for Sick Children and edited that report. In 1993, she completed, with colleagues, a survey of provision and purchasing of mental health services for children and young people throughout England, funded by the Department of Health, and is currently carrying out a related project to develop models of services to meet differing population needs.

Dr Gregory Richardson

Dr Gregory Richardson led this NHS Health Advisory Service Thematic Review on The Commissioning, Role and Management of Child and Adolescent Mental Health Services. He is a Consultant in Child and Adolescent Psychiatry in the York Health Services NHS Trust. Prior to becoming a consultant, he worked in Sudan and Canada. He is particularly interested in the management of mental health services and has published works on management topics relating to mental health services. He is currently chairman of the Royal College of Psychiatrists' Management Special Interest Group. He is currently the Deputy Regional Advisor in Psychiatry for the Yorkshire part of the Northern and Yorkshire Regional Health Authority, and is an honorary lecturer at the University of Leeds.

Dr Michael Shooter

Dr Michael Shooter came late to medicine via a history law degree and years spent as a newspaper reporter and a secondary school teacher. He is currently a Consultant in Child and Adolescent Psychiatry for the Gwent Community Health NHS Trust and was formerly the clinical director of the sister service in South Glamorgan. He is Deputy Registrar of the Royal College of Psychiatrists and a member of the Executive Committee of its Child and Adolescent Psychiatry Specialist Section. Dr Shooter has an interest in working with children who have a chronic physical illness, in liaison with paediatricians. He has run hundreds of experiential workshops for people who are in front-line contact with dying and bereaved people, both in the UK and abroad, and has written extensively on the subject.

Mr Richard White

Mr Richard White is a partner in White and Sherwin, solicitors of Croydon. The practice specialises in the law relating to children. He is co-author of a Guide to the Children Act, 1989, and co-editor and an author of the Concise Guide to the Children Act 1989, and editor of Clarke Hall and Morrison, an encyclopedia on child law. He was a member of the NHS Health Advisory Service/Mental Health Act Commission/Department of Health Social Services Inspectorate Team which reviewed Adolescent Forensic Psychiatry Services in 1993-94.

Dr Richard Williams

Dr Richard Williams is the present Director of the NHS Health Advisory Service (HAS). Upon appointment in 1992, he was required to reposition the HAS so that it worked in accordance with the reformed health service. One of the new activities of the HAS, which he has developed, are the Thematic Reviews. Three of these have been completed and another seven are either close to completion or in progress. Richard Williams is also a Consultant Child and Adolescent Psychiatrist at the Bristol Royal Hospital for Sick Children, where he developed an extensive liaison and consultation service, with other community childcare workers and the child health services. His particular clinical interests include the psychological impacts and treatment of life-threatening and chronic physical disorders and he has extensive experience of working with families which have experienced psychological trauma. He has been involved in service management over a number of years and has a particular interest and experience in the theory of leadership and the selection and development of leaders. Along with the Director of the Institute of Health Services Management, he inspired the creation of a Leadership Development Programme for Top Managers in 1994. Consequent on his work with the HAS, he has developed particular experience in the challenges posed to health authorities in purchasing comprehensive health services for mentally ill and elderly people.

Additional Authors

In addition, the NHS Health Advisory Service and the editors of this report are grateful to:

Dr Michael Berger, Consultant Clinical Psycologist

Professor Peter Hill, Head of the Section of Child and Adolescent Psychiatry and

Dr David Walk, Consultant Child and Adolescent Psychiatrist

all of St Georges Hospital Medical School for supplying Annex B, *A Suggested Framework for Outcomes in Child and Adolescent Mental Health Services*, and to:

Mr Bob Sang

of the Kings Fund Centre

for his contributions to the analysis of documents in the HAS *Library of Commissioning Documentation* and for contributing material in Chapter 6, *The National Survey of Commissioning of Child and Adolescent Mental Health Services*.

When work on this thematic review started, Dr Richard Williams established a wide ranging steering committee to advise him and share the task. Dr Richard Williams takes this opportunity to thank its members for the generosity of their time, their commitment and their wisdom.

In addition to the authors of this review, the steering committee consisted of:

Mr Roy Atkinson

Roy Atkinson was educated at Bolton County Grammar School and followed graduate and postgraduate studies at the Universities of Leeds, Nottingham and Birmingham. His main studies have been in psychology and he is a holder of the Diploma in Management Studies. Following teaching experience at Colne Valley High School, further professional training at the University of Birmingham and experience in the counties of Durham and Gwent, he became Principal Educational Psychologist to the County of Staffordshire, in 1976. During his service with Staffordshire, he moved into educational administration, being first Principal Assistant Education Officer for Special Services and then for Schools in the Northern part of the County. In November 1984, he moved to Northamptonshire to the post of Deputy County Education Officer and succeeded Michael Henley to the post of County Education Officer, now the Director of Education and Libraries, in September 1986.

Dr Hugh Barnes

Dr Hugh Barnes is a Consultant Child and Adolescent Psychiatrist in the United Bristol Healthcare NHS Trust and he is based at the Bristol Royal Hospital for sick children. Presently, he is the consultant in charge of the Lumsden Walker House children's psychiatric day and inpatient unit and resource centre. His clinical commitments also include paediatric liaison, and he provides community outreach services from a clinical base in the south of Bristol. His special interests include consultation and family therapy.

Dr Wendy Casey

Dr Casey is Head of the Clinical Psychology Service for Children in the West Herts Community Health NHS Trust and she is responsible for the development and provision of all child clinical psychology services in that trust. She graduated from Queen's University Belfast and took her Ph.D. at London (Birkbeck University College) in 1974, and her Diploma in Clinical Psychology in 1975. Originally working in learning disability, she moved on to work with children with special needs in Haringey and Barnet, finally settling in Hertfordshire in 1988. Her main professional interest is children under five years old and she is a firm believer in the prevention of later problems through early intervention.

Ms Jane Christian

Ms Jane Christian has worked in the field of non-statutory provision of services for people who misuse substances since completing a degree in social policy and administration in 1979. The following year, she joined Turning Point, the UK's largest charity providing alcohol, drug, mental health and learning disabilities services. Jane Christian has worked in a range of drug misuse services: a residential rehabilitation project; a central London street agency; and in a partnership project with health authority, social services department and probation services. Currently, she is the manager of community drug services in Staffordshire, placing a particular emphasis on developing services to meet the needs of young people. Jane has been involved in the work of the NHS Drug Advisory Service since 1988.

Dr John Coleman

Dr John Coleman trained as a clinical psychologist at the Middlesex Hospital, London and worked for 14 years as a senior lecturer in the department of psychiatry in the Royal London Hospital. Since 1988, he has been the Director of the Trust for the Study of Adolescence, an independent research and training organisation based in Brighton. Currently he is the editor of the *Journal of Adolescence* and the editor of the Routledge book series, *Adolescence and Society*. He has published a number of books, the most well-known being *The Nature of Adolescence*, now in its second edition. He is a Fellow of the British Psychological Society and acts as a consultant for many organisations, including the World Health Organisation and the Prince's Trust.

Professor Ron Davie

Ron Davie, Consulting Child Psychologist, is Visiting Professor at Oxford Brookes University and Honorary Research Fellow at UCL. His positions, as recent past President of the National Association for Special Educational Needs and, until 1990, as Director of the National Children's Bureau, have given him a very close familiarity with current legislation and practice in the child care and special needs fields. He has particular expertise on children's emotional and behavioural problems. He now writes and lectures extensively in these areas and draws on this knowledge for his forensic practice and in consultancy for a range of statutory agencies.

Dr Martyn Gay

Dr Gay is a Consultant Child and Adolescent Psychiatrist based in the Department of Family Psychiatry at the Royal Hospital for Sick Children and in the Weston Health NHS Trust. He is also a consultant to the Regional Secure Unit at Kingswood in Bristol and has a special interest in child and adolescent forensic psychiatry services and in the delivery of drug and alcohol services to children and adolescents. Previously he worked in the prison and probation service in the United States of America at Temple University, Philadelphia prior to coming to Great Britain in 1968 to take up his present post. His research interests have covered the fields of children in residential care, the impact of secure accommodation upon young people and the outcome of Section 53 serious young offenders. From 1984 to 1987 he was involved in an extensive DHSS funded research project when he was Research Director of the Avon Drug Abuse Monitoring Project. This surveyed the extent of drug misuse in a city population and identified key indicators of drug misuse within the local community.

Dr Eilish Gilvarry

Dr Eilish Gilvarry is Clinical Director and Consultant Psychiatrist in the Northern Regional Alcohol and Drug Service in Newcastle-upon-Tyne. Her particular interests are in the fields of preventive and treatment interventions for substance misuse among young people. She was instrumental in the re-establishment of the Centre for Drug and Alcohol Studies in Newcastle and helped to establish the North East Addiction Services Alliance in conjunction with the Leeds Addiction Unit and the economics department at York University. Both these organisations foster research, emphasising audit and evaluation. In particular, Dr Gilvarry has developed services for young people in conjunction with child and adolescent mental health services and the voluntary sector. In collaboration with child psychiatrists, she has published work on epidemiology in the field of youth substance use.

Ms Mary Hancock

Ms Mary Hancock is a Social Services Inspector within the policy division of the Social Services Inspectorate of the Department of Health. After a brief career teaching in New Zealand and England, Mary Hancock qualified as a psychiatric social worker, and worked in Islington and Southwark as a mental welfare officer, and, subsequently, as a generic social services team leader. Later, she took a joint appointment with Goldsmiths College, as a senior lecturer in social work, and as a training officer in Lambeth, where she specialised in mental health, staff and student supervision and handicap, and organised field and residential placements. In the Department of Health, she covers mental health policy, including that relating to adult and child and adolescent mental health services and mental health legislation.

Ms Olga Kurtianyk

Ms Olga Kurtianyk qualified as a Registered Sick Children's Nurse (RSCN) in 1974. In 1988, after holding posts in neonatal intensive care and general paediatrics, she was appointed to be Director of Nursing Services at the Queen Elizabeth Hospital for Children in London. Her interests include the effects of cultural influences on the approach of individuals to health services and education. In particular, she is interested in how this affects the psychological and physical well-being of children.

Professor William Ll. Parry-Jones

William Ll. Parry-Jones is Professor of Child and Adolescent Psychiatry at the University of Glasgow. Previously, he was consultant in charge of the Oxford Regional Psychiatric Adolescent Unit and Fellow of Linacre College, Oxford. His clinical and academic interests include psychological traumatisation, adolescent psychiatry, chronic illness and adolescent health care. He was a member of the HAS Steering Committee responsible for the Report, *Bridges Over Troubled Waters*, (1986). Recently, he directed a European Community project to develop child and adolescent psychiatry in Hungary and, currently, he is involved in establishing psycho-social programmes for traumatised children in former Yugoslavia.

Dr Martin Smith

Dr Martin Smith trained at the Universities of Cambridge and Birmingham. He has been a GP in Toxteth in Liverpool for the last seven years. His special interests are working with problem drug users and working with children and adolescents.

Dr Eddy Street

Dr Eddy Street is Consultant Clinical Psychologist with Llandough Hospital NHS Trust and Honorary Senior Research Fellow in the Department of Child Health, of the University of Wales College of Medicine in Cardiff. His clinical work is focused on the provision of services to abused children and their carers. He has published widely on issues related to the theory, practice and service development of family therapy.

Mr Peter Wilson

Mr Peter Wilson started work as an unattached youth worker for the National Association of Youth Clubs, and then trained to be a social worker at the London School of Economics. He worked in New York, USA, from 1964-67 as a psychiatric social worker in a residential treatment centre for emotionally disturbed children and, subsequently, returned to England and trained as a child psychoanalyst at the Anna Freud Centre. Qualifying in 1971, he spent many years practising as a child psychotherapist in child guidance clinics in London and a walk-in centre for adolescents, and occupied the role of a senior clinical tutor at the Institute of Psychiatry and Maudsley Hospital Children's Department. During the 1980s, he was Director of the Brandon Centre and the Consultant Psychotherapist to the Peper Harow Therapeutic Community. Since April 1992, he has been the Director of Young Minds.

The service visits were undertaken by teams of professionals drawn from the steering committee and enhanced by a specially recruited group of key people. They have concentrated their minds on understanding the work and functioning of many different services and agencies in a diverse range of settings. The HAS is grateful to them for their skilled contribution to this review. The additional visitors were:

Ms Sue Croom

Ms Sue Croom obtained her ENB 603 in the psychological care of children and adolescents at the Fleming Nuffield Unit in Newcastle in 1983. She practised as a group leader there and initiated, and published, a paper on social skills training. She has worked in health visiting and developed behaviour management groups with parents and counselling sessions in high schools. As a clinical nurse specialist at the Fleming Nuffield Unit since 1991, she has facilitated audit and community nursing links. She is, currently, studying for a MSc. in health science research focusing on evaluating nursing practice and management in child and adolescent mental health services.

Dr Victor Doughty

Dr Victor Doughty has been a Consultant Child and Adolescent Psychiatrist in Hull and East Yorkshire for 22 years, witnessing many changes in the management of the NHS and in clinical practice. He has been responsible for the adolescent unit serving the whole of Humberside for 15 years, and planned for its move into its present community setting six years ago.

Mr Stephen Harrison

Mr Stephen Harrison is a community nurse working for South Tees Community and Mental Health NHS Trust. He has worked with young people and their families for the past 15 years and is currently engaged in developing community-based services.

Mr Geoffrey Lake

Mr Geoffrey Lake is currently Director of Quality Performance at Leeds Healthcare where he has a commissioning responsibility for child and adolescent mental health services. These services in Leeds are currently being redesigned. Previously, he was Deputy Director of Social Services in Humberside County Council. In this role, he had a responsibility for day-to-day management of services. During his career, he has been involved in the general management of all social services including residential, field work, and day services for children and adults.

Mr Martyn Pritchard

Mr Martyn Pritchard currently works as a healthcare purchasing manager for West Yorkshire Health Authority. His main responsibilities are commissioning mental health services for adults, acute sector contracting, community care planning and contracting with voluntary sector organisations. Before entering the NHS, he worked as a researcher at the School of Geography in the University of Leeds where he studied the spatial distribution of healthcare resources.

Mr Ted Riley

Mr Ted Riley is originally from Liverpool. He obtained a business degree from the University of Sheffield and worked in industry for a number of years. Subsequently he trained as an occupational therapist and worked predominantly within hospital and community mental health services. Following his clinical experience, Ted moved into general management and held operational and managerial posts in occupational therapy, mental health and acute services (general surgery, operating theatres). He has also worked within planning in the acute services. His present post is with the Avon Health Commission in which he commissions and purchases mental health, substance misuse and learning disabilities services. He has also worked extensively for the NHS Health Advisory Service on several of its Thematic Reviews.

Dr Guinevere Tufnell

Since 1986, Dr Guinevere Tufnell has been a Consultant in Child and Adolescent Psychiatry in East London. She supervises senior registrars on placement from the Royal London Hospital training scheme and contributes to the scheme's academic programme. She is also lead clinician for child mental health within the Forest Healthcare NHS Trust. She is a member of the Executive Committee of the Child and Adolescent Specialist Section of the Royal College of Psychiatrists, for which she acts as a Public Education Officer, and is a member of the College's Public Education Committee. She is a co-author of a document for Purchasers of Child and Adolescent Psychiatry Services in the North East Thames Region and edits Points of Law for the Association of Child Psychology and Psychiatry Review and Newsletter.

Ms Judith Young

Ms Judith Young has recently become Director of Health Care Purchasing for West Yorkshire Health Authority. Judith Young started her career, after her first degree in psychology, in residential social work in Hertfordshire and then worked as a clinical psychologist with people with mental health problems and people with learning disabilities for 12 years. In 1991, she moved into health commissioning and enjoys the challenge of strategic planning and purchasing.

With special thanks to:
The children and staff of
Crockerne Pill Church of England Infants School,
Pill Nr Bristol
for help with the front cover illustration.

Printed in the United Kingdom for HMSO
Dd 300660 C40 4/95 321311